GREAT IDEAS FOR YOUR HOME

JULIAN CASSELL • DAVID HOLLOWAY
MIKE LAWRENCE • JOHN McGOWAN
PETER PARHAM • TONY WILKINS

NEW
BURLINGTON
BOOKS

Authors: Julian Cassell, David Holloway,
Mike Lawrence, John McGowan, Peter Parham, Tony Wilkins

A New Burlington Book
Conceived, edited, and designed by Marshall Editions
The Old Brewery, 6 Blundell Street, London N7 9BH, U.K.
www.quarto.com

ISBN 1 84566 051 X

1 3 5 7 9 10 8 6 4 2

Printed and bound in China by Midas Printing Limited

Design for this edition: Alchemedia

CONTENTS

PART ONE:
RENOVATING AND REFURBISHING

GETTING STARTED

F rom time to time we all look at different rooms in our homes and decide that it is time to make a few changes to improve their appearance and generally remodel and refurbish them to keep pace with fashion, style, and changes in personal taste. This process can be carried out on a large scale with a complete overhaul of the room, or it can be a matter of adding a few details here and there to give a new look. This section of the book covers a range of remodelling ideas—large and small—and provides the technical know-how, illustrated with clear step-by-step instructions, to help you make all manner of home improvements. Never before have manufacturers offered so many materials and tools all aimed at producing particular styles and looks in the home—the choice of finishes and effects has never been greater. Much of the fun of improving your home is in the decision-making process, combining your ideas with professional advice on how best to produce results that will be beneficial to the look of your home and very rewarding in terms of personal achievement.

BUDGETING FOR A REVAMP

The main concern with any home improvement is to decide on its extent and how much time and money you are prepared to commit to the job. The personal pleasure you will get from a new look should be balanced against such facts as whether you intend to stay in the house for a long time, or if you plan to move in the near future and will therefore only get a short-term return. However, while it is nice to be able to enjoy the fruits of your labour for as long as possible, remember that any home improvement will usually add to the value of your home. This is one good reason to go into any remodelling job with the attitude that you want to produce the best possible finish, regardless of whether you intend to stay in the house for a long time or plan to move shortly—the result of your work will be beneficial one way or another.

ESSENTIAL FIXES

Chapter 1 acts as a directory that demonstrates the most effective ways of carrying out many of the most common household repairs and maintenance tasks in the home. The home safety and maintenance checklists will ensure that you always have the systems in your home functioning at optimum level. After all, not every area of home improvement is concerned with looks, and the essential areas of maintenance and safety should always be given careful attention.

ADDING CHARACTER

Once the essential repairs in your home have been carried out, you can turn your attention to the more creative task of adding style to the rooms. Chapter 2 illustrates many ways in which it is possible to add character to existing schemes. All the techniques in this chapter aim to take the basic shell of a room and achieve a different look by adding various embellishments to the walls, ceilings, or woodwork.

RENOVATING FLOORS

Try to keep in touch with modern developments, as the choice and variety of floorcoverings are constantly increasing. This area of refurbishment has become much more accessible to the home decorator since manufacturers have made it easy to lay all kinds of floorcoverings. Chapter 3 provides a whole range of flooring choices, demonstrating how they can be laid to the best possible effect and the best techniques for doing this.

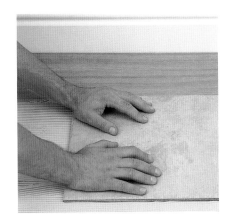

FIXTURES AND FITTINGS

All homes have a selection of fixtures that fulfil relatively straightforward functions but are essential for the running of the household. Chapter 4 covers all the essential aspects of this important area of any refurbishment project, guiding you through the choices. The finishing touches of home improvement are essential to the final look. This chapter also covers all kinds of finishing ideas, demonstrating the best techniques for adding a variety of features, such as pictures, mirrors, and lights.

EFFECTIVE STORAGE

Improving or adding to storage areas is an essential part of refurbishment since it can completely transform the general functioning of the household and improve its overall look. Chapter 5 explores this exciting area of home improvement with lots of good ideas for turning wasted space into storage areas and innovative suggestions for storage systems in general.

DEALING WITH PRIORITIES

Home improvements can include so many areas in the home that there needs to be a priority list. After dealing with the essentials, it is always best to turn your attention to the most lived-in areas of the home, since these are the places where you will spend time and gain most benefit from improvements. Always try to finish one job or project before beginning the next, otherwise there is a danger of the whole house turning into a building site.

1
ESSENTIAL REPAIRS

Before starting to remodel your home or to undertake any decoration, it may be necessary to carry out some basic structural repairs. This chapter explains how to fix commonly damaged surfaces and fixtures, as well as giving advice on general maintenance, and the best way to keep your home functioning efficiently. The repair projects detailed in this chapter use the simplest and most time-efficient techniques but without any compromise on quality and finish. Make sure you leave yourself adequate time to carry out these basic tasks before beginning on your refurbishment plan as a little time and money spent now will result in savings later. These repairs are the building blocks of your refurbishment scheme.

REPAIRING FLOORBOARDS

Where the general condition of floorboards is poor, the best option is total replacement. However, in many cases it is possible to repair damaged areas by cutting out the old boards and replacing them with new ones. The technique varies according to whether the boards have flat edges or a tongue-and-groove design.

FLAT-EDGED FLOORBOARDS

These floorboards are simply planks of wood used to cover the floor joists. Replacing a damaged part of one of these boards is quite straightforward.

1 Use a brick chisel to lever up the damaged area of board. In this example, the split begins at the end of the board; however, even if the damage is more central to the board length, it is best to begin by lifting the board at one end.

2 Place a length of batten under the damaged area of board to hold it up above the floor. Saw through the board at a point where it is no longer damaged and is above a floor joist.

3 Remove the damaged section of floorboard, then hammer the end of the undamaged section of board back in position.

4 Cut a new length of board the same size as the damaged section of board. Hammer the new section in place at the joist.

TONGUE-AND-GROOVE BOARDS

This design of floorboard requires a slightly different technique when it comes to replacement. Because the edge of each board locks into the adjacent one, it is not possible to simply lever up a board at the end, as shown, with flat-edged boards. It is necessary to free the edges before the board can be removed.

Cutting the tongue: in order to remove a tongue-and-groove board, use a saw to cut through the board tongue. Allow the saw blade to run down the edge of the board, but be careful not to damage any wires or supply pipes that may be below floor level. Once the board edges are cut, follow Steps 1–4 opposite—it is difficult to use a tongue-and-groove board as a replacement so, in this case, use a flat-edged board instead.

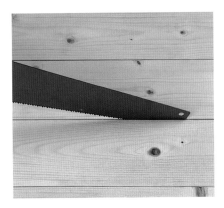

FLOORBOARD PROBLEMS

Aside from the more extensive damage that floorboards can experience, there are a number of minor problems that can be overcome with relative ease. There are also a few extra tasks that can be carried out when floorboards are replaced, in order to help things like the decoration and the general look of the floor.

- Squeaky boards: the remedy can be a simple case of screwing or nailing down any loose boards. However, in many cases, these may not be very obvious, but a generous sprinkling of talcum powder along board edges and joints often solves the problem of squeaking boards.
- Dealing with gaps: on a decorative level and in terms of drafts, gaps between floorboards can cause a problem. Use thin wedges of wood to fill these areas and plane them until they are flush with the floor surface. If the floor is going to be covered, the look is not important and you can use a wood filler to fill the gaps before laying the new floorcovering on top.
- Using the access: if floorboards do have to be taken up, draw a plan of the pipe and wire network below floor level. This knowledge will be useful for knowing where cuts can and cannot be made for any future refurbishing projects.
- Like for like: where a damaged board is in the centre of an exposed floor area, replacing it with a new board will result in the repair standing out against the surrounding floor and this will spoil the overall look. In cases like this, take up an old, but sound, board from under an item of furniture or a rug and use this to make the repair. A new board can then be used to patch the area below the furniture or rug where it will not be seen.

REPAIRING SKIRTING BOARDS

S kirting boards provide the decorative trim for most rooms and, if they are to show off the room to best advantage, they need to be in good condition. Therefore, repairing any damaged sections of skirting board is essential. The technique required to repair it depends on whether it is minor or major damage.

SMALL HOLES

Minor damage such as small nicks and scrapes, all of which are the result of everyday wear and tear, can be simply filled with an all-purpose filler, then sanded back to a smooth finish before decorating. For slightly larger holes, it is advisable to use a different technique to ensure that the repair will be a long-lasting one. Such repairs are needed when fixtures are removed from a skirting board position or, as shown in the example below, some pipes have been rerouted, leaving unsightly holes in the skirting.

1 Mix some proprietary wood filler and press it firmly into the holes. Wood filler is much harder than all-purpose filler and does not shrink when applied in areas such as this. Because it dries to such a hard finish, make sure that the filler does not sit higher than the holes, as it can be a lengthy process to sand it back.

2 Once it has dried, use some fine-grade abrasive paper to remove any excess filler from the skirting surface and provide it with a key for the next step.

3 Apply a thin skim of fine surface filler over the holes to give the best possible finish. Leave the filler to dry, then sand again with fine-grade abrasive paper before painting.

Large Holes

For large holes in the skirting, or areas that are damaged beyond a simple filling repair, some form of replacement will be necessary. While it is possible to cut out sections of skirting, this can be a difficult and very time-consuming process. It is much easier to replace the entire length of skirting. Unless the skirting is particularly ornate, it is relatively inexpensive to buy and, by using a new length along a wall, the finish is certain to be much better than trying to camouflage a patched area.

1 Use a hammer and brick chisel to prise the skirting away from the wall. Try not to damage the wall area above the skirting while carrying out this process.

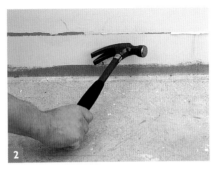

2 Remove any old nails from the skirting area, otherwise these will interfere with the new length once it is attached. A new section can now be cut and secured; if lengths need to be joined, it will be necessary to follow Steps 3 and 4, below.

3 If you need to join lengths of skirting, mitre the joining end of the new length and secure it to the wall. Apply some wood glue to the cut end of the length.

4 Attach the next length, and join it to the first board, having measured and cut the opposite mitre so that the two pieces fit together. Hammer in small nails or brads to make the joint secure and prevent it from splitting open at a later date.

REPAIRING DAMAGE TO A CEILING

A ceiling can suffer the same wear and tear as a wall, but it may also be damaged by a leak. Make sure you repair the cause of the leak and let the ceiling dry before making a repair to it.

PATCHING PLASTERBOARD

A small hole can be covered with plasterer's glass-fibre patching tape and coated with a cellulose filler, but a hole larger than 9 cm (3½ in) requires a backing piece to serve as a base for the filler.

1 Cut a plasterboard patch 2.5 cm (1 in) larger than the damaged area, and drill a hole through the middle. Slip a length of string 15 cm (6 in) long through it, and tie a nail to the string on the back side of the board. The nail will prevent the string exiting the hole.

2 Apply plaster filler around the edges of the front of the plasterboard, then slip the piece through the hole—the front side of the board should face outward. Use the string to pull the board against the back of the plasterboard surrounding the hole, then pull the string taut and let the filler set.

3 Apply a layer of plaster filler to bring the patch almost flush with the surface. Allow the filler to nearly set before cutting off the string and adding a final filler layer flush with the surface. After the filler is dry, sand it smooth (see pages 16–17).

REPAIRING LATH AND PLASTER

Most older houses were constructed with lath-and-plaster ceilings. How a hole is filled depends on its size and the condition of the laths. If the laths are not broken, coat them with diluted PVA adhesive before filling the repair. If the laths are broken and the hole measures less than 7.5 cm (3 in) across, simply push scrunched-up newspaper into it to serve as a backing before plastering the hole. Where a hole is more than 7.5 cm (3 in) across, you'll need to use fine expanded metal mesh as a backing, as below.

1 Use an old paint brush to remove any dust and debris from the areas to be repaired, wearing safety goggles and a dust mask.

2 If the laths are damaged, use tinsnips (a metal cutting tool) to trim some expanded metal mesh to size. Then fit the mesh in place by curling its edges around the back of the laths. The mesh is flexible, so this should be easy to do.

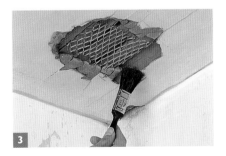

3 Use a bolster chisel and club hammer to undercut the edges of the hole so that the plaster will have a better grip (see pages 16–17). Make sure you do this gently to avoid creating any further damage. Once again, use the old paint brush to remove any debris.

4 Place an excess of plaster filler onto a float and push it up into the repair until it is flat against the ceiling, forcing the paster through the holes in the mesh; slide the float over the repair. Scrape off as much excess plaster as you can and sand it smooth when the filler is dry.

DEALING WITH CRACKS AND STAINS

S uperficial cracks and small dents in plaster can be repaired quickly with a cellulose or acrylic filler. If there are a lot of fine hairline cracks, cover a plaster surface with lining paper.

REPAIRING CRACKS

Not all cracks should be filled with cellulose fillers. Normal seasonal movement of the house structure can cause cracks at joints. If cracks are where the walls meet the ceiling, the real answer is to hide them by attaching coving (see pages 44–45). Cracks above a skirting board or around window and door frames need a mastic sealant. It remains flexible, so it keeps the gap closed despite any further movement. Minor damage in a decorative plaster cornice or ceiling rose can be repaired using a small artist's clay-modelling tool and a cellulose filler. However, most ornate repairs are best left to the professional.

1 Using the edge of a pointed putty knife, "undercut" the crack—the idea is to widen the crack below the surface, forming an inverted V cavity, with the point of the V exposed to the surface. This will help the filler stay in place.

2 Remove any loose debris from the work area with an old paint brush. Using a flexible putty knife, firmly press the filler into the crack, forcing it into the cavity.

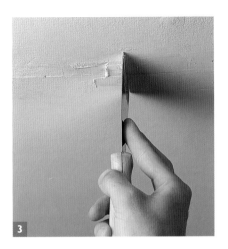

3 Hold the putty knife at an angle perpendicular to the work and scrape away the excess filler, but leave it slightly protruding from the surface. A more experienced person can smooth the filler level with the surface. Let the filler dry.

4 A wood or cork sanding block will help you achieve a smooth finish. Wrap a piece of fine wet and dry sandpaper around the sanding block and, holding it flat against the work, sand the filler until it is flush with the surface.

TREATING STAINS

Most stains are due to water damage or tobacco smoke. Stains seep through paint, but you can prime a water stain (see below). For a room stained by tobacco smoke, try a strong sugar soap solution on painted surfaces. If it doesn't work, you'll have to remove the paint. Wallpaper must be stripped (see pages 184–185).

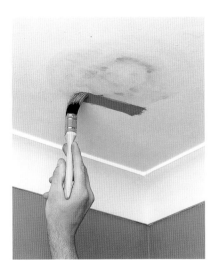

For a water stain, you can apply a coat of aluminium primer sealer, available in large cans or small aerosols. However, first deal with the cause of the problem, such as a plumbing leak, and allow the ceiling to dry before applying it. The primer will seal the surface and form a good base for paint.

REPAIRING WOODEN WINDOWS

W et rot, which softens the wood, usually attacks window sills and the lowest frame member (rail) of softwood windows, where rainwater can collect. If the damage is serious, the only solution is to replace the frame; however, you can repair the damage if you catch it early by using a wood repair kit. Dry rot requires specialist help.

DEALING WITH WET ROT

1 First determine the extent of the damage by poking the rotten area with a sharp pointed tool such as an awl. This will go easily into rotten areas. Use a chisel to remove all the affected wood until you reach solid wood (this ensures that all the rotten wood is removed).

2 If the wood is still damp, use a heat gun to dry it out, but keep it away from the glass to avoid cracking it. Brush on a wood hardener (follow the manufacturer's instructions); let dry. If necessary, apply a second coat. Some wood hardeners contain a preservative; work it into the wood.

3 If the kit provides preservative pellets, drill holes in the sound wood. The holes should be the same diameter and slightly longer than the pellets. Insert the pellets into the holes, pushing them just below the surface. Fill the holes with an exterior filler, allowing it to slightly protrude from the surface.

4 Whether or not you use pellets, mix together the resin-base wood filler and its hardener; apply it with a putty knife, leaving it just raised from the surface. You may have to apply the filler in two layers; mix a little at a time, and wait for the first layer to set before applying the second one. When it has dried, sand it flush with the surface.

GENERAL MAINTENANCE PROBLEMS

- Rising damp: moisture coming up from the ground causes rising damp. Symptoms are damp patches low on the wall, often accompanied by a "tidemark." A house has an impermeable layer, called a damp-proof course (DPC), built into the walls 30 cm (12 in) above ground level to help prevent rising damp. If you suspect your DPC is damaged, there are some do-it-yourself treatments but it is best to opt for a professional company to install a new course where needed.

- Penetrating damp: other places where water can enter a house are through a damaged roof, around windows and doors, and through older masonry. The signs of penetrating damp are often worse after rain. Remedies include replacing roofs tiles and leaking gutters, for example, or painting exterior walls with a silicone or polyurethane sealant.

- Condensation: although a different problem, condensation is sometimes incorrectly diagnosed as penetrating damp. It occurs when warm, moist air contacts a cold surface—such as an outside wall or glass window pane—and is cooled, depositing water droplets. The typical symptoms of condensation are mildew and random damp patches on walls, which usually become worse in cold weather. Treatment will depend on the cause. It may simply be a matter of heating a cold room, adding ventilation in a bathroom or kitchen (or a blocked chimney), or insulating an attic or cold water pipes.

- Woodworm: this is a type of insect that will attack all structural wood in the house. The exit holes are easy to spot and an infestation is simple to treat with manufacturer's liquids if caught early.

- Wet rot: this is a type of fungi and occurs in damp wood, such as in window frames and exterior wood. After treating the cause of the damp, dig out the damaged wood and replace it.

- Dry rot: this is also a fungi but is more serious. Once established, it can transfer from wet wood to dry wood. It can cause severe structural damage and should be treated only by a professional. Signs of its presence are cracks across the wood grain, a musty smell, and growths like cotton wool and mushroom on the wood. It is often discovered in poorly ventilated areas such as basements or under floorboards.

- Subsidence: two of the causes of subsidence are the ground below the house drying out in a drought and the roots of a nearby tree draining water from the ground. The signs are wide cracks in the walls, especially near windows and doors, and splitting bricks. You must call in professional help and may need to have the foundation of the house underpinned.

REPLACING WINDOW PANES

Replacing cracked or broken glass isn't difficult, but it takes time and great care is needed to avoid cutting yourself. If you doubt your ability to do the job, cover the opening securely (for example, with plywood), remove the window from its frame, then take it to a glazier for replacement panes. Even if you feel capable of replacing the pane yourself, have the glass cut to size where you buy it. There are several thicknesses of glass, so make sure you buy the right type.

1 Remove the window from its frame, and lay it down (exterior side up) on a worktop covered with a protective cloth. Using a chisel or a glazier's knife, remove the old putty. You'll come across glazier's clips holding the glass in place; remove them with pincers. Wearing thick gloves, pull the glass from the frame.

2 Wearing safety glasses to protect your eyes, use a chisel and mallet to remove the remaining large pieces of old putty from the bottom of the rebates in the frame—make sure you avoid cutting into the wood.

3 Use a scraper to clear the thin residue of putty from the frame rebates. When completely clean, carefully gather up and dispose of the old broken glass. Give the rebates a coat of wood primer. Measure for the new pane of glass, allowing 3 mm (1/8 in) clearance on all sides.

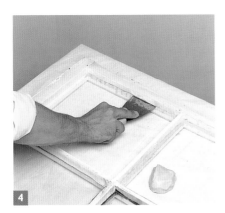

4 When the primer has dried, knead the putty in your hands until it is pliable; run a bead 3–5 mm (⅛ inch to ¼ inch) thick around the bottom of the rebates. Use a putty knife to press it down flat, trimming off any excess that hangs over the edge.

5 Insert the glass into the frame, leaving a 3 mm (⅛ in) gap all around. Gently press the glass firmly into place along its edges—never the centre—until putty squeezes out of the inside of the window. Use glazier's sprigs or clips to secure the glass in place. Using the flat end of a hammer, press the clips into place (do not hit them as you would nails).

6 Knead the putty and roll it into a thin sausage shape. Starting at one corner, lay the putty down and push it against the sides of the rebates in the frame. Continue in this way completely around the frame.

7 To make a smooth bevel in the putty, hold a putty knife at a 45° angle, with its straight edge on the putty, and pull the knife along. To mitre each corner, place the knife diagonally in the centre, and pull it away from the corner. Use the knife to remove any putty left on the glass. Allow the putty to dry for at least a week before painting.

REPAIRING DOOR FRAMES

M ost repairs to internal door frames are usually simple. For example, problems with rattling doors or damaged door frames are easy to solve with basic carpentry skills.

COMMON DOOR PROBLEMS

- Rattling door: a rattling door can be repaired by repositioning the striker plate of the door latch. Unscrew the plate, then use a chisel to enlarge the width of the recess on the side closest to the door stop. Drill out the screw holes and glue in dowels. After the glue dries, drill new pilot holes and screw in the plate.
- Loose frame: first try tightening or replacing any existing screws. If the frame has been nailed in place, add a few screws. In a masonry wall, you'll also need to add wall plugs. If the frame is fitted to a partition wall, drill and countersink a hole into the door stop. Have a helper hold the frame in place; drill a smaller diameter hole through the frame into the stud, then drive in a 7.5-cm (3-in) long screw. Cover the screw

head with wood filler; once dry, sand and paint it.
- Loose hinge screws: first try tightening them. If they won't hold, fit bigger screws—either the same gauge but longer or, if the hinge holes are big enough, a larger gauge of the same length. If you can't get the screws tight, drill out the holes and add dowels. Drill pilot holes into the dowels to take new screws for the hinges.
- Sticking door: A door may bind if the hinge is recessed into the door frame too deeply. To rectify this, so the door hangs farther away from the frame, remove the door from the frame. Cut a piece of cardboard the same size as the hinge leaf and insert it into the recess; then rehang the door. See also page 49.

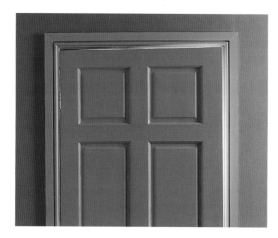

NEW FOR OLD
With a coat or two of paint, a new architrave can improve the overall look of a tired door frame.

REPLACING THE ARCHITRAVE

Old architrave surrounding a door may eventually need replacing. When buying new architrave, remember to measure each length to the end of the mitred corner.

1 Insert the tip of a utility knife blade between the architrave and door frame. Slowly pull the knife down to break the skin of the paint. Repeat on the other pieces of architrave. Use a broad-blade chisel to pry off the architrave. Clean the exposed area with sandpaper.

2 Mark a right angle 6 mm (1/4 in) away from the top corner of the frame. Align a length of architrave at the vertical line, with its end above where the horizontal length will be. Make a mark on the piece at the point where the two pencil lines meet. Repeat at the other side of the frame.

3 Use a mitre frame and saw to cut mitres at the marks—they indicate the lowest end of the mitre. Nail the lengths in place. Hold a length of architrave across their tops. With a ruler at the outside edge of one vertical length of architrave, mark the top of the horizontal length. Repeat at the other side; use these marks to cut mitres.

4 As with the vertical lengths, drive nails through the front of the horizontal length and into the frame. To hold the corners together, nail down through the top of the horizontal length into the vertical one at each side. Drive the nail heads down with a nail punch, and cover them with wood filler. After it dries, sand and paint the architrave.

REPAIRING STAIRS AND BALUSTRADES

T he staircase and its accompanying balustrade is the most complex piece of carpentry in the house, and, as time goes by, it can develop a variety of faults, primarily caused by daily wear and tear.

FIXING A SQUEAKY STEP

1 If you cannot get below the stairs, drill a hole smaller than the screw through the tread and into the top of the riser. Drill a larger hole into the tread for the shank of the screw, then countersink the top of the hole to accept the screw head. Install the screw.

2 You can use a store-bought wood plug to cover the screw head, or make one yourself—use a bit specifically designed to cut plugs. Dab some wood glue onto the plug and tap it into place; then chisel it flush with the tread.

FIXING A DAMAGED NOSING

1 Mark out the area to be removed, making sure the back edge is parallel with the nosing but does not reach the riser. Using a jigsaw, cut into the nosing and, to release the strip, along the back edge. Then use a tenon saw to make cuts at right angles to the back edge.

2 Cut a patch of replacement wood, with the grain running lengthwise, to fit the shape of the cut-out, then glue and screw it into place, countersinking the screws. Using a block plane or wood rasp, shape the patch to match the profile of the nosing.

SECURING A LOOSE BALUSTER

If a baluster is loose, you can tighten it by skew-nailing. Drive an oval nail into the stringer below or handrail above at a 45° angle. Use a nail punch to sink the nail below the surface. Cover the nail head with acrylic filler if the repair will be painted or wood filler if it will be varnished.

REPAIRING A SPLIT BALUSTER

A strong impact is usually responsible for cracking a baluster. To repair it, open up the split and squirt in some wood glue. Then bind the split firmly by wrapping utility tape around it. Leave the tape in place for 24 hours, until the glue is dry.

REPLACING A BALUSTER

1 Pry out the broken sections. Using a sliding T bevel, transfer the angles of the stringer and handrail to the new baluster. Finding one that matches can be difficult. If a mismatch will be noticeable, remove one from a less conspicuous area, but first make sure it will fit in the new site.

2 Trim the baluster along the marks with a tenon saw. Then work it carefully into place and skew-nail it to the stringer and handrail (see Securing a loose baluster).

HOME MAINTENANCE

O ne of the most important aspects of home improvement is ensuring that your house is well maintained and that all the services and warning systems are working. Many of the areas of concern are listed below, with suggestions for how to check them.

HOME CHECKLIST

- Water meters: it usually becomes apparent very quickly when there is a water leak in the home, but outside the home this can be less obvious. A monthly check of your water meter to see how many units are being used will soon show if there might be a leak between the main water-supply pipe and where it enters your home.
- Electrics: the fuses in the electrical wiring system act as the warning for any problems with outlets or appliances. Most electricity suppliers offer a free electrical check service and advice on whether any wiring should be updated or renewed.
- Gas: any problems with gas become apparent very quickly because of its smell. Never take any chances with gas, and if you do detect a leak, call your local supplier immediately. All gas appliances should be regularly maintained. Central heating systems should be serviced once or twice a year, depending on the make. Read the installation and instruction manuals for all your gas appliances to check when they need servicing. Never try to service appliances yourself—always use a professional.
- Security alarms: intruder alarms are becoming a very popular addition to most homes, and it is important that they function properly so that they can do their job should the need ever arise. The maintenance of such systems varies, but most are very simple and quick to check. Use your operation manual for guidelines.
- Smoke alarms: these are one of the simplest yet most effective safety mechanisms and are essential in every household. Battery-operated alarms tend to have an alert noise if the battery is running low. As a further safety check, they can be tested manually with a button that will set off the alarm briefly to make sure that it is working. Don't take risks—check alarms weekly.
- Carbon monoxide alarms: because carbon monoxide has no aroma, high levels in the home cannot be detected by smell. Special alarms have been developed to solve this problem. Most are electrically operated, and it is important to pay particular attention to the manufacturer's guidelines on where they should be installed in the home. As with smoke detectors, the alarm can be tested manually with a button that will set off the alarm briefly to check that it is working correctly.

Simple Maintenance

Many household problems can be avoided by following simple maintenance guidelines. Some have already been discussed on the opposite page, but the examples below show other areas where general maintenance can help to prevent problems from occurring at a later date.

MAINTENANCE GUIDELINES

- Lubrication: it is always a good idea to keep your water supply valves well lubricated. Then if you have to turn off the water in an area of the home, or for the whole house, the water supply valve will turn easily. Proprietary aerosol lubricants are best for this purpose. This method of lubrication can also be applied to household locks, to ensure they remain in good working order.
- Drainage systems: make sure that all the drains and the flow of waste out of the house is an efficiently functioning system. Use a proprietary drain cleaner from time to time to keep the waste pipes in good working order.
- Gutters and downspouts: these areas must keep water flowing, otherwise blockages and drips can cause damp problems on internal walls. Make sure that the gutters are cleared seasonally to ensure that water flow is always maintained.
- General cleaning: on a decorative level, painted and papered surfaces will deteriorate much faster if they are not kept clean. This also applies to floorcoverings. Regular cleaning will increase the life span of all these surfaces in the home.

Emergencies

However vigilant you are about maintenance in your home, from time to time it may be necessary to deal with an emergency, and it is important to have some sort of action plan to deal with such occasions. The following checklist provides excellent guidance, showing you the best way to be prepared for any unwelcome emergencies.

EMERGENCY CHECKLIST

- Telephone numbers: keep a list of emergency telephone numbers in a safe place that is known to all the household members. As well as emergency services, this list should contain numbers for professional plumbers and electricians.
- Supply switches and valves: stay aware of the places where all the household supply systems can be turned off in an emergency.
- Escape routes: make sure that the household is able to deal with fire emergencies and that escape routes are kept clear. Your local fire safety officer can provide advice on the particular needs of your home and any necessary improvements.

DEALING WITH LEAKING TAPS

Leaky taps are a frequent and annoying problem in bathrooms and kitchens. Fortunately, they are usually an easy problem to fix, and one that takes little time and expense. The most common cause of a leaking tap is a broken or corroded washer, or one with a hairline crack. No matter what the tap design, the water must be turned off at the shutoff valve (stopcock) that feeds the tap. The tap can then be opened to drain off any water in the pipe system. Only when this is done, can you work on the tap to replace its washer.

REMOVING THE TAP HEAD

Designs vary, but in most cases the actual tap head is held on by a small grub screw, which can be undone to release the head. The screw may be hidden by a cover cap, as shown below. Once the head is removed, the internal workings are revealed. Some taps will have an extra cover, or shroud, that will need to be unscrewed before you can replace the washer.

1 Prize off the cover cap with a straight-bladed screwdriver, and undo the retaining screw that holds the tap head in place.

2 The washer is still hidden by the headgear of the tap. Use an adjustable wrench to grip the headgear nut and undo it slowly to remove the headgear. If the nut does not move easily and greater effort is required, make sure that you support the rest of the tap mechanism with your other hand to avoid damaging any of the tap parts.

CHANGING THE WASHER

Once the headgear has been removed, the washer can be clearly seen, and replacing it is straightforward. In some cases, the old washer can be prized directly off the bottom of the headgear; in the example below, a small fixing nut is used to hold the washer in place.

1 Undo the fixing nut with long-nosed pliers. Because this nut is so small, it is easily lost so be sure to put it in a safe place before refitting.

2 Carefully prize out the damaged washer with a straight-bladed screwdriver.

3 Clip in a new washer, making sure that it is the correct size, and fits tightly in position. Refit the fixing nut, and screw the headgear back into the main tap body. Once the tap head is back in place, close the tap before turning the water supply back on. If the washer has been installed correctly, the drip will be cured.

ADJUSTING TOILET CISTERNS

The main problems found with toilet tanks either involve constantly dripping overflow pipes, or insufficient water to expel all material from the bowl when the toilet is flushed. Both cases are linked to the water level in the tank; this is easily adjustable since nearly all tank levels are based on the same system, built around an air-filled float. This float rises and falls with the water level, shutting a valve to prevent water from flowing into the tank when the water level is high, and opening the valve when water level is low (after flushing). The air-filled float is positioned on the end of an arm, and there are two main methods of adjusting the level at which the arm shuts off the incoming water flow.

Traditional ball cocks: traditional air-filled floats, often called ball cocks, can be adjusted by bending the metal arm so that the ball cock changes its level in the water. Alternatively, as shown here, its height can be adjusted by loosening a small nut, which then allows the ball cock to be moved up and down a small vertical stretch of the arm, again changing its level in the water.

Plastic arms: some air-filled floats are held in position with plastic arms. In this case, adjustment tends to be at the other end of the arm, close to the valve controlling water flow. These arms are normally adjusted by using long-nosed pliers to change the position of a small nut on the arm, which increases or decreases the level at which the air-filled float will shut off the water supply to the tank.

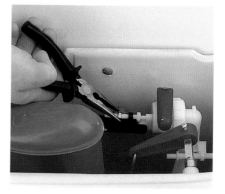

BATH WASTE SYSTEMS

B ath waste systems vary considerably, but most are based on a design which takes water out of the bath through a U-bend or trap and out into the main sewage system. Blockages and leaks occur because of problems in this simple system. Dealing with any problems is relatively simple as long as you understand the way in which such systems interconnect. This diagram shows a standard bath waste system and the areas that can cause potential problems.

Bath Waste System

Leakages can be caused by:

Holes or corrosion of the overflow seal. The solution is to unscrew the overflow outlet system and run a bead of silicone around the overflow hole, before repositioning the overflow outlet system.

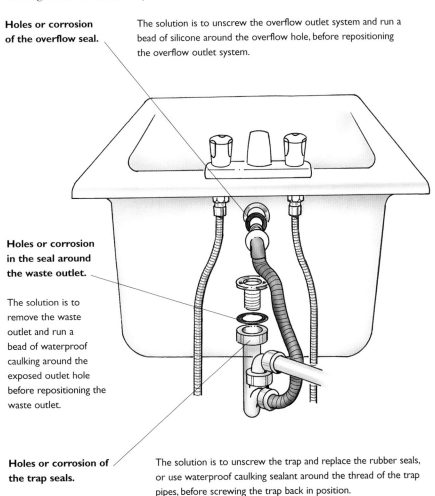

Holes or corrosion in the seal around the waste outlet.

The solution is to remove the waste outlet and run a bead of waterproof caulking around the exposed outlet hole before repositioning the waste outlet.

Holes or corrosion of the trap seals. The solution is to unscrew the trap and replace the rubber seals, or use waterproof caulking sealant around the thread of the trap pipes, before screwing the trap back in position.

GENERAL BATHROOM MAINTENANCE

There are many simple plumbing jobs that come under the heading of general maintenance, and these small tasks can help to keep the bathroom functioning efficiently. Problems occur when water is either not flowing at all, or not flowing as well as it should be.

DESCALING A SHOWERHEAD

Most shower flow problems result from the showerhead becoming blocked with mineral deposits—this is particularly common in areas with hard water. Fortunately, there is a simple way of clearing this problem and returning the showerhead water flow back to its proper efficiency level.

1 Unscrew the showerhead to remove the perforated plate.

2 Wearing protective gloves, scrub the plate with some descaling fluid using an old toothbrush. If it is badly blocked up, soak the entire plate in a bowl of descaling fluid overnight. Rinse the plate thoroughly after it has been in contact with descaling fluid.

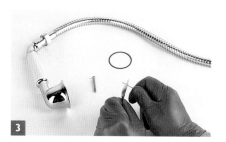

3 Use a pin to remove any small deposits in the perforations of the plate, but do not use this method if the plate has an integral plastic diaphragm, as this could be damaged by a pin. Reassemble the showerhead to see if waterflow has improved.

UNBLOCKING TOILETS

Toilets are one of the more common bathroom outlets that become blocked from time to time. As soon as you notice that flushing is less efficient than normal, or waste is not being carried away with the usual ease, it is likely that a blockage is building up. It is always best to rectify the problem right away—leave the blockage too long and major work will almost certainly be required. The solution is usually very simple.

Using a plunger: a simple plunger can often deal with minor blockages. Push it down into the bottom of the toilet bowl and plunge the handle up and down vigorously to create suction between the plunger head and the sides of the bowl. This puts water pressure on the blockage in the pipe and eventually moves it out of the way.

SINK WASTE

It is worth clearing sink waste traps from time to time since they do become blocked with small bits of debris and a buildup of silt. The design of the waste pipe does vary, but in general there are obvious areas in the trap that are meant to be unscrewed to dispose of any debris and dirt buildup.

1 Unscrew the trap, taking care not to twist the rest of the outlet pipe structure and risk fracturing any of the seals.

2 The bottom of the trap should contain water but it ought to be relatively clean. If the water is dirty or there is debris at the bottom, clear it out, then screw back the trap.

RE-ENAMELLING A BATH

Re-enamelling a bath sounds like a daunting task, and, until recently, this would have been a fairly accurate sentiment, since there were no easy-to-use systems available for carrying out this recoating process. However, the situation has changed and various proprietary products are now available. Before trying one, make sure that the new enamel coating is suitable for your bath—most should only be used on previously enameled surfaces or porcelain ones.

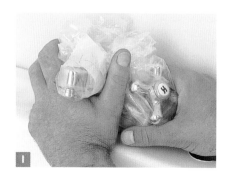

1 Mask all taps and other fixtures on the bath, using plastic dust sheets. This has two functions: firstly, it keeps the taps clean and, secondly, it stops any enamel drips from falling on the bath surface.

2 Use an electric sander to rub down the entire bath surface. Use the finest grade abrasive paper, as you do not want to make deep cuts in the bath surface. Wear a respiratory mask while carrying out this process.

3 Clean the bath surface thoroughly with a mild detergent, then rinse with clean water. Leave the bath to dry completely before finally wiping over the surface with a rag dampened with mineral spirits. This evaporates quickly to leave a totally clean bath surface ready for painting. Mask off the surrounding bath area with some masking tape.

4 Use proprietary bath enamel to spray even coats over the entire bath surface. Wear a respiratory mask while applying the enamel. Manufacturers' guidelines vary, but normally three or four thin coats will produce a good finish. Allow plenty of drying time between the coats. Remove the masking tape when the last coat has dried.

BATH RESTORATION
Re-enamelling is particularly appropriate for older roll-top baths that have suffered surface deterioration over the years. Restoring them to their original look can be a very satisfying process. The process does not have to be confined to baths—sinks and shower trays can be re-enamelled as long as they have a suitable surface.

TOUCHING-IN

In many cases, re-enamelling the bath is too extreme a measure, especially if the damage is slight. Any small nicks or scrapes in the surface can normally be touched-in very effectively with a small paint brush, using the appropriate colour of oil-based eggshell-finish paint. It may be necessary to add an extra coat, since it is better to apply two thin coats than one thick one.

PLUMBING SOLUTIONS

W ith plumbing systems, it is always good to know how the basic system works so that, when there is a problem, the correct course of action can be taken. In some cases, you will need to call in the professionals, but there are other situations where you may be able to solve the problem yourself.

SOLVING PROBLEMS

- Corroded nuts: if you are trying to undo any pipe joints that are particularly stiff, try loosening them with some proprietary aerosol easing spray.
- Cold radiator: if a water-filled radiator is not giving off much heat, it is possible that the thermostat is turned down too low or is broken. Before replacing it, bleed the radiator to check that there is no air trapped in the system, preventing the radiator from warming up. In a pressurized central heating system, take care when bleeding radiators as it may be necessary to build the pressure back up in the system once it has been bled. Check your boiler instructions to see if this is the case.
- Frequent washer trouble: when washers on taps keep giving trouble, it can be due to excess water pressure. Try turning down the stopcock slightly to reduce this pressure.
- Water too hot or cold: all water-heating systems have a controlling thermostat. Temperature problems with hot water can normally be traced to the thermostat, which should be adjusted as required. Check your heating installation instructions for detailed advice on thermostatic control in your system.
- Testing stopcocks: in emergencies, it may be necessary to turn off the water supply. It is vital to test stopcocks from time to time to check that they are functioning correctly; otherwise, when an emergency does arise, it may not be possible to turn the water off.
- Knowing a plumber: plumbers are well-trained professionals, and most plumbing jobs should be left to them. Find a plumber through personal recommendation, and keep the phone number handy for both emergencies and advice. Always remember that, if you are in any doubt about attempting a plumbing job, it is best to call a professional.

2
ADDING CHARACTER TO YOUR HOME

Once the essential repairs are complete, it is time to turn to the areas of your home where you can get creative in your attempts to add character and style. While most houses have the essential basics, improving on them can produce a much more comfortable living environment, reflecting your personal preferences and tastes. Many changes can be achieved with very straightforward projects that can be completed in a relatively short time. Even simple changes can be very effective, illustrating that it is not always necessary to undertake major structural work in order to achieve an exciting new look.

WOODEN RAILS

A dding a picture rail or dado trim to a room is one way of breaking up wall surfaces and adding interest to the decoration as a whole. A picture rail is particularly appropriate in rooms with high ceilings since it can be used to help "bring down" the level of the ceiling. Wooden dado trim can be used in nearly all rooms and makes an excellent division for separating different wall finishes and colours, or it can be seen simply as a design feature in its own right.

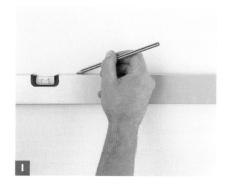

1 Draw a level guideline around the perimeter of the room. For dado trim, a suitable position is one metre (yard) from the floor.

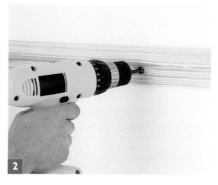

2 Hold the dado trim with its base along the pencil guideline and drill through it into the wall. Open up the entrance to the drilled hole with a countersink drill bit.

3 Insert a wall anchor and screw, knocking it into place with a hammer. Leave about one-third of the length of the screw visible.

4 Screw it into place, ensuring that the head of the screw sits below the level of the wood.

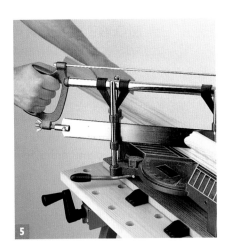

5 Measure and cut any corners in the trim using a mitre saw.

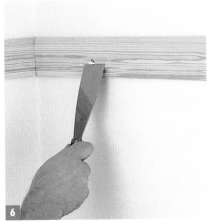

6 Fill the screwhead holes using all-purpose filler. Apply it so that it is slightly higher than the surface to allow for shrinkage as it dries.

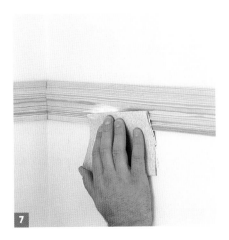

7 Sand the filled holes to give them a smooth finish that is level with the rest of the wooden trim.

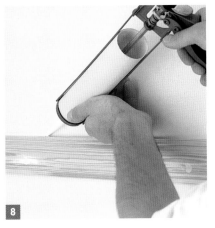

8 Run a bead of caulking around the top and bottom edges of the trim and along the corner junctions, then smooth it with a wet finger to give a neat finish, ready for painting.

SKIRTING

M ost rooms need skirting boards because they act as decorative trim or division between walls and floors. There are different styles of skirting—your choice is a matter of personal preference. It is a straightforward job to remove existing skirting and replace it with new, and although it might be necessary to redecorate wall surfaces afterward, this can be seen as part of the remodelling process.

CUTTING CORNERS

In order to fit new skirting, you need to be able to cut corners in it. Internal corners are cut in exactly the same way as dado trim (see page 39). At external corners, the skirting should be measured and attached as shown below.

1 To measure the corner accurately, position the skirting board for one wall at a time in place, and mark the exact apex of the corner on the board with a pencil.

2 Using a mitre block or specially designed mitre saw, cut the marked lengths of skirting.

3 Hold the two mitre joints together at the external corner by nailing panel pins along the joint. This will prevent the skirting joint from easing open over time.

SCRIBING SKIRTING BOARDS

Floors that undulate, or are not level, can pose a problem because the factory-made edge of the skirting will not sit flush along the floor surface. This makes it necessary to fit the bottom edge of the skirting board more precisely to the uneven floor profile. This is achieved by a process known as "scribing."

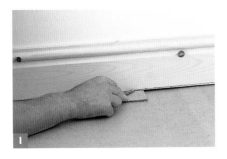 

1 Cut a small block of wood the same height as the largest gap between the base of the skirting board and the floor. Hold a pencil on top of the block and run the block along the entire length, making a guideline that should imitate the curvature of the floor.

2 Clamp the skirting board to the workbench, and use a wood plane to remove shavings of wood as far as the pencil guideline. Attach the skirting to the wall, with the base of the length of board flush with the undulating profile of the floor.

SECURING SKIRTING BOARDS

Skirting can be secured with nails or screws, depending on the nature of the wall that it is being fixed to. Wire nails are ideal for drywall, whereas masonry nails are ideal for solid block walls, although there can be a tendency for skirting boards to "bounce" away from the wall surface if the nails do not hold it securely. Wall plugs and screws, although more time consuming, tend to produce a firmer, longer-lasting attachment.

Using screws: drill some pilot holes and use all-purpose concrete anchor screws, or wall plugs and screws as shown here. Knock the plug and screw into place with a hammer before finally screwing tightly in position.

Using nails: make sure that you punch in nails after they have been hammered in. This way the holes can be filled and sanded to a flat, smooth surface before the skirting boards are painted.

PANELLING

P anelling is another method of adding character to wall surfaces. It can be applied over entire walls, or just up to dado level. Most panelling needs to be secured to a framework that acts as a level base, otherwise any slight unevenness in a wall surface will be accentuated by the finished panel.

MAKING A FRAME

A framework needs to be substantial enough to support the panelling, but not so intrusive that it brings the panelling too far away from the wall surface. The ideal material for frame construction is 5-by-2.5-cm (2-by-1-in) battens.

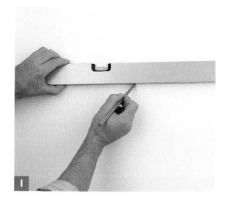

1 Make a level pencil guideline on the wall at the height you want your panelling to reach.

2 Attach a length of wooden batten horizontally, using the pencil line as a guide for the top of the batten.

3 Continue to add battens down the wall, ensuring that they all run parallel. For dado panelling, three or four battens are all that are required. Make sure that the bottom batten sits close to the floor surface.

INSTALLING PANELLING

There are different types of panelling available, but tongue-and-groove provides an effective and neat finish. It can either be applied as single strips, joined to make a continuous surface, or specially routed medium-density-fibreboard (MDF) sheets can be cut down to size and installed.

Secret nailing: apply single tongue-and-groove lengths vertically, slotting the groove of each new length over the tongue of the previous one. Secure each length in position by nailing at a 45-degree angle through the tongue and into the wooden batten below. Use a punch to push the nailhead below the surface of the wood, so that every fixing is hidden when the next tongue-and-groove length along is added.

Using sheets: large sheets of tongue-and-groove MDF panelling can be used to cover frameworks very quickly, but they can be more expensive, so you need to weigh the cost against the time advantage.

FINISHING OFF

Whichever type of panelling is used, you will always need to make finishing touches to complete the effect before you decorate it. As well as adding skirting board to the base of the panelling, creating a decorative edge at dado trim height is also important.

1 Attach another length of batten along the top edge of the panelling. Screw it directly into the top horizontal batten used for the initial frame.

2 Pin a half-round decorative moulding to the front edge of the batten to create an attractive curved edge. Fill the panelling surface and edges, as required, before decorating.

COVING

In much the same way that skirting boards add a decorative edge at floor level, coving complements this finish at ceiling level. It also rounds off the sharp edge of a wall/ceiling junction, giving a more elegant and shapely look to a wall surface. There are many different types and styles of coving available—they can be made from polystyrene, or various plaster bases, but the most authentic period styles tend to be made from fibrous plaster. Always use the adhesive recommended by the manufacturer for applying coving to the ceiling. The tricky part of coving application is mitring the corners, whether external or internal. However, manufacturers usually supply a custom-made template or mitre block, which can be used for making whichever mitre is required for a particular joint.

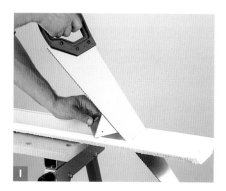

1 Measure the length of coving required and cut it to size, using the mitre block positioned across the coving width. Keep the saw tight against the block as you cut, to ensure the correct angle of cut and gradient through the length of coving.

2 Apply coving adhesive generously to the top and bottom edges of the length. A scraper is the ideal tool for applying the adhesive.

3 Press the length of coving firmly in position at the wall/ceiling junction, making sure that the edge of the coving on the ceiling extends onto the ceiling the same distance as the edge of the coving on the wall extends onto the wall.

4 Hammer in a number of nails below the coving to support its weight while it dries.

5 Use a damp sponge to remove excess adhesive from the coving surface before it dries.

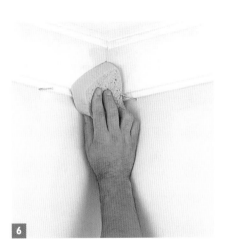

6 Fill in all the cracks at the ceiling and wall junction with adhesive. Fill any gaps at the mitred junction of the corner once the next length of coving has been applied.

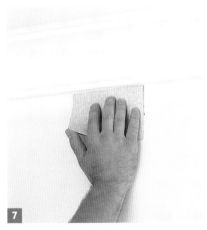

7 Once the adhesive is dry, remove the supporting nails and fill any holes. Finally, sand away any rough areas of adhesive before decorating the walls and ceiling.

PLASTER FRAMES AND ROSES

O ther plaster-based accessories that can be used to add character to rooms include frames and ceiling roses. Most are applied with coving adhesive, but some need extra support to keep them in place.

MAKING A FRAME

Plaster frames are a good way of highlighting features, or creating display areas on a wall space. They can be used around alcoves to add greater depth; on a flat wall area, they can be painted to provide an excellent decorative detail on an otherwise bland surface.

I Draw a wall panel with a pencil, ensuring that it is totally square by using a level.

2 Cut the horizontal and vertical lengths to size, apply adhesive, and position them using the pencil lines as guides. Hammer in nails to support each length, as required.

3 Apply adhesive to the corner blocks and position them. Once the frame has dried, remove the nails and fill any holes, as required.

ATTACHING A CEILING ROSE

Options for ceiling decoration are often limited, but adding a plaster rose is one way of adding extra interest to the vast open area that is characteristic of most ceilings. Lightweight plaster roses can be secured using coving adhesive, but heavy-duty ones need the extra support of screws as well, to hold them in position on the ceiling. The screws must be screwed into ceiling joists.

1 Use a joist detector to find the position and direction of the ceiling joists. Using this information, mark the ideal position for your ceiling rose—usually this is in the centre of the room.

2 Apply generous amounts of the coving adhesive to the back of the ceiling rose, being careful to cover it completely.

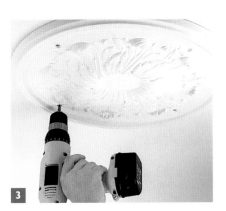

3 Position the rose on the ceiling and drill through it into the ceiling joist, using a screw for fixing. Repeat this process all around the circumference of the rose, fixing a screw in any area that the detector shows to have joist support.

4 Fill all the screw holes with some all-purpose filler, to create a neat finish on the ceiling rose, then sand with fine-grade sandpaper for a smooth finish.

DOORS

D oors help to form the overall look of a room, and they should be considered as one of the main features in the room. As well as performing their functional role, they can make a style statement. In this way, they can contribute dramatically to the decorative scheme.

CHOOSING A DOOR STYLE

Door decoration, such as leaded windowpanes, or the way they are painted, is often the most influential factor in their appearance. Doors that have a large wooden surface area lend themselves to various paint or natural wood finishes that show them off to good effect.

The rustic look: old doors often need little decoration—their natural grain plus the effects of wear and tear over a long period of time produce a very authentic, rustic appearance.

Using glass: doors that contain glass panels or panes let more light into rooms, whether the doors are exterior or interior ones. Using leaded windowpanes or coloured glass can also create an attractive and individual look.

Paint effects: any number of door finishes can be created with paint effects—a marbled finish is a very inventive way of producing a new and interesting look.

STICKING DOORS

Whatever doors you choose to have in your home, it is essential that they open and close smoothly. In modern houses, because central heating is common and makes temperatures vary, doors can expand and contract over time. Slight structural movement of the house can also lead to doors sticking and becoming difficult to open. Fortunately, this is a simple problem to solve.

1 Make a pencil guideline along the edge of the door in the places where it is sticking. This can be done by holding the shaft of the pencil against your finger as you run it down the edge of the door to produce a straight line.

2 Use a wood plane to shave away the edge of the door as far as the pencil guideline. If the door is sticking closer to the bottom, it may be necessary to take it off its hinges to plane it.

LOOSE DOORS

The opposite problem may occur where a door fails to shut properly because it has shrunk slightly. Since it is not easy to add wood to the edge of the door, an alternative method is required. The hinges can be built out from the doorstop, or, as shown here, the striking plate can be built out slightly in order to engage the latch and close the door.

1 Unscrew the striking plate from the door frame. Cut a piece of thick, stiff cardboard the same size as the striking plate and position it on the door frame before reattaching the plate.

2 When the plate is screwed back in place, use a craft knife to cut out the central area of cardboard to allow the latch to close. You may find that you need to experiment and add more cardboard until the door shuts firmly.

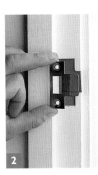

RENOVATING FLUSH DOORS

F lush doors have very little character and they benefit from some form of refurbishment to add an extra dimension to their bland appearance. Repainting the door or changing the handles are two simple methods of remodelling the look of a flush door. For a more dramatic transformation, you can add panels to its surface.

ADDING PANELS

When adding panels to a door, you need to work out how many panels you want on it, and whether the panel sizes will vary across the door surface.

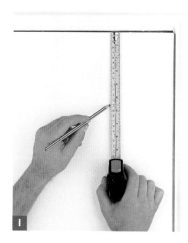

1 Mark out the panel sizes on the door, pencilling in the corner positions of each panel. Take time to double check the measurements as any mistakes will be very obvious on the finished door.

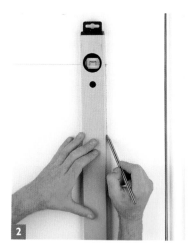

2 Using a level, join up all the corner measurements and provide a complete pencil guideline for the panel layout. For a crooked door frame or a sloping room, you may need to adjust the level of the panels by eye and balance their position against the unlevel elements of the door position.

3 Use a mitre saw to cut moulding beads down to the required size. Use some fine-grade abrasive paper to sand the cut edge to remove any rough areas before attaching them.

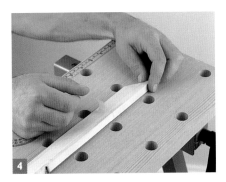

4 Attach double-sided tape to the back of each moulding in turn, applying the tape along the central area of the moulding.

5 Stick the moulding in position along the pencil guideline on the door. There will be a little time to adjust its position before the tape adheres to the door permanently. Once positioned correctly, press firmly on the moulding to ensure a strong bond.

6 Continue to add mouldings until all the panels are complete. Finally seal along the edge of each moulding with decorator's caulking, using a wet finger to smooth it to a neat finish. Paint the door once the caulking is dry.

PANEL TRANSFORMATION
Panels can totally change the look of a flush door. The moldings can be painted the same colour as the main body of the door, as shown here, or they can be picked out in a contrasting colour for an impressive effect.

FIREPLACES

F ireplaces—whether they are used or not—create an attractive focal point in a room and revamping your old fireplace or installing a new one is a good way of changing the look of a room. Installing an inactive fireplace and surround is a simple job that requires little time and endeavour. Some fireplaces are supplied by manufacturers in kit form; alternatively, you can build one from your own plan.

LAYING A HEARTH

Most fireplaces require a hearth area in order to complete the effect. This can simply be a cutaway section out of the carpet, or a material such as a marble slab can be laid to make a hearth, but this will need to be secured in place with mortar, as shown below.

1 Measure along the wall to find the central point for the position of the marble slab. A fireplace tends to look best when it is centred on the wall.

2 Mix some mortar (five parts sand to one part cement). Add water to make it a firm but smooth consistency. Place six fist-size piles of mortar, one at each corner and the two midpoints of where the slab is to be positioned.

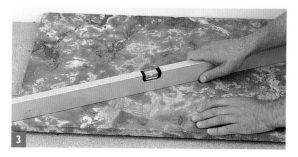

3 Position the marble slab, twisting the slab slightly as you bed it into the mortar. Use a spirit level to make sure that the slab is sitting perfectly level across all dimensions.

ATTACHING THE SURROUND

If you are not using a kit-form surround, it is possible to buy complete fire surrounds that are quite simple to attach to the wall. When choosing a surround, make sure that its base dimensions match the width dimension of the hearth area, so that a neat, balanced effect is achieved.

Screwing in position: a wooden surround can be secured with two to four screw fixings. Depending on the design, try to hide the fixing points so that they are not obvious when the mantel is in place. The best method is to attach a glass plate fixing to the back of the surround and then fix through this into the wall.

REAL FIRE SURROUNDS

Installing a mantel for a real fire, or installing a real fireplace on its own, is a longer process. The extent of work that is required will depend on your choice of fuel.

- Gas fireplaces: these have a real fire effect without the need to clear away ashes, or physically lay and light the fire. A gas supply is essential, as is a flue or an existing chimney. Once installed, a gas fire is an efficient, attractive asset to a room. All gas fireplaces should be fitted by a fully qualified installer and in accordance with the manufacturer's instructions.
- Electric fireplaces: like the gas fireplaces, these are made to imitate the effect of a real fire, but use electricity as their power source. No flue or combustible fuel supply is needed.
- Solid fuel: changing the hearth or the mantel around an existing solid-fuel fireplace can be simple or complex, depending on the fireplace design. Seek professional advice before working on complex designs.

THE DRESSED LOOK
Once fixed in place, a simple combination of a hearth and surround makes an excellent focal point in any room.

TEXTURED PLASTER

A dding texture to wall surfaces is an easy way of adding character to a room. This can be achieved by paint effects or embossed wallpapers, but by far the most authentic way is to actually add a coat of textured plaster to the walls. Proprietary brands of textured plaster are available or you can achieve the finish with simple one-coat plaster. The wall can be painted, or colour-washed, to add depth to the surface.

APPLYING TEXTURED PLASTER

One-coat plaster can be applied over rough or smooth surfaces with equal effect. Make sure that the floor is covered with drop cloths since some plaster will fall away as it squeezes out around the edge of the plaster float.

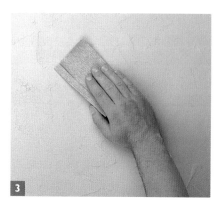

1 Apply a PVA solution (five parts water to one part PVA) to the wall surface to prime and seal it.

2 Mix some plaster to a firm, pastelike consistency. Apply it to the wall with a plaster float, using large sweeping motions. Combine moving the float across the surface with firm downward pressure. Leave grooves and ruts in the surface of the plaster to ensure a textured finish.

3 Once the plaster has dried, use fine-grade abrasive paper to remove any high points on the finish—these will only fall away with time so it is best to remove them before decorating. The surface can then be painted, or you can use a paint effect such as a colour-wash.

3
RENOVATING AND LAYING FLOORS

Floors are an important consideration when revamping your home because they have a major influence on the look of rooms and their overall decorative effect. Refurbishment can be a simple matter of replacing the carpet or vinyl. For a more dramatic effect, you can change the look completely. When choosing a floorcovering, remember to consider the rest of the decoration in the room, as well as the practical aspects of the flooring you select. This chapter contains many options for floor renovation, plus a variety of finishing techniques.
For tiling floors, see pages 357–78.

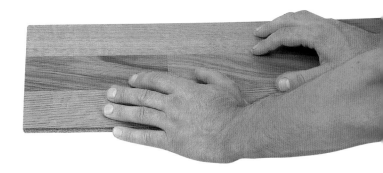

CHOOSING A STYLE

Y our choice of flooring will almost certainly be dictated by the overall look you are going for. The questions of wear, noise, moisture (such as in kitchens and bathrooms), and dirt will also inform your decision. Cost is also a relevant factor, with floorboard and carpet, for example, being less expensive than tiles or hardwood flooring.

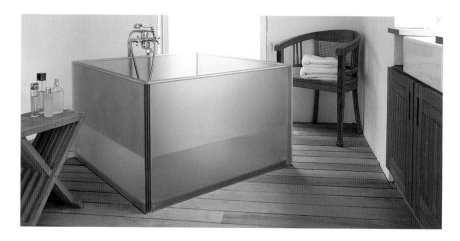

Wooden flooring: the natural beauty of wood has made it a popular choice as a flooring material. Floorboards may be left uncovered (but stained, painted, or varnished) if they are in good shape. Alternatively, a wood floor covering may be laid over existing floorboards, chipboard sheeting, or concrete floors. Laminated wood flooring or more expensive mosaic wood flooring are just some of the many options.

Tiled floors: solid and hard-wearing, tiles are a popular and practical choice in kitchens and bathrooms. But carpet tiles and other soft tiles, such as linoleum and vinyl, can also be a dramatic and cost-effective choice in other rooms. For more on tiling floors, see pages 357–378.

Carpeted floors: carpets are a comfortable option for most rooms in the home. Most carpets have a wear rating that indicates their suitability for use in different areas. They are also generally described by the type of backing they have (foam and hessian) and the way in which the fibres are connected to it, known as the pile. The fibres may be natural wool or manmade. Natural floor coverings, such as coir, sisal, and sea grass, are also increasingly popular.

Sheet vinyl and linoleum: these popular roll floorcoverings are hard-wearing and easy to clean, making them ideal for kitchens and bathrooms. Laying sheet vinyl is an easy job (see pp.74–75), but putting down linoleum is best left to a professional. Both materials are available in a huge range of colours and patterns, making them a versatile and modern choice. However, some vinyls can be slippery when wet.

SANDING FLOORS

T o create any sort of finish on bare floorboards you need to sand
them first to provide a good surface. For a large area, it is worth
renting a drum floor sander. Before using the sander, make sure that
the floor is totally clear of obstacles and that any protruding nails are
punched in below the surface. See pages 10–11 for repairing floorboards.

ORDER OF WORK

In order to produce an even finish, it is important to stick to a particular
sequence of work when using a drum sander.

First, sand at a 45-degree
angle to the boards.

Next, sand at 45 degrees
in the other direction.

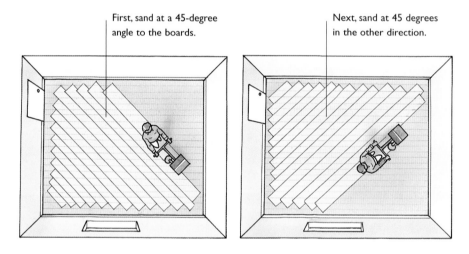

Finally, sand with the grain of
the boards.

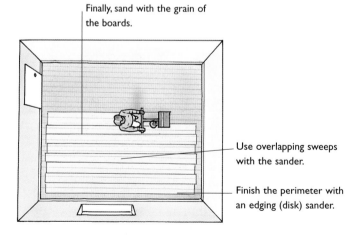

Use overlapping sweeps
with the sander.

Finish the perimeter with
an edging (disk) sander.

USING A FLOOR SANDER

Floor sanders are fairly straightforward to use as long as you follow the manufacturer's instructions and the directions shown opposite. Make sure that you wear a dust mask because the machine causes a lot of mess.

Starting the sander: tip the sander back slightly before starting it, otherwise the sanding drum will dig into the floor surface. Once started, lower it gently onto the floor and work with an even pace in the required direction. Do not linger in one area for any length of time.

Grades of sandpaper: depending on the nature of the floor, you may need to use different grades of sandpaper. To remove several layers of old coatings, begin with a coarse grade of sandpaper and gradually work down to a fine grade.

USING AN EDGING SANDER

Edging (disk) sanders are used to get close to the skirting and reach the areas that cannot be covered by the larger drum sander. They are also messy, so it is still essential to wear a dust mask.

Sanding technique: hold on tightly to the handles of the sander, since they can produce quite a kick as they progress across the floor surface. Allow the edge of the sanding pad to get right up to the floor edge in order to remove the old coatings.

Grades of sandpaper: an edging sander works with an orbital action and uses round sheets of sandpaper. Again, gradually reduce the grade of sandpaper as you remove all the old layers of paint and/or varnish from the floor.

STAINING AND VARNISHING

S tain and varnish give a hard-wearing coating while allowing the natural grain of the wood to show through. Traditionally, stains and varnishes were fairly limited in their choice of colour and finish, but in recent years the range has increased to include all sorts of options for the final look of a stained or varnished floor.

TECHNIQUE

Varnish can be applied to floorboards as a finish in its own right, following the steps below. Stains usually need to be protected with coats of varnish after they have been applied. Always read the manufacturer's guidelines to check that the stain or varnish you have bought is suitable for floor use—some may not have the hard-wearing properties that are essential for floor coatings.

1 Clean the entire floor surface with a cotton rag dampened with mineral spirits. This removes dust and debris and, once the mineral spirit evaporates, it leaves a totally clean and particle-free surface.

2 Apply stain with the grain of the wood, brushing it out thoroughly to ensure even coverage. Treat each floorboard as a separate surface, otherwise the overlaps in stain from one board to another will show up as rather patchy and ruin the finish. Apply extra coats of stain, if they are needed—two full coats is usually sufficient for floorboards.

3 Once the stain is totally dry, apply varnish to seal and protect the stain finish. Again, brush with the grain of the wood, ensuring that the varnish covers the entire floor surface. A second, and sometimes third, coat will be required to give the floor surface a tough and hard-wearing finish. When applying coats of varnish, sand the wood lightly between each coat.

VARYING COLOUR AND PATTERN

When staining floorboards, it is possible to be quite adventurous and achieve a more extravagant look, or simply a very individual one. Colour can be used to add greater vibrancy to a floor finish, and this idea can be taken one step further if some sort of pattern is also introduced into the design.

1 Stain every other row of boards with the same colour—a vivid blue makes a change from more traditional natural wood colours.

2 Once the blue has dried, apply a strong contrasting colour to the other boards in order to produce a simple striped effect. Apply extra coats, if necessary, as well as varnish to protect the finished floor.

ALTERNATIVE NATURAL WOOD FLOOR FINISHES

There are various alternatives to stain and varnish for producing a natural wood floor finish.

- Wax: this is one of the more traditional finishes for floors. Wax produces an excellent effect, especially on older floorboards, which tend to have more character than modern equivalents. However, waxing floors can be an arduous process requiring frequent recoating and buffing for the floor to look really good. Using a proprietary sealer on the bare wood surface before waxing reduces the number of wax coats required to produce a good finish.

- Stain varnishes: there are proprietary stain varnishes that can be used as an all-in-one floor treatment. These are applied to the floorboards in the usual way, but require no varnish coatings as final protection.
- Water-based alternatives: traditional floor coatings have always been oil-based. They take a long time to dry between coats and make the overall process fairly lengthy. Nowadays, when choosing floor finishes, there are various water-based products to choose from. These are just as durable but their shorter drying time means that the job can be completed much more quickly.

LAYING A SUBFLOOR

S ubfloors, as their name suggests, are a base on which finishing
floorcoverings are laid, although they can be painted to provide a
finished look in their own right (see page 65). They are most often used
to smooth over a previous floorcovering in readiness for the new one.
Hardboard, chipboard, and plywood can all be used for a subfloor.

LAYING HARDBOARD

Hardboard is a thin, flexible board that is used to cover floorboards and
provide a sound surface for a new floorcovering. It is supplied in large and
small sheets—the smaller 120-by-60-cm (4-by-2-foot) sheets are easiest to use.
It has a rough side and a smooth, shiny side, and it is always best to lay the
board shiny side up. Make sure that the hardboard is stored in the room it
is to be laid in for a few days before you actually secure it in place. This
allows it to acclimatize to the atmospheric conditions of the room.

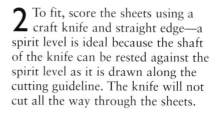

1 Butt the edges of the hardboard
sheets up against each other, and
either nail them to the floorboards
or use a staple gun, as shown here.
Stagger the joints and secure each
board along the edges and every
15–20 cm (6–8 in) in all directions.

2 To fit, score the sheets using a
craft knife and straight edge—a
spirit level is ideal because the shaft
of the knife can be rested against the
spirit level as it is drawn along the
cutting guideline. The knife will not
cut all the way through the sheets.

3 Turn the board over and fold it
upward so that it snaps along the
scored line. Use the craft knife to
finally cut through the board on the
opposite side of the scored line.
Position the cut piece of board and
nail or staple it in place.

LAYING CHIPBOARD

Chipboard is thicker than hardboard and is generally used to make floor surfaces in new homes, rather than using traditional floorboards. It can be used over old floorboards to provide a flat, level surface, but its most common use is to provide a solid subfloor for carpets or vinyl flooring.

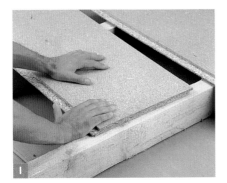

1 Chipboard has a tongue-and-groove jointing system which means that each new board edge is fitted into the previous one in order to make a strong flush joint.

2 It can be fixed to the joists with nails, but screws make a more solid fixing and reduce the risk of loosening with age. Stagger the board edges and cut them so that they join on a joist and not in between them.

LAYING PLYWOOD

Plywood is another building board that has many general uses, including being used as a subfloor in some situations. Where hard tiles or block flooring are to be laid, it is important to ensure that there is little or no flexibility in the subfloor. Laying plywood on top of the existing floor, whether it be traditional floorboards or chipboard, reduces flexibility and provides a sound surface.

Attaching plywood: for a subfloor, the sheets of plywood should be about 18 mm ($\frac{3}{4}$ in) thick. They can be either screwed or nailed down, and as with all forms of subfloor, the edges should be staggered.

PAINTING FLOORS

O ne of the most straightforward methods of refurbishing a floor is to paint it, but this is only possible if the surface has been well prepared. Floorboards, subfloors, and concrete floors can all be revitalized by being painted.

FLOORBOARDS

Floorboards should be sanded to remove the previous coatings (see pages 58–59). Once prepared and cleaned, they can be painted to produce a hard-wearing surface that is easy to keep clean. It is always advisable to use proprietary floor paints since they tend to be the most durable, although gloss paint and some all-purpose water-based paints, which should be coated with varnish to give a final protective layer, can also be used.

1 Prime the floorboards before paint application, to ensure that the surface is sealed and to provide a good base for the subsequent coats of floor paint.

2 Apply the floor paint, brushing with the grain of the boards. Use a generous amount of paint on the brush and brush the paint into the surface, making sure that it does not "pool" in any areas. Two coats of paint should be sufficient for most floors, although hallways and other areas that have a lot of wear and tear may need more coats.

The grained look: instead of priming and applying each coat of paint all over the floor, simply paint each floorboard and then wipe away the excess paint with a cotton rag as you proceed across the floor. In this way, the grain of the wood is exposed, to give a timber-rubbed effect, which offers an alternative to the opaque finish of most painted floors.

PAINTING SUBFLOORS

It is possible to paint subfloors, as long as you have made sure that the surface is totally clean and free from dust and particle debris. Prime the floor surface first to make sure that it is sealed, as this will give the best possible top coat adhesion. Because of their relatively flat surface, subfloors offer the opportunity to paint intricate designs and patterns that would be difficult to carry out on any other floor surface. The example here shows how to paint a border stripe—simple to do and very effective.

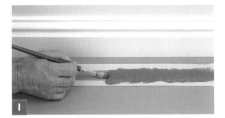 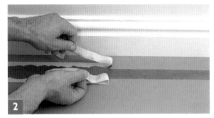

1 Paint the floor its base colour and let dry. Apply two strips of tape around the edge of the room, 2.5 cm (1 in) apart. Paint between the strips with a contrasting colour.

2 While the paint is still wet, pull away the masking tape strips to reveal a contrasting stripe bordering the entire room.

CONCRETE FLOORS

Concrete floors are not common inside the home but there is sometimes a storage room that has no other floorcovering than bare concrete. Garages and basements are also areas where there may be a concrete floor. Painting these floors can add a touch of "finishing," while reducing dust and making the floors easier to keep clean. However, you should not paint new concrete screeds until you are sure they are totally dry; this may take weeks or even months—always use a moisture meter to check the floor before painting it.

1 Sweep the floor thoroughly, then remove any grease spots or impurities from the floor with a proprietary solvent.

2 Apply floor paint directly onto the concrete— some manufacturers may recommend thinning the first coat slightly in order to seal the surface, although this will not be necessary in most cases. A roller covers the floor quickly, then a brush may be used to finish off around the edges.

STENCILLING FLOORBOARDS

S tencilling your floorboards is a great way of giving an unusual and highly individual look to your room. Before stencilling, repair any surface damage to your floorboards, sand them down, and use steel wool with white spirit to remove any wax or grease.

MAKING A REPEATING STENCIL PATTERN

You can buy ready-made stencils or make your own. A transparent acetate sheet is the best material to use: lay it over a pattern for tracing, then cut out the design, leaving "bridges" so parts of the design don't fall out of the stencil. The best tool for cutting the stencil is a craft knife with a sharp blade. A continuous pattern requires a registration mark to align the stencil: use an element in the design or draw a line on the stencil.

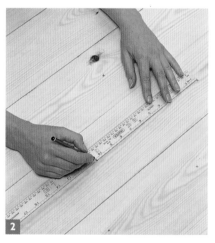

1 Plan out your pattern on a scale drawing of the floor, starting at the centre of the room and using small squares to indicate how often the pattern is repeated. On the floor itself, find the centre using two lengths of string tied to small nails tapped partway into the floorboards.

2 Measure and mark the positions for several of the surrounding patterns. By marking the patterns as you go, you can make slight adjustments if you start to go off course. With each new group of marks, double check for overall appearance before you commit yourself by applying the paint.

3 The easiest way to secure the stencil to the floor is to spray the back with a spray mount adhesive. This will hold the stencil in place while you paint, but allow you to peel it off and reposition it afterward. Or you can use painter's masking tape.

4 Load a stencil brush with some of the paint and dab it on a sheet of white paper to find the right amount to use (a little stencil paint goes a long way). Apply the paint to the floor, using a short dabbing motion to prevent the paint from going under the edges of the stencil.

5 If you want to use a second colour, allow the first one to dry completely (water-based paints will dry quickly). If using more than one stencil sheet (some ready-made stencil kits have a separate sheet for each colour), make sure the stencil is correctly aligned over the previous image before applying the new colour.

6 Remove and reposition the stencil, continuing until you finish the room. When the paint has completely dried, cover the final result with three coats of floor-grade varnish, painting the full length of a few planks at a time.

LAYING LAMINATE FLOORING

Wood stripped floors are difficult to lay, but it is now possible to create the same effect by using laminated flooring, which mimics the effect of its more traditional counterpart. Laminated floors tend to be laid as a "floating" floor, so called because the individual boards are not stuck directly to the subfloor below. Instead they are laid on a foam underlay that adds acoustic and thermal insulation to the floor, as well as levelling out any rough areas on the subfloor. The latter point is particularly important when laying laminated floors on concrete screeds that are not totally smooth. Overall, the "floating" floor system makes this surface very easy to lay and combines interlocking tongue-and-groove boards with adhesive to create a hard-wearing and easy-to-clean floorcovering.

1 Roll out the foam underlay onto the subfloor surface. Make sure that it is totally flat with no folds or kinks in it, and that its edge is butted up against the skirting. The underlay can be cut quite easily with scissors or a craft knife in order to fit it where required.

2 Lay the sheets of laminated flooring on the underlay and against the skirting, inserting wedges along its edge. These wedges, which are usually supplied with the flooring as part of the kit, ensure an expansion gap for the entire floor. Make sure that they are all inserted to the same level.

3 To join the next sheet of flooring, run some adhesive along the tongue of the previous sheet. Lock the groove of the new sheet over this tongue to join them together. Make sure that the ends of the boards are staggered as you build up each new row of sheets.

4 To ensure a tight joint, use a hammer and block to knock each laminated sheet firmly in place. If no block is supplied with the flooring, use a scrap piece of laminate. Never directly hammer the edge of the sheet or you will damage it.

5 Wipe away the excess adhesive that is squeezed out of the joint with a clean rag. Make sure that this is done immediately, before it has a chance to dry. Continue to build up sheets, row by row, across the floor until the surface is completely covered. At some stage you will need to cut some boards to finish off along the edges. This can be done with an ordinary handsaw. Once the floor is completely covered, remove the wedges and use some quadrant beading to cover the floor/skirting junction.

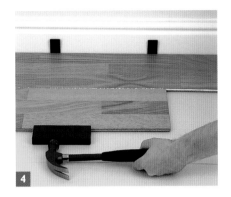

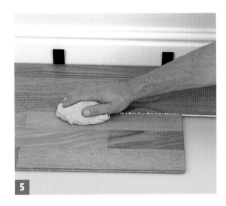

LAMINATE FLOOR CONSIDERATIONS

Laminated floors are relatively easy to fit, but there are a few considerations that need to be taken into account before you decide to lay them.

- Suitable areas: laminated floors are suitable for most areas in the home, except those places which are prone to damp or rooms with a high amount of moisture. Bathrooms, for instance, are not ideal for this type of flooring.
- Concrete floors: as long as the floor is old and well established, there is no problem in laying a laminated floor on a concrete surface.

However, new screeds must have dried totally before a laminated floor can be laid on them. Test the moisture content of a new screed with a moisture meter to ensure that it has dried before you start.

- Covering edges: the expansion gap around the edge of a laminated floor can be covered with some quadrant beading as suggested in Step 5, above. However, a neater alternative is to remove the skirting board before the floor is fitted, then you can replace it afterward and it will cover the expansion gaps.

CARPETING FLOORS

C arpet still remains one of the most popular floorcoverings, due to its comfort factor. There are many different types with varying qualities to choose from. Most carpets are either burlap-backed or foam-backed. Burlap-backed carpets tend to be better quality, but are more difficult to lay. Foam-backed carpets, which are often less expensive, can be very hard-wearing. They also have the advantage of being relatively simple to lay.

FIXING THE EDGE

The way the carpet edges are dealt with is one of the main differences between laying burlap-backed or foam-backed carpets. Both types of carpet need to be secured around the perimeter of the room, but the methods by which this is achieved are very different.

Foam-backed carpets: the foam backing of these carpets means that the harsh structure of a "gripper rod" cannot be used to hold it in place. The best way to secure it is simply by using double-sided carpet tape. Stick this around the edge of the room and peel away the top layer before sticking the trimmed carpet in place. Carpet joints in central areas of the room may also be secured with double-sided tape.

Burlap-backed carpets: this type of carpet requires "gripper rods" to be positioned around the edge of the room. The carpet is then stretched over and behind the rods in order to hold it taut and in position. The metal teeth on the gripper rods dig into the carpet's burlap backing and hold it tightly in position. The gripper rods are attached to the floor by simply hammering in nails along its length—for concrete floors, use masonry nails. It is a good idea to hold a piece of scrap board by the skirting to prevent it from being knocked by the hammer while the gripper rods are installed.

STRETCHING CARPET TO FIT

Burlap-backed carpets need the help of a carpet stretcher to ensure that they are held tautly in position. Underlay is usually laid across the floor surface first because this increases the insulation and the comfort factor of the carpet. Underlay should be rolled out, butt-joined at the edges, and trimmed where it reaches the gripper rods. Do not allow it to encroach onto the gripper rods.

1 Cut the burlap-backed carpet into the skirting/floor junction using a craft knife. Be careful not to cut into the skirting. It does not matter if the cut is not totally accurate since the carpet fitting process is not yet complete.

2 Using the carpet stretcher, work outward from the centre of the room to the edges, ensuring that the carpet is stretched out and perfectly flat. Hold the carpet with the gripping end of the carpet stretcher, while using your knee to knock against the broad pad at the base of the stretcher to force the carpet toward the edge of the room.

3 Use a brick chisel to force the edge of the carpet over and behind the gripper rods around the edge of the room. Again, be careful not to damage the skirting—just use the broad face of the chisel to mould the carpet into position.

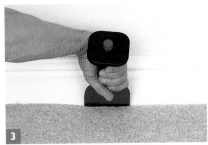

Entrances: finishing carpets at doors or other room entrances is always a problem. The easiest way is to attach a threshold strip, which acts in the same way as a gripper rod, securing the carpet in place. The type you use will depend on the floorcovering in the next room. Here, a chrome edge provides a boundary between the carpet and a wood-planked floor.

LAYING STAIR CARPET

There are two methods of carpeting a staircase: fitting the carpet to cover the stairs completely or laying a "runner" with a gap along each side. A stair runner is easier to lay, and you can easily move it to distribute wear evenly at the front edge, or nosing, of the steps. A fitted carpet will always look better, but is more difficult to lay.

MEASURING STAIRS

To find the length needed for straight stairs, add together the depth of one tread (front to back) and the height of one riser; multiply by the number of steps. If the stairs turn a corner, measure from the deepest part of the tread. Carpets are sold by the metre (or yard); order the next highest metre (or metre yard) above your measurement.

1 After doing repairs and painting, nail down gripper strips at the angles between the treads and risers. Use L-shape stair strips, with tacks pointing toward the angles (use a spacer between the strip and the wall). Or use normal strips: nail a strip on the riser, then a strip on the tread, both of them 12 mm (1/2 inch) from the angle.

2 At a landing, cut the tackless strips to length with a tenon saw, and fit them as you would fit gripper strips around a room. Fit all the gripper strips for the complete staircase before going on to the next step.

3 Cut the underlay to the width of the carpet and into short lengths the width of a tread plus 25 mm (1 in). Position a length on the top tread, letting it overhang the nosing. Use carpet tacks or staples to secure the underlay, fastening it along the back and side edges. Continue until all the treads are covered.

4 Take the carpet from the landing above and cut it so that it covers the top riser, using a utility knife fitted with a carpet-trimming blade. Push the carpet firmly into the gripper strip (see step 6), then trim off the excess.

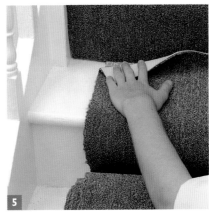

5 While balancing the runner on the step below, position the top of the runner so that it's centred on the tread. Push the end down into the gripper strip and secure it in place with a chisel and mallet (see step 6). Allow the roll to move down, one step at a time, as you secure the carpet to the tackless strips.

6 For each step, check that the carpet is properly aligned, and reposition the roll if necessary. Use an carpet-layer's stair tool to push the carpet onto the gripper strips, working along the angle from end to end; then secure the carpet by hitting the stair tool with a rubber mallet as you, once again, work along the angle.

7 At the end of each flight, trim off the excess carpet using the utility knife, then return to the top of the steps to trim off any excess at the top of the run. Fit the carpet at the landing in the same way that you would fit standard carpet in a room.

LAYING VINYL FLOORING

Vinyl bridges the gap between hard tile floors and carpets. Hard-wearing and water-repellent, it makes an ideal bathroom or kitchen flooring, which, although slightly cold underfoot, has a more cushioned feel than hard tiles but is not as soft as carpet. Sheet vinyl is tricky to fit, so take the time to measure and cut carefully to avoid mistakes.

MAKING A TEMPLATE

To get a roll of vinyl into a manageable size to fit in the room, you need to make a template of the floor and transfer it onto the vinyl. This makes the trimming and fitting process much easier and allows for approximate positioning of the vinyl before it is finally secured in place.

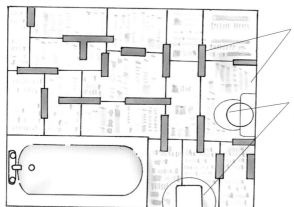

Use sheets of newspaper and masking tape to make an exact template of the floor.

Cut precisely around the edges of the pedestals of basins and toilets.

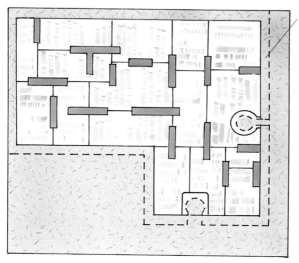

Place the template on the unrolled vinyl and cut around the edge, adding 5 cm (2 in) onto the template size to allow for final fitting when positioned in the room.

INSTALLATION GUIDELINES

Vinyl is not a totally flexible floorcovering because it will not stretch; therefore, accurate cutting is vital. Even the most experienced floor layers take extra time when laying vinyl, as it is very difficult to rectify mistakes once an incorrect cut has been made.

Straight lines: use a sharp craft knife to accurately cut straight edges next to skirting boards. Crease the vinyl as firmly as possible into the floor/skirting junction to ensure an accurate cut.

Cutting curves: around curved areas such as toilet pedestals, cut small slits in the vinyl to help to mould it around the pedestal profile, then trim it with the craft knife. Vinyl does not have to be stuck down around the edge, but it is a good idea to use double-sided tape or proprietary vinyl adhesive.

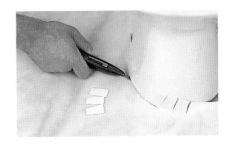

Joining: in larger rooms it may be necessary to join sheets of vinyl. In these cases, always join two factory-finished edges, and use double-sided tape to make sure that both pieces are stuck firmly to the floor.

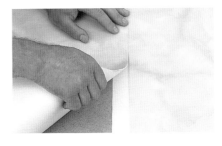

Extra sealing: because of the moisture in bathrooms and kitchens, it is a good idea to run a bead of waterproof caulking around the perimeter of the vinyl to prevent water from seeping under it. For a neat finish, mask the floor/skirting junction with two strips of masking tape, apply the caulking, then remove the tape immediately.

BATHROOM AND KITCHEN FLOORCOVERINGS

I t can be useful to weigh all the pros and cons of the different floorcovering options before making a final decision about your bathroom or kitchen floor. As well as taking into account the flooring techniques shown in this chapter, and in the "Tiling Floors" chapter (pages 357–378), the good and bad points of the various floorings themselves will affect your decision.

PROS AND CONS OF KITCHEN AND BATHROOM FLOORING

FLOOR TYPE	Durability	Ease of cleaning	Preparation	Laying/ Finishing	Expense
	poor ✔ excellent ✔✔✔✔✔	difficult ✔ easy ✔✔✔✔✔	lengthy ✔ quick ✔✔✔✔✔	difficult ✔ easy ✔✔✔✔✔	high cost ✔ low cost ✔✔✔✔✔
Burlap-backed carpet	✔✔✔	✔✔✔	✔✔	✔✔✔	✔✔
Foam-backed carpet	✔✔	✔✔✔	✔✔✔	✔✔✔✔	✔✔✔✔
Vinyl flooring	✔✔✔✔	✔✔✔✔✔	✔✔	✔	✔✔
Stripped flooring	✔✔✔✔	✔✔✔	✔✔✔	✔✔✔✔✔	✔✔✔✔✔
Painted flooring	✔✔✔	✔✔	✔✔✔✔	✔✔✔✔✔	✔✔✔✔✔
Hard tile	✔✔✔✔✔	✔✔✔✔✔	✔	✔✔	✔

4
FIXTURES
AND FITTINGS

Certain fixtures are essential for the day-to-day smooth running of the household; others, such as mirrors and pictures, add character and style to your home. This chapter is full of ideas for revamping and improving your fixtures in a way that suits your personal taste and requirements. This chapter also demonstrates the benefits to be gained from carrying out these tasks and explains what is involved, so that you can decide whether the job is one that you want to attempt. It explains the importance of prioritizing areas such as home security and insulation, for example, so that your home is safe and you save on fuel bills.

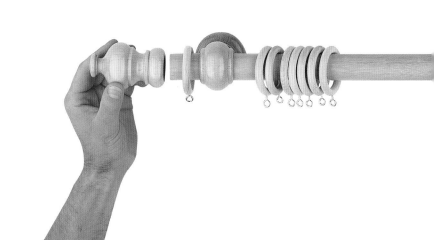

DOUBLE GLAZING

D ouble glazing on windows reduces heat loss, sound transmission, and the buildup of condensation, thereby acting as an efficiency mechanism for the whole household. It uses two panes of glass, separated by an air gap, in place of the standard single pane. The opening and closing mechanism on double-glazed units is more efficient than that of single-glazed units. Double-glazed windows differ in style, quality, and efficiency, so it is important to weigh these differences when deciding on the best system for your needs.

CHOOSING A STYLE OF DOUBLE-GLAZED WINDOW

The early days of double glazing provided unimaginative functional units, aimed at efficiency rather than any aesthetic appeal. In recent years, this position has changed and double-glazed-window manufacturers now provide a wide range of styles to suit all tastes. The major criticism of double glazing has sometimes been its lack of character, but nowadays it is possible to install units that give the appearance of more traditional, and arguably more attractive, designs. Natural wood double-glazed windows, for instance, are becoming increasingly popular. These are usually made from hardwood.

PVC frames: these window units are low maintenance while providing excellent heat-retaining qualities and reduced sound transmission from outside. They are easily cleaned and require no painting, inside or out. They are also very secure, with most designs having locking casements.

Dealing with doors: units that replace existing door systems, whether they be front or back doors, or sliding patio units as shown in this example, may have an aluminium finish that requires very little maintenance, but provides maximum efficiency.

DOUBLE GLAZING CHOICES

- Entire windows: double-glazed units in a PVC frame are a common option for people renovating their home. This tends to be the most expensive option because all the windows in the house are usually replaced at the same time because replacing single windows has little effect on efficiency. Although expensive in the short term, savings will be made in the long term. It does require more advanced do-it-yourself skills to install these.
- Real wood double-glazed windows: these cross the barrier between traditional windows and earlier, less attractive versions. Hardwood double-glazed windows require only coats of stain or varnish from time to time as maintenance.
- Single-sealed units: as an alternative to replacing entire windows, frames and all, it is possible just to replace the glass itself with single double-glazed units. The existing frames do need a large rebated area to fit these thick panes, but as long as they are of

sufficient size, the process is a simple matter of replacing the old single panes with the new double units.
- Secondary double glazing: this involves attaching glazed units to the existing windows. The old frame is used as the base on which large panes of glass, secured in a PVC frame, are attached. They are usually hinged to allow you access to the original window. These units are less of a job than total replacement with double-glazed window units.
- The budget option: the simplest form of double glazing is to use proprietary plastic film or sheeting, secured around the window frame with double-sided tape. Going over the positioned film or sheeting with a hair dryer tightens it slightly to give a taut, neat final appearance. The drawback is that it is not possible to get to the windows to open them, so this method should only be used if this limitation is acceptable.

INSULATING

Insulation plays an important role in retaining heat in a house, as well as eliminating drafts and creating a more efficient home. Double-glazed windows play an important part in this process, but it is also possible to target other areas that benefit from insulation. The cost of insulation can range from a few pounds to a very large sum of money, depending on the scale of the work and the available budget.

AREAS TO INSULATE

Attics
Attics are one of the most important areas to insulate because a great deal of heat can be lost through the roof of your home. You can use loose-fill insulation, which takes the form of granules that are poured between the joists in the roof space, or blanket insulation. Blanket insulation (shown opposite) tends to be a neater process, with large areas being covered quickly and at relatively low cost.

Floor
The space between floor levels can also be insulated. This involves taking up the floorboards, so it can be a fairly lengthy project. However, it can be beneficial, especially if the floor in question is above a basement.

Walls
In new houses, the exterior walls are insulated; in older houses, this may not be the case. External cavity walls are insulated by an injection process; an insulating chemical is forced, under pressure, through a number of drilled holes into the cavity. Once completed, the holes are filled. This technique is really the domain of the professionals,

and is one area where you should seek a specialist's advice and help. When erecting new internal stud walls, blanket insulation can be used inside the cavity during construction.

Doors
Doors can be fitted with antidraft strips to make them more efficient barriers once they are closed. This form of insulation is relatively simple to install and can be carried out very quickly (see opposite).

Windows
Aside from double glazing, a window's insulating efficiency can be improved by using antidraft strips in a similar manner to that used for doors, to reduce the flow of air around the edges of the windows. Curtains are good window insulation, especially if they are thick ones or have an insulating lining.

Pipes
All pipes in the attic must be insulated to protect them from the effects of extreme cold temperatures. Insulation specially designed for this purpose is easy to install and relatively inexpensive (see opposite).

USING INSULATING MATERIALS

Insulating materials are by design fairly unattractive. In most cases this is not a problem for the overall look of your home because the insulation is hidden from view. However, in places where it can be seen—such as around windows or doors—try to make sure that the insulation is installed as neatly as possible. With the less structured methods of insulation, the installation process is fairly simple. It can be achieved in a relatively short space of time and the beneficial effect will be very noticeable, but it is necessary to stick to a few straightforward rules in order to gain the maximum benefit from your efforts.

Blanket insulation: this insulation is manufactured in rolls and is applied between the joists in the attic. Because it can irritate the skin, you need to wear a dust mask, protective gloves, and a long-sleeved shirt when rolling it out. Be careful not to crush the blanket since much of its effectiveness is in its depth. Position it very lightly, rather than forcing it.

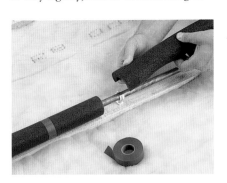

Pipe insulation tubes: those pipes in the attic that are not covered by blanket insulation (see above) must be covered with pipe insulation. Always use the pipe insulation tubes specially designed for this process. They open along one side, allowing you to mould a tube around the entire pipe. Secure the pipe tubes in place with tape—this is especially important at joints and corners.

Draft eliminators: draft eliminators for doors consist of a metal or plastic fixing plate with a fibrous brush strip. The strip can be attached to the door with screws. Make sure that the ends of the bristles overlap onto the floor surface when the door is closed, thus preventing a draft. Because the bristles on the brush strip are flexible, they allow the door to be opened easily but retain the draft-eliminating properties when shut.

DOOR FURNITURE

D oor furniture (or hardware) is designed to look good and be practical. Like other fixtures around the home, the cost varies according to the quality. However, one very quick and easy way of updating the appearance of a door is to simply replace the handles.

CHOOSING A STYLE OF DOOR HARDWARE

There is a vast selection of door hardware available, which makes choosing a style quite difficult. However, the choice is narrowed down by the type of doors you have in your home and the handle mechanism that they require. The style should also be chosen with the design and decoration of the room in mind. The selection below gives an idea of the variety of styles.

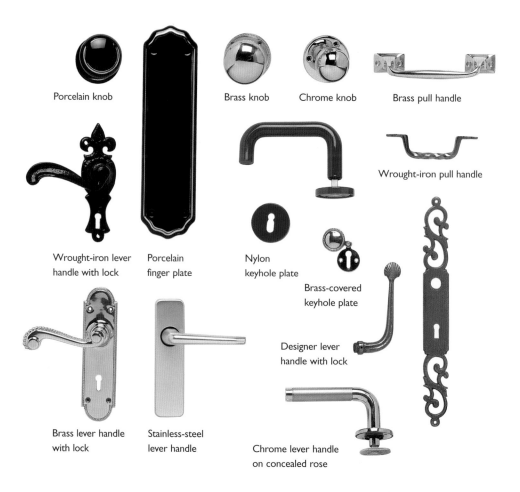

Porcelain knob

Brass knob

Chrome knob

Brass pull handle

Wrought-iron pull handle

Wrought-iron lever handle with lock

Porcelain finger plate

Nylon keyhole plate

Brass-covered keyhole plate

Designer lever handle with lock

Brass lever handle with lock

Stainless-steel lever handle

Chrome lever handle on concealed rose

CHANGING DOOR HARDWARE

Most handles are held in place by retaining screws that go directly into the face of the door. However, in some cases, small grub screws are used to secure the handle in position. Whatever the design, it is usually easy to determine how the handle is fixed in place and how to remove it.

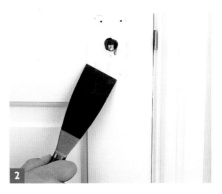

1 Remove the old lever handle with a screwdriver. If you are going to replace the corresponding handle on the other side of the door, remove that one as well.

2 Fill the old screw holes with all-purpose filler, and sand it to a smooth finish when it is dry. Leave the old spindle in place as this is already cut to the right size for the door; only replace it if the new door hardware will not fit it.

3 Position the new door knob on the door and make pilot holes for the new screws with a bradawl. Remove the new knob.

4 Paint over the repaired screw holes and leave to dry. Secure the new knob in position, inserting the screws into the pilot holes.

SECURITY FIXTURES

S ecurity should always be considered when making improvements. Windows and doors are two areas where these considerations are particularly appropriate, since it is always possible to update or add to the security systems you are using. Although security is the main concern when installing these devices, it is possible to use systems that do not detract too much from the room decoration.

WINDOW SECURITY

Most home security is based on a system of deterrents—although window locks may not deter the most determined of intruders, they certainly ward off the casual ones. Installing window locks is a simple process that can be carried out very quickly.

I Remove the old pins from the window frame and then replace them with locking pins that match the finish to your existing stays.

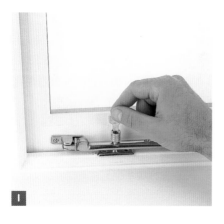

2 Use a key to fasten a locking bolt on top of the pin. This prevents the stay from being lifted, so that the window cannot be opened.

Casement locks: screw one part of the lock into the casement frame and the other into the window frame. A key is used to clamp the two parts of the lock together, preventing the window from being opened. This lock can be installed in minutes with four screws. For extra security on large windows, have one lock at the top part of the casement and one at the bottom.

DOOR SECURITY

Exterior doors should always have a key locking system, whether it be a mortise deadbolt lock, cylinder lock, or other similar security feature. Always change the locks when you move into a new house, since you can never be sure how many people have had access to the existing set of keys. In addition to secure locks, there are other simple security measures that can be used to back up the primary locking systems on the door. These help to provide peace of mind by adding to the overall security of your home. Some of the simplest measures to install are peepholes or viewers, door chains, and mortise door bolts. Peepholes or viewers are the best way of seeing who is knocking at the door without having to open it. They come in a range of sizes, so choose an appropriate one for your door. Door chains allow you to see who is outside while opening the door only a little.

1 Drill a hole in the door the same size as the threaded part of the peephole. Insert half of the peephole on the exterior side of the door.

2 From the inside of the door, join it up with the other half of the peephole. Use the flat edge of a screwdriver to tighten it.

Mortise door bolts: these should be positioned at the top and bottom of the door. They take a little longer to fit than standard door bolts, but they tend to provide better security. The locking system is operated with a special key.

Door chains: these chains can be fitted quickly with just a few screws, and they offer extra protection when opening the door to strangers.

WINDOW FURNITURE

A s with door furniture (or hardware), there is a wide choice of styles and types of fixtures for use on windows. Window mechanisms tend to vary a bit more than those for doors, so it is important to choose fixtures that will operate correctly on your particular window.

Choosing A Style Of Window Hardware

Always remember the practical issues when choosing a style of window hardware—just because something looks good, doesn't necessarily mean it will be easy to use. Try to choose something that will complement the colour and design of other accessories in the room—the door hardware especially—as this will help to create a balanced decorative scheme.

Fanlight catch

Wrought-iron fanlight opener

Fanlight catch plate

Brass screw-up casement stay

Wrought-iron stay and pins

Brass casement fastener

Brass opening stay and fastener

Telescopic friction casement stay

Locking steel casement fastener

Wrought-iron casement fastener

Locking chrome casement fastener

Brass sash fastener with ceramic knob

Brass sash lift

Brass stay and pins

CHANGING CASEMENT WINDOW HARDWARE

As long as you make sure the window hardware you buy is suited to the design of the windows in your home, the attachment process is relatively straightforward. Casement windows are usually secured with fasteners along the side and with stays and pins along the bottom of the casement frame.

1 Remove the old fasteners. Hold the new ones in place and mark the position for the new screw holes with a pencil. Draw a line around the fastener catch to see if it will need to be recessed slightly into the frame.

2 If it is necessary to cut a recess for the fastener catch, use a chisel to cut out the recess in the window frame. Be careful to remove shavings of wood only as far as the pencil guideline—do not go beyond it.

3 Make pilot holes for the fastener catch plate with a bradawl. Screw it in tightly in position in the recess.

4 Make two more pilot holes for the fastener itself, then screw that in place on the window.

STAYS AND PINS

For the stays and pins, use a similar procedure to that used for fasteners (see the steps above). However, it is not necessary to recess the pins into the window frame. Fill all the old fixing holes made for the previous window hardware and paint the repaired area before attaching the new fixtures.

WINDOW SHUTTERS

S hutters are an increasingly popular mode of window dressing, particularly when the choice of window treatment is limited by the amount of available space. Window shutters are an attractive option since they do not take up much room and can be very effective when limited to half the overall window size, in a café-curtain style.

1 Measure the exact width and height of the window recess to establish the required dimensions of the shutters.

2 Make the two doors out of fretwork panelling by cutting the panel to the exact size of the doors, allowing in the measurements for two lengths of 5-by-2.5-cm (2-by-1-in) wooden batten to be positioned on each side of the window recess for hinging the shutter doors.

3 Attach four lengths of 5-cm-by-12-mm (2-by-½-in) batten all around the perimeter of each cut fretwork panel, using brads.

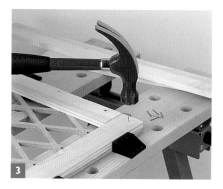

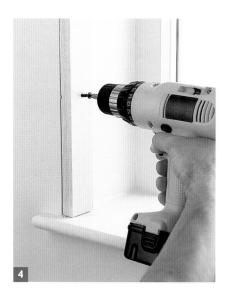

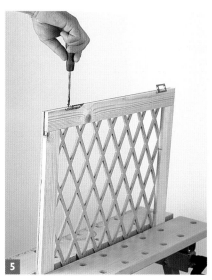

4 Cut two 5-by-2.5-cm (2-by-1-in) lengths of batten to exact door height and fix them securely on each side of the window recess.

5 Attach two hinges to each fretwork panel door.

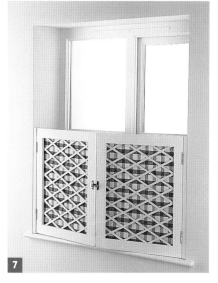

6 Attach a lever catch to the centre of the doors.

7 Mark and attach the hinges onto the lengths of batten on each side of the window recess. Paint the shutters, and staple fabric to the inside of the panels for extra privacy.

FITTING BLINDS

B linds are a popular window treatment since they offer flexible light-control, take up little room, can be highly decorative, and are easy to fix in place. Blinds are particularly suitable for kitchens and bathrooms as they are easy to clean, although more elaborate fabric blinds, such as Austrian and festooned types, will collect moisture in damp rooms.

Roller blinds: these are the easiest way of controlling the flow of natural light into a room. Plain or highly patterned, they can fit well into most schemes. Because they can be rolled up completely onto their retaining pole, it means that the window can be totally exposed during the day so that the maximum amount of light can be let in, which is ideal for small or dark rooms.

Roman blinds: these operate by the material being gathered upward in folds as the blind is opened. They are slightly more complicated than rolling window blinds, but if plain colours are used they can have a great effect on a simple scheme.

Venetian blinds: these have always had a classical appeal because of the unique way in which they break up the natural light source in a variety of mood-creating ways, as well as providing total privacy when the slats are closed at night.

NO-SEWING BLINDS

It is easy to create different types of blinds very quickly, without even the hint of any complex stitching. Making a simple blind from some favorite material has never been easier, especially since the invention of hook-and-loop tape.

1 Measure the exact dimensions of the window frame. Make sure the width measurements come in fractionally from the wall recesses so that the finished blind will be able to fall easily at the frame edge. Add 15 cm (6 in) onto the height measurement to allow 7.5 cm (3 in) at each end of the blind for attaching a length of wooden dowel. Mark the material, and cut it to size using dressmaker's scissors.

2 Cut two lengths of wooden dowel to slightly less than the window recess width and place one at each end of the cut material. Fold over the material at one end and secure it in this position with self-adhesive hook-and-loop tape. Apply the corresponding side of the hook-and-loop tape 7.5 cm (3 in) farther onto the material. Apply two more strips of tape in corresponding positions at the other end of the material (on each side of the other batten). Fold the tape over each batten.

3 Screw two hooks into the window frame, in order to support one of the battens. The other batten is used to weigh down the blind and keep the material taut.

THE STITCHLESS LOOK
The simplest of blinds can often produce the most attractive effect. Here, the blend of colours and the intensity of the light combine to give the window a stylish finish.

CURTAIN TRACKS

Tracks are one of the simplest mechanisms for hanging curtains or draperies. They are designed purely as functional items and have no real aesthetic value since the curtain heading covers the track once it has been installed. Although track design varies, most work on the principle of using a number of specially designed plastic brackets that hold the track securely in place.

ATTACHING THE TRACK BRACKETS

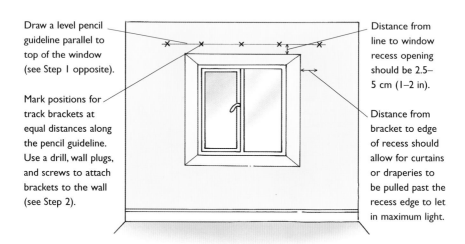

Draw a level pencil guideline parallel to top of the window (see Step 1 opposite).

Mark positions for track brackets at equal distances along the pencil guideline. Use a drill, wall plugs, and screws to attach brackets to the wall (see Step 2).

Distance from line to window recess opening should be 2.5–5 cm (1–2 in).

Distance from bracket to edge of recess should allow for curtains or draperies to be pulled past the recess edge to let in maximum light.

ATTACHING THE TRACK

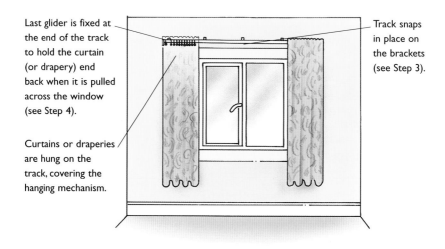

Last glider is fixed at the end of the track to hold the curtain (or drapery) end back when it is pulled across the window (see Step 4).

Curtains or draperies are hung on the track, covering the hanging mechanism.

Track snaps in place on the brackets (see Step 3).

INSTALLING A TRACK

Tracks can be attached directly to the window frame, but this will cut down the distance the curtains or draperies may be drawn back from the window, especially when the window is recessed as shown here. Attachment on the wall surface, outside the recess, is usually the best option.

1 Use a level to draw a line above the window recess, parallel to the top of the recess and the ceiling. Bracket positions may then be marked out along this line to ensure that the track will run straight, without any kinks or bends.

2 Secure the track brackets to the wall, making sure that they are the right way up. The brackets must be attached securely in place so that they are able to take the weight of both the track and the curtains or draperies.

3 Clip the track onto the brackets, then tighten up the retaining screws on the brackets to make sure that the track cannot fall off and that it is secure enough to take the weight of the curtains.

4 Hang the required number of gliders on each end of the track, before securing the final gliders in place at each end of the track. Touch in any visible pencil marks on the wall with the appropriate paint and leave to dry. The curtains can now be hung on the gliders.

CURTAIN POLES

Curtain poles are a more decorative alternative to curtain tracks. The curtains are hung from rings rather than gliders, with the idea that the poles are meant to be seen and form part of the window dressing decoration. Poles are usually wooden but some are made from metal or plastic composites.

ATTACHING THE POLE BRACKETS

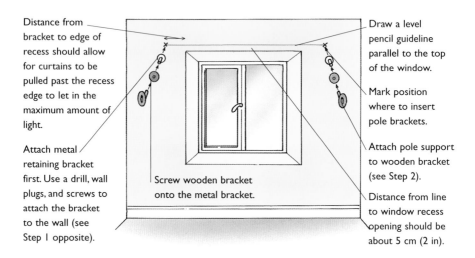

Distance from bracket to edge of recess should allow for curtains to be pulled past the recess edge to let in the maximum amount of light.

Attach metal retaining bracket first. Use a drill, wall plugs, and screws to attach the bracket to the wall (see Step 1 opposite).

Screw wooden bracket onto the metal bracket.

Draw a level pencil guideline parallel to the top of the window.

Mark position where to insert pole brackets.

Attach pole support to wooden bracket (see Step 2).

Distance from line to window recess opening should be about 5 cm (2 in).

ATTACHING THE POLE

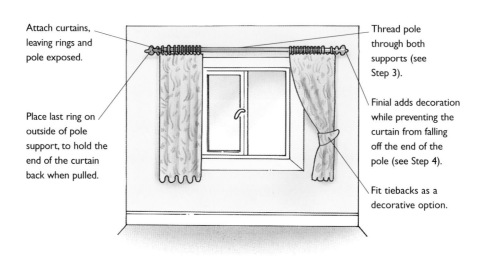

Attach curtains, leaving rings and pole exposed.

Place last ring on outside of pole support, to hold the end of the curtain back when pulled.

Thread pole through both supports (see Step 3).

Finial adds decoration while preventing the curtain from falling off the end of the pole (see Step 4).

Fit tiebacks as a decorative option.

INSTALLING A CURTAIN POLE

Curtain poles are simple to install since they usually have just two wall fixings (though longer poles may require more). However, the brackets and pole must be positioned correctly; if they are not level, the curtains will hang unevenly, spoiling the finished look.

1 Once a level guideline has been drawn (see page 93, Step 1), attach the metal retaining brackets at the end of the guideline. Make sure that the threaded central column of the bracket is positioned precisely on the pencil guideline.

2 Screw the wooden bracket onto the metal one and fit the pole support into the wooden bracket. Fix the pole support in position by tightening the retaining screw on top of the wooden bracket, screwing it through into the pole support.

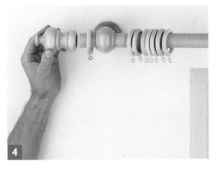

3 Thread the curtain pole into the wooden pole supports.

4 Once rings have been threaded onto the pole, attach a finial to each end. These prevent the final rings from falling off the end of the pole and add a decorative touch.

EASY KITCHEN FIX-UPS

Totally redesigning a kitchen is a major operation that most people carry out on a very infrequent basis. An alternative is to find ways of improving and updating your kitchen's appearance without incurring a heavy work load and major expense.

SIMPLE TECHNIQUES FOR CHANGE

Making changes to kitchen cabinets is a very simple process because most of them are designed along similar lines at the basic level; therefore, changing one component for another is usually a relatively straightforward operation.

REVAMPING OPTIONS

There are many options for remodelling the look of a kitchen. Using one or more of the following ideas will help to change its overall look and improve the practical facilities.

- Cabinet fronts: most kitchen cabinets are constructed of carcass base units that are of a very similar size and dimension, only varying according to their specific function—in other words, a wall cabinet base unit made by one manufacturer is very similar to one produced by another. The more decorative aspect of the kitchen is achieved by the actual doors and drawer fronts that are attached to these units. Therefore, the appearance of the entire kitchen can be changed by replacing existing unit fronts with new ones. When choosing this option, always check that the new fronts will fit the older base units—sometimes some slight adjustments need to be made to make them fit accurately.
- Painting cabinets: instead of replacing cabinet fronts, it is possible to paint them instead. The exact method of achieving this will depend on the actual surface of the cabinets. If the cabinet has a non-wooden surface, it will be necessary to use a proprietary surface preparation compound to ensure that the surface will accept coats of paint.
- Changing a worktop: in spite of their hard-wearing properties, worktops tend to be the areas that wear out the fastest in the kitchen and this detracts from the smart look of the room. For instructions on how to entirely replace a worktop, turn to page 98. But a much simpler option is to tile the worktop, eliminating the need for the more extensive task of completely replacing the units. Furthermore, the tiling can be extended to cover the old tiles above the worktop and produce a more complete makeover.
- Lighting: in any room, the lighting has a great effect on its mood and atmosphere. By experimenting and changing the source of directional lighting, or by simply adding to the existing arrangement of lights, you can produce a completely different feel in the room.

Replacing doors: most kitchen cabinet doors are hinged in a similar way and are simple enough to unscrew and change for a different design. In most cases, it is possible to use the existing hinge on the base unit to secure the new door.

Changing door hardware: this is usually secured with a single threaded bar or screw that extends from the handle side of the door through to the interior side. Changing the handle on a cabinet is a simple case of unscrewing the old one and changing it for the new one.

Changing a plinth: plinths on kitchen cabinets tend to be secured in place with a clip-on bracket system. It is easy to pull the old plinth away and replace it with a newer design or finish.

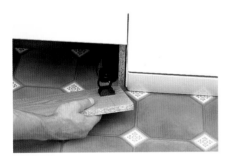

THE MADEOVER LOOK
Simple remodelling in an old kitchen, such as changing handles or painting cabinets, can breathe new life into it, altering its appearance and extending its overall life span.

REPLACING A WORKTOP

K itchen worktops have to put up with more wear and tear than any other surface. Hot pans are placed on them, potentially staining sauces are spilled on them, and all manner of food items are chopped and sliced on them. The look of your kitchen can be brought dramatically up to date with the installation of a new worktop.

EASY INSTALLATION

The easiest type of worktop to install is a slab of chipboard covered with a durable layer of plastic laminate. The front edge is usually rounded off—a detail known as post-forming, where the laminate is shaped and bonded to the rounded-off board edge. It can be bought in a wide range of designs and two standard lengths—2 m (6 ft 6 in) and 3 m (9ft 10 in). The same techniques can be used to fit a top to a vanity unit in the bathroom or to create a work station.

1 If the worktop has an inset sink or hob, disconnect their supplies. Release the clips holding them to the worktop to lift them out. Undo the screws holding the worktop to the base cabinets. Tape the screws you remove to the inside of the cabinet near their mounting position (use them to attach the new worktop).

2 Lift the old worktop off the base cabinets—it may come off in sections—and set it aside. Clean away any old strips of sealant from the walls where the worktop was fitted against them.

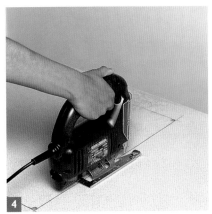

3 You can use the old worktop section as a template to measure and mark out the new one. Mark any holes needed for inset sinks or hobs. Rest the worktop, underside face up, on a work-bench, with clearance below the inset. Drill a hole at each corner of the inset, making sure you bore the holes in the waste area.

4 Insert the blade of a jigsaw into one of the holes, and start to cut out the inset. Continue until all four sides have been cut.

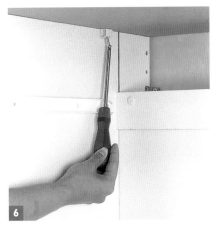

5 With the worktop underside face up, clamp a straightedge as a guide for a circular saw, and trim the end of the section to the correct length, if necessary. If an end will be exposed, finish it off with specially shaped metal trim.

6 Lift the worktop into place, and secure it to the base cabinets with screws and fixing clips. If you're using more then one section, join them with specially shaped metal trim. Seal the gap at the corner between the worktop and the walls using a silicone sealant.

SHOWER AND BATH SCREENS

S hower and bath screens are used to prevent splashes of water from covering bathroom surfaces while the shower is being used. A screen is required where a bath and shower are integrated—when they are separate, a shower is more likely to have its own screen housing. Whichever variety is suitable, most manufacturers supply adequate, although varied, guidelines for installation.

Bath screening: bath screens are quite straightforward to install, and clear glass varieties provide a relatively unobtrusive mechanism for containing a bath and integrated shower. Many consist of two main screens, one of which can slide out across the bath rim to extend the overall screen length and so prevent any overspray onto the bathroom floor when the shower is in operation.

Shower cubicles: separate showers are best housed in an enclosed cubicle to prevent water from spraying over the floor. Any number of designs and screen shapes are available, but make sure that your chosen screen fits the shower tray dimensions. Access to the shower can be by means of a customized (watertight) hinged door, or a sliding door similar to the mechanism on bath screens.

INSTALLING AFTER TILING

If possible, fit a bath screen before tiling the bathroom; if installing after tiling, you will need to use a tile drill bit to make holes in the tiles for the screen fixings.

INSTALLING A BATH SCREEN

Since the function of a bath screen is to create a watertight barrier, this must be the primary consideration when installing it—concentrate your efforts on keeping the screen completely vertical, easily operational, and fitted in the correct position according to the shower requirements. Make sure that the base of the retaining bracket sits central to the bath rim so water will run down onto the rim and back into the bath once the screen is in place.

1 Use a long spirit level to ensure that the bath screen retaining bracket is positioned precisely vertical, and that the base sits central to the bath rim. Use a pencil to mark its position on the wall and also where the retaining screw holes should be drilled.

2 Remove the bracket, and drill holes ready to house the retaining screws. Depending on the wall surface and the method of fixing, wall anchors may be required. If this is the case, insert them at this stage, making sure that drill bit size, anchor size, and screw size all correspond.

3 Hold the bracket back in place, checking that it is vertical once more, and screw the bracket in position on the wall.

4 Fit the screen into the bracket, following the manufacturer's guidelines. Apply caulking around the wall screen junction to provide a watertight seal.

SHOWER CEILINGS

S hower ceilings are always under constant attack from moisture and can, therefore, deteriorate very quickly after painting. Tiling a ceiling is one way of getting around this problem, although gravity makes this a difficult task to achieve. Alternatively, a sheet of plastic (PVC) can be cut to fit the ceiling area, providing an easily cleaned, moisture-resistant surface that will not deteriorate like a painted one.

1 Measure the area directly above the shower, whether it be in a cubicle or above a bath.

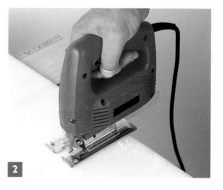

2 Cut a sheet of plastic to size, using a jigsaw. Remember to follow manufacturer's guidelines on safety when using a jigsaw, and at no time place any part of your body in front of the blade.

3 Apply a generous amount of silicone adhesive to the back of the sheet, making sure that there is plenty of adhesive at the edges.

4 Press the sheet into position above the shower, twisting it into place to ensure good adhesion between the sheet and the ceiling.

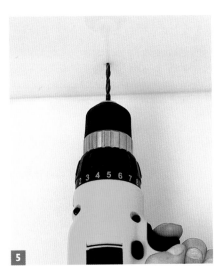

5 Some screw fixings are required to attach the sheet securely. Drill pilot holes around the edge of the sheet at 20-cm (8-in) intervals, being careful when drilling into the ceiling not to damage service pipes or wires, and, more importantly, not to risk injury to yourself.

6 Insert the screws and fit plastic screw cover caps over them to give a neat finish. Apply a band of silicone around the edge of the sheet to ensure a watertight finish.

DEALING WITH DAMP AND CONDENSATION

Damp and condensation can be a problem in bathrooms—the hot water from showers and baths is the main cause of this problem. Having an exhaust fan fitted is the best method of removing moist air from a bathroom, but there are other measures that can also help.

- After a bath or shower, simply opening windows helps to reduce the moisture content of the air in the bathroom.

- Wiping off the moisture on walls helps to prevent the development of mould, which will always attack the decorations and lead to a rapid deterioration in their finish.
- Use proprietary bathroom paints that are more resistant to moisture than standard varieties.
- If your windows are single paned, consider installing double glazing since this will reduce condensation.
- Keep the room adequately heated.

TONGUE-AND-GROOVE PANELLING A BATH: 1

MAKING THE FRAME

Before a bath can be panelled, you need to build a frame onto which the panelling can be attached. Use 5-by-2.5-cm (2-by-1-in) wooden battens for this purpose since they are sturdy enough to provide a sound base while being easy to work with. For the best results, build a frame that combines vertical and horizontal struts, with supporting diagonal lengths to brace the entire framework and keep it firmly in position.

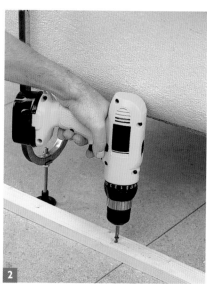

1 Cut a scrap of board the same thickness as the panelling you are going to use, to the height of the bath so that it just fits under the bath rim. Lay a piece of 5-by-2.5-cm (2-by-1-in) batten along the floor, parallel with the bath rim. Use a level and the board scrap to adjust the position of the batten so that it lies directly below the bath rim. Make a pencil guideline all the way along the batten.

2 Cut the batten to the length of the bath, and screw it into the floor, using screws that are long enough to bite into the floorboards below, but not so long that they might go through the boards and damage any service pipes and wires below the floor, and, more importantly, injure you.

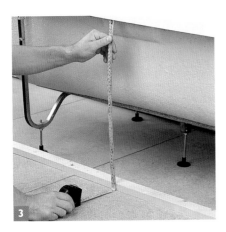

3 Measure the height from tight under the rim of the bath to the top of the floor batten. Cut four or five pieces of batten to this length, for vertical supports. Some baths have a horizontal batten fixed under the rim, but it may be necessary to wedge another length of batten under the rim for fixing on vertical battens.

4 Attach the vertical battens at equal distances along the length of the bath, securing at floor level and under the rim. When attaching below the bath rim, be careful not to screw into the bath itself.

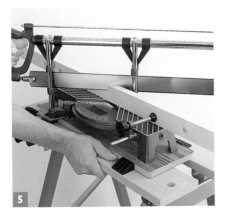

5 Use a mitre saw to make angled cuts in another four or five pieces of batten to use as diagonal supports. Take care when measuring these mitred lengths to fit, as they must be accurate in order to keep the frame in the correct position for attaching the panelling.

6 Secure the diagonal batten supports between all the vertical lengths of batten on the frame.

TONGUE-AND-GROOVE PANELLING A BATH: 2

Once the panel frame has been made, the panelling itself must be cut to
fit. Using large sheets makes the job quicker, but cutting accurately is
that much more important, since small measurement mistakes in one area can
lead to a larger mistake in another. Take time to measure carefully.

ATTACHING THE PANEL

When measuring the tongue-and-groove panelling, remember that the panel
should fit just under the rim of the bath. Do not cut the panelling too
large or you will not be able to get it under the rim.

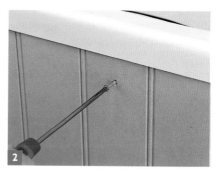

1 Use a jigsaw or panel saw to cut
the bath panel to size. Once in
position, drill six pilot holes in the
panel, one at each corner, one in the
centre of the panel at the top (as
shown here), and one in the centre
of the panel at the bottom.

2 Screw a mirror screw into each
of the pilot holes. For a totally
professional finish, before inserting
the mirror screw, make each hole
entrance slightly larger with a
countersink drill bit, so that the
screwhead will sit flush with the
surrounding panel surface.

3 Attach a mirror screw cap to
each screw. (Always remove
mirror screw caps before painting the
panelling and replace them once the
paint has dried.)

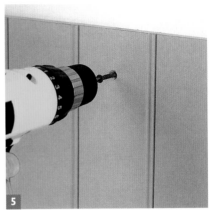

4 For the rest of the bath border, attach panelling as required. Using panelling the same height as the bath panel itself produces a well-balanced effect. Drill pilot holes every 20 cm (8 in) along the top and bottom of the panelling.

5 Use a countersink drill bit to open up the entrance to each hole before securing the panel. Concrete anchor screws, which bite equally well into wood or masonry, are shown here. If you are using normal screws, insert wall plugs before screwing in the screws.

DECORATIVE BATH BORDERS
Once painted, a tongue-and-groove panelling provides a decorative and hard-wearing bath border.

6 Finally, attach a length of quadrant beading around the top of the panelling to provide a smooth finish to the edge. Decorate, then seal the bath edge with silicone.

BATHROOM ACCESSORIES

B athroom accessories can transform the look of the room, so accessory style is an important design element. Whether the accessories are essential or optional, large or small, make sure that they blend with the room's decoration and add to its overall appeal.

TOWEL RAILS

Most bathrooms require something to hang towels on to dry, and heated towel rails are ideal for speeding up this process. The functional role of the towel rail can combine with the look of other accessories in the room—whether traditional, or more modern and innovative—to provide a well-integrated scheme.

Traditional rails: simple in construction and style, a traditional rail fits well into an established bathroom surrounding. Whether it is powered by electricity, or is part of the central heating system as shown here, a traditional towel rail is practical as well as smart.

Modern systems: in recent years, rail designs have become more varied and innovative. Using the heat from radiators to dry out items on a fixed framework of rails is a way of extending the function of the radiator, while producing an unusual alcove design which fits well into a modern bathroom design.

CHANGING FIXTURES

All the smaller bathroom fixtures are quick and simple to change, making it easy to alter the appearance of wall surfaces. Bathroom makeovers do not have to be complex and time consuming to achieve a change in style.

Fitting the fixtures: many essential wall fixtures come supplied with a paper template that makes marking for drill fixings much easier. Simply position the template and mark the appropriate points on the wall.

The simplest of changes: cord pulls for lights or shades are often a neglected area of change. Many variations on the standard plastic theme are available, and can be attached in seconds.

DOOR LOCKS

Bathroom locking systems come in all manner of designs—choosing one is a matter of personal choice and what suits your bathroom. Locking systems that are separate to the handle mechanism are one option, although a fully integrated handle and locking system can often provide the neatest solution.

Operating the lock: integral systems work on a locking screw centrally positioned on the bathroom handle.

Child safety: the beauty of an integral system is that most can be opened from the outside with a special safety key. This means a trapped child can easily be freed with little fuss.

DECORATING BATHROOM ACCESSORIES

M ost bathroom accessories can be transformed with paint, varnish, and all manner of other standard decorating materials, whether you are renovating older items or starting from new.

NEW TOILET SEATS

One of the last outposts of mundane practicality has at last been reached by the modern world of design and progress. Toilet seat style, colour, and finish are now as important a part of bathroom makeovers as any other fixture. The natural wood look is one option for a seat finish; it is very easy to recoat with varnish, giving it excellent life expectancy as well as attractive looks.

Installing seats: most seats are designed with universal fixtures that slot into the retaining holes at the back of the toilet bowl. These fixtures can be adjusted to fit the size of most toilets, but it is always worth checking that this is the case with your chosen design before you buy it.

RENOVATING AN OLD SEAT

Old plastic seats have little character of their own, but a quick change of colour can integrate a seat into a specific bathroom scheme. Remove the seat before painting to protect the bowl and allow access to all areas of the seat itself.

1 Plastic seats need to be cleaned thoroughly before painting, using a proprietary surface preparation solution. This should be wiped onto the seat and then polished off to remove all dirt.

2 Spray the seat with several coats of acrylic paint, keeping the aerosol about 15 cm (6 in) from the seat surface. Work in smooth sweeping movements, applying several thin coats rather than a few thick ones. Follow the manufacturer's guidelines on aerosol safety; at the very least, you will need to wear a respiratory mask.

BATHROOM CHAIRS

Room for furniture is often severely limited in bathrooms because of their size; however, there is often space for the odd item, such as a bathroom chair. These can be used as a movable decorative item, which can either complement the surrounding decoration or provide a contrast. Aerosol paint effects, such as crackle glaze, are ideal for painting awkwardly shaped items.

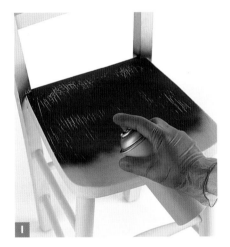

1 Sand down the chair surface, and use a damp cloth to wipe off any dusty residue. Holding the aerosol about 15 cm (6 in) from the chair surface, work across the chair. Turn the chair around and then over to reach all the less accessible areas.

2 Allow the glaze to dry and the crackle effect to develop. When it is dry, spray the entire chair with a protective aerosol varnish.

THE AGED EFFECT
The crackle glaze on this chair provides a wonderfully aged look, which would look good in almost any bathroom scheme.

CHANGING TAPS

Changing old taps for new is a relatively easy procedure and could dramatically alter the appearance of your kitchen or bathroom. First, carry out all the relative checks to ensure that the new taps will fit your plumbing. Taps are literally secured onto the end of the water pipes by simple connectors: changing them is just a matter of unscrewing these connector joints to remove the old faucets, fitting the new faucets in place, then screwing the connectors back in place.

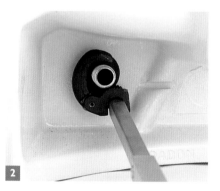

1 Once the water supply is shut off, take off the water supply pipe to gain access to the back nut on the tap. Use a sink wrench to undo the nut at the top of the supply pipe, which connects the pipe to the tap above.

2 With the water pipe removed, undo the tap's back nut. Repeat the process to disconnect the water pipe to any other taps. The taps are now free to be removed from above and new taps installed. Depending on tap design, it may be necessary to disconnect the pop-up rod for the waste pipe. This is normally a simple matter—check the manufacturer's guidelines to see whether a new sink stopper needs to be installed.

CAUTION

Before any tap can be installed, the water supply must be turned off. Most modern water systems have shutoff valves that are situated close to the taps themselves—often they are a short way along the tap supply pipes below the sink. The sink taps can then be turned on to drain off the small amount of water left in the end section of the pipe.

INSTALLING THE NEW TAPS

Tap tails should be lowered through the appropriate holes.

Washers or silicone should be used to cushion the tap block onto the sink surface. Check manufacturer's guidelines for the taps you are using.

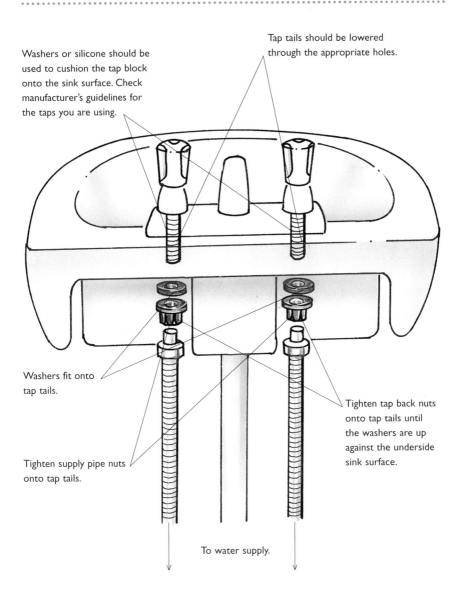

Washers fit onto tap tails.

Tighten tap back nuts onto tap tails until the washers are up against the underside sink surface.

Tighten supply pipe nuts onto tap tails.

To water supply.

(Only turn on water when all joints are tightened.)

LIGHTING

L ighting is one of the major elements for creating atmosphere and
mood in a room, so it is important not to overlook it when you
carry out any sort of makeover. Try to assess the practical needs of the
room in terms of its lighting, before exploring your own ideas on the
kind of light effects you wish to achieve. Always consult a qualified
electrician if any rewiring work is required for the type of lighting you
want to install.

Downlighting: ceiling downlighters
always provide excellent light for
work areas and also produce good
overall lighting for any room. Some
spotlights are fixed, but it is possible
to install "eyeball" types, which can
be moved in their sockets to provide
an alternative direction for the light.
Combining spotlights with other
directional lighting above the table
adds to the atmosphere created by
the lighting in this room.

Simple uplighting: uplighters can
be floor or wall-mounted. Another
option is to use a movable lamp
such as this one, which has a shade
that funnels light upward.

Traditional lamps: these are the
most versatile of all lighting systems
since the shade can be changed to
give a new look, and they can be
moved around the room to create a
different ambiance. Height is an
important factor when positioning a
lamp—low-level lighting produces a
more intimate, cosy atmosphere than
a light source at a higher level.

BATHROOM LIGHTING

Lighting can have a profound effect on any bathroom scheme. It requires careful thought to decide what best suits the atmosphere of the room and its decoration. Also think about what will best fulfil the practical requirements of the room, bearing in mind how you tend to use the room and the sources of natural light. For safety reasons, electrical work should be carried out by a qualified electrician.

Focusing light: downlighting can be aimed directly at a certain part of the room so that a specific task can be carried out. Experimenting with varying levels of light can produce different moods while retaining the directional function.

DIRECTIONAL LIGHTING

Everyday bathroom activities necessitate light sources that are directional and can be used to clearly light up certain areas. This function may be included in the overall lighting setup in the room, but in many cases it can be confined to more direct-task lighting, designed to direct light exactly where you want it.

Downlighting: rather than aiming light at one particular part of the room, overall downlighting tends to give even light throughout the room, making all areas relatively consistent in terms of their light level.

HANGING PICTURES

Most people have a variety of pictures in their homes. The size of the picture, the type of frame, and the place where you want to hang it will all influence the way it is hung on the wall. It is therefore important to choose the right fixing and to attach it to the wall using the correct technique. Although there are some revolutionary designs in this area, which can be helpful in certain situations, the traditional methods are usually more than adequate.

GROUPING PICTURES

Hanging single pictures is usually a straightforward case of holding the picture in the desired position, marking the spot on the wall, and inserting a hook, as required. However, the process is slightly more demanding if a number of pictures are used to form an arrangement, or specific grouping, as shown in this example.

1 Once the first picture is in position, the remaining ones can be measured from this point. Hooks will go into most wall surfaces if you use a hammer to knock them into place.

2 Use a level and a tape measure to position the next hook, adjusting your calculation to account for the picture size, whether you are using an even or a staggered design, and how many pictures are going to be in the final grouping. Continue to position hooks until the required amount are inserted into the wall.

A GROUPED IMPRESSION
A group of pictures that are all the same size gives a decorative and well-ordered finishing touch to a room.

USING FLUSH FIXINGS

In some cases, it may be necessary to hang a picture so that it sits flush and secure against the wall surface. This is usually the case in corridors or any areas where the picture may be easily knocked; standard hooks would allow the picture to be moved out of place, or possibly even damaged.

Fixing in place: the best attachments to use for pictures that need to sit flush are glass plate fixings. These flat plates are screwed to the back of the picture and then the remaining hole houses the screw that fixes the plate (and therefore picture) to the wall, as shown. The number of plate fixings required will vary according to the size of the picture.

HEAVY PICTURES

Standard picture hooks are fairly robust, but with heavier pictures you may want the added peace of mind gained from using more substantial fixing mechanisms. There is no simpler method than using a straightforward wall anchor and long screw. As well as the fixing, make sure that the string or wire on the picture itself is strong enough to take its weight.

1 Drill into the wall surface at the required position in order to make a hole for the screw fixing. Hold the drill at a slight angle so that the screwhead, when inserted, will be pointing ceiling-ward slightly.

2 Knock in the appropriate size plug and screw with a hammer, before screwing into position with a power driver. Leave enough screwhead showing to loop the picture wire over it. Make sure that the screwhead is large enough to hold the picture wire on the screw.

HANGING MIRRORS

A lthough mirrors are generally hung on the wall like pictures, their hanging system varies slightly from the more traditional hook mechanisms. It is preferable to have the mirror secured flush against the wall surface, so that its reflective qualities can be used to the best possible advantage.

FLUSH FIXINGS

There are a number of types of flush fixings available, and indeed in some cases the glass plate fixings shown on page 117 can be used. However, one of the best methods to attach a plain mirror securely on the wall is to use the flush fixing-brackets shown here.

1 Hold the mirror in the required position on the wall, making sure that the mirror is precisely level, then draw a light pencil guideline around its edge. Once the guideline is drawn, put the mirror to one side.

2 Screw four flush fixing-brackets into the wall, two along the bottom edge of the guideline and two along the top edge. The bottom brackets are designed to fit rigidly in one position; the top ones can move slightly.

3 Fit the bottom edge of the mirror into the two lower brackets and push it flat against the wall. The sliding mechanism on the top two brackets allows them to sit higher than the edge of the pencil guideline until after the mirror is inserted. It is then possible to slide these upper brackets over the top edge of the mirror and secure it firmly in place.

HIDDEN FIXINGS

Where a mirror has predrilled holes, it is possible to use a different type of discreet fixing mechanism—mirror screws. These differ slightly from the standard screw fixing in that they have a threaded hole that runs down the central shaft of the screw. This is used to house a chrome cover cap, which hides what would otherwise be an unattractive finishing detail on the mirror.

1 Mark and drill the required number of holes for the mirror, using a drill bit that corresponds to the size of the mirror screws you are using.

2 Mirror screws come supplied with rubber rings, which should be positioned in the mirror holes on the reflective side. These help to prevent the mirror from cracking as the screw is driven into place.

3 Drive the mirror screw into place, being careful not to overtighten it. Apply just enough turns to ensure a secure fixing, allowing the screwhead to nestle inside the rubber ring.

4 Screw the chrome cover cap into the head of the mirror screw to cover the screw and provide a more attractive fixing. Apply more mirror screws and caps to other holes in the mirror, as required.

HANGING TEXTILES

R ugs, throws, and textiles in general provide a particular problem when they are being hung on the wall because they do not have a rigid structure and cannot be treated in the same way as pictures or mirrors. In order to display such items in a way that will show them to full effect, they should be hung using the methods shown here.

USING GRIPPER RODS

In most cases, carpets are placed on the floor, but they can be displayed on the wall, making an attractive feature in a room. Gripper rods can be used to hold the carpet in position, but should not be used for valuable antique carpets.

2 Attach the edge of the rug to the gripper rod, pressing it into position along the serrated edge of the rod. Be careful not to scratch your fingers when positioning the rug as the gripper rod teeth can be very sharp.

1 Cut a gripper rod to the precise width of the rug you want to hang. Nail it into the wall at the appropriate height, using a level to make sure that it is straight.

COMBINED DISPLAY
A combination of pictures and textiles across a wall surface provides a dramatic and impressive wall display.

USING A DOWEL

In some cases, it is possible to hang a rug using a piece of wooden dowel. This method can only be used when the rug has looped tassels, so that the dowel can be threaded through them and then hung on the wall to hold the rug in position.

Cut a length of dowel to the width of the rug and carefully thread it through all the tassels on the end of the rug. Insert two hooks in the wall, slightly less than the width of the dowel apart, and position the dowel in the hooks.

UNUSUAL FEATURE
Rugs and carpets like this one, usually found on the floor, make an extremely attractive feature when they are hung on the wall.

HANGING A THROW

The flimsy nature of a throw means that it needs a larger number of fixing points to keep the material taut and in a good position to display it properly. The exact number of fixing points will vary according to its size.

1 Take each corner of the throw and use some nylon thread to bind around the material, making a securely tied-off section.

2 Position hooks on the wall, and loop the nylon thread over the hooks, adjusting the material, as necessary, to produce the best effect.

HOOKS AND PEGS

H ouseholds can never have enough hooks and pegs for hanging up all manner of everyday clothing. However, they are often forgotten until the rest of the room has been redecorated. In many ways, this is an advantage because you can then position them where they will be useful but still incorporated into the decorative scheme.

MAKING PEGS

Pegs are an attractive hanging system that can add a pleasing finishing touch to a room, as well as being practical. Use a 12.5-by-2.5-cm (5-by-1-in) plank as the base for the pegs and some simple wooden dowel for the pegs themselves.

1 Cut a piece of 12.5-by-2.5-cm (5-by-1-in) planking to the length you require for the base. Draw a pencil guideline centrally along its length. Make a further series of guidelines bisecting the central one at equidistant intervals along its length. Each bisection of the central line represents the position of a peg.

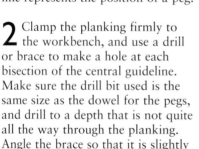

2 Clamp the planking firmly to the workbench, and use a drill or brace to make a hole at each bisection of the central guideline. Make sure the drill bit used is the same size as the dowel for the pegs, and drill to a depth that is not quite all the way through the planking. Angle the brace so that it is slightly off perpendicular to the planking, maintaining this angle for each separate hole.

3 Cut the required number of dowel pegs. Apply a generous amount of wood glue to the pegs and insert them into the drilled holes. Wipe away the excess glue once they are positioned. Leave to dry. The rack can be painted before or after it is fixed to the wall. For a natural wood finish, rub out the guidelines before applying stain and/or varnish.

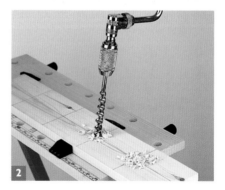

USING HOOKS

As with pegs, hooks tend to look best if they are mounted on a wooden base before they are fixed to the wall. Softwood planking can be used (see opposite); alternatively, a length of hardwood, as shown here, makes an excellent base that contrasts well with the metallic finish of the hooks themselves. To maintain the decorative appeal of this storage system, the fixings used to position the hardwood base on the wall can be hidden behind the hooks, giving a neat and attractive finish.

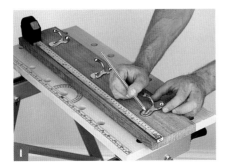

1 Cut a piece of 12.5-by-2.5-cm (5-by-1-in) hardwood planking to the length required. Place the hooks at equal distances along its length. Lay a tape measure along the wood; mark the screw holes for the hooks.

2 Drill a series of pilot holes in the hardwood at each pencil mark, making sure that the drill goes into the surface of the wood vertically.

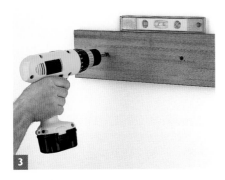

3 Position the wooden base on the wall using a level, and drill fixings between the pilot holes for each of the hooks. Screw the base firmly in position on the wall. Then, before proceeding, oil the wood to give it a good finish.

4 Finally, screw the metal hooks in place, covering the fixings that are holding the wooden base securely on the wall.

INTEGRATING A DOORMAT

A small but very effective home improvement can be achieved by integrating a doormat into the carpet by the front door. Not only does it create a better finish than simply having a separate mat, it can also be cut to the exact size you require. Although the mat will give the appearance of being fixed in place, it will still be possible to remove it for periodic cleaning. The example shown here is for a carpeted floor, but the technique can easily be adapted for wooden or tiled floors by simply following the basic principles of the procedure.

1 Measure the required area for the mat, using a piece of chalk to mark the carpet in the required places. The precise design will vary according to taste, although a straight edge usually gives the best finish. For a slight variation, the corner areas can be cut across the angle to add some extra interest to the final mat shape.

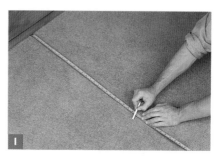

2 Cut through the carpet using a craft knife. Do not worry if you cut into any underlay below the carpet as this will also have to be removed in order to accommodate the new mat. A straight edge, such as a level, can be used as a guideline for cutting, although this is unnecessary if you have a steady hand and can cut accurately along the chalk line.

3 Remove the excess piece of carpet and underlay, then use a hacksaw to cut a section of carpet-edging strip to correspond with the length of the cut carpet edge. If you have an angle or corner in the mat design, it will be necessary to join sections of the strip with mitred joints. Nail the strip in position precisely along the cut edge of the carpet and underlay.

4 Use a bolster to feed the edge of the carpet into the serrated edge of the carpet-edging strip. Make sure that there are no hollow areas under the carpet, as any bumps or dips will ruin the whole effect—it is important to force the carpet edge firmly into the carpet-edging strip.

5 Finally, cut some core matting to the size of the hole and fit it into the hole, making sure that its edge is tightly butted against the carpet strip. Depending on the type of mat, it can either be cut using scissors or a craft knife. With some matting, it may be worthwhile making a template for cutting, in order to achieve a neat finish.

THE INTEGRATED FINISH
Installing a built-in mat by the front door provides a practical and attractive way of stopping mud and dirt from being trailed through the rest of the house.

ALARMS

H ousehold alarm systems were often considered to be an optional choice, but in recent times their popularity has escalated. The growth of this market has resulted in a range of systems that can be easily installed, rather than having to turn to professional installers.

BURGLAR ALARMS

All burglar alarms are based on a system of sensors that either detect room movement or are alerted when contacts are broken around house entrances. Once a contact is broken or sensor alerted, a siren raises the alarm. A wired system requires the components or sensors in the system to be connected and relayed back to the control panel. A non-wired system doesn't need a physical connection between the sensors and the control panel, although there may need to be a connection from the control panel to the outside siren.

SMOKE ALARMS

These are essential in every household. They should be positioned at ceiling level outside bedrooms, to wake occupants in an emergency, and any areas where a fire might start. Smoke alarms wired into the electricity supply should be left to an electrician. However, battery-operated ones are simple to install.

1 Unhinge the lid of the battery-operated alarm and mark the position of the two screw holes on the ceiling with a pencil. Drill two pilot holes and position wall plugs, if necessary. Hold the alarm back in position and secure it with screws inserted in each drilled hole.

2 Once the alarm is in position, insert the battery, close the lid, and test the alarm following the manufacturer's guidelines.

CARBON MONOXIDE ALARMS

This form of alarm is becoming more popular due to a greater awareness of the risks of carbon monoxide poisoning. They are simple to install—most designs simply need to be plugged into the electricity supply.

5
INTELLIGENT STORAGE

Most of us are constantly trying to make more space in our homes and reduce the everyday clutter. It is therefore important to devise storage systems around the home that can counteract the clutter and produce a sense of order. Storage systems vary in size and specific function, which makes them an interesting area of home improvement. This chapter shows you how to find creative solutions for particular storage problems and demonstrates innovative ways to make these systems attractive as well as practical. In addition to standard storage solutions, there are many ideas for transforming existing systems into interesting and attractive storage areas.

SHELVING OPTIONS

A fter painting, putting up shelves is the one do-it-yourself activity that everyone tackles. Display and storage space is a necessity in virtually every room in the house, and there are several options you can choose to meet your needs. These range from open wall shelving to alcove shelving to freestanding units. Use different paint finishes and clever lighting to place your individual stamp on the shelves you choose to make, as well as on ready-made ones from stores.

Alcove shelving: colour is used here to blend in the alcove shelves with their surroundings. The combination of the shelves with the cupboards turns the shelving into a piece of built-in furniture.

Custom-made shelving: built-in shelving makes efficient use of space and is inexpensive to install. These two units are fitted in the same way as traditional alcove shelving, but the top arches were custom designed. Because it's supported by walls on three sides, you can use this type of shelving to store large, heavy books. Store lighter items on high shelves to avoid lifting heavy objects above your head.

Free-standing units: deep storage shelves can look dark. However, you can make them seem lighter by having no back on the unit (as long as it won't be supporting heavy items) and by painting bright colours inside the unit.

Simple shelves: add a splash of colour by painting your shelves in shades that contrast with your wall. The curve of these shelves is not hard to achieve if you use the right material, such as MDF, and cover the edges with a veneer.

Display shelving: open shelving can be as simple as two brackets and a plank of wood—or as intricate and ornate as these, where the shelves are as interesting as the items on display.

SIMPLE SHELVES

S omething simple is often the most effective kind of shelving. There
is no specific design for a simple shelf, except that it should be as
uncomplicated as possible and provide enough support for the objects
it will hold. Make sure that the finished shelf is level on the wall and
choose a finish that will complement the decorative style of the room.

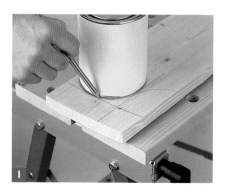

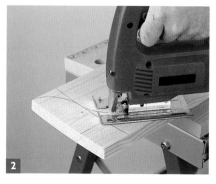

1 On a length of 12.5-by-2.5-cm (5-
by-1-in) softwood, measure 6 cm
(2½ in) in from each corner. Draw
lines at right angles to these marks to
make a cross, then use a paint can to
draw three curves in a bracket shape.

2 Use a jigsaw to cut along the
curved pencil guideline. Follow
the manufacturer's safety instructions
when using a jigsaw, and never stand
in front of the blade. Repeat Steps 1
and 2 to make a second bracket.

3 Cut another length of 12.5-by-
2.5-cm (5-by-1-in) prepared
softwood to the required length for
your shelf. Hold a bracket 12.5 cm
(5 in) in from the cut end, drawing a
pencil guideline along the point
where the bracket meets the shelf.

4 Hold the bracket securely on the
guideline and drill a pilot hole
through the bracket into the shelf.

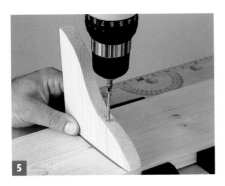

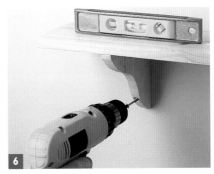

5 Drive a screw into the hole (see below), making sure that it bites firmly into the shelf, but does not go all the way through to what will be the shelf top. For extra strength, apply some wood glue to the bracket before positioning it on the guideline. Attach the other bracket to the shelf in the same way.

6 Drill two more holes in the brackets for wall attachment. Position the shelf using a level, then screw through the brackets into the wall, using wall plugs, if necessary. For added strength, drill and fix two screws at a 45-degree angle through the top of the shelf (at the back), through the brackets, and into the wall. Fill all screw holes. Round the corners of the shelf with sandpaper.

DECORATIVE
STORAGE SYSTEM
Once decorated, a
simple shelf provides
an attractive decorative
storage system for
ornaments or items
in everyday use.

FIXING THE SCREWS

Use a countersink drill bit to open up the entrance to the drilled hole on the bracket, so that the screw will fit below the wood surface.

WALL-SUSPENDED SHELVES

A llowing the majority of the weight of a shelf to be supported from above, rather than below, produces an interesting effect quite different from the more traditional shelves. Combining wood with rope, and using large obvious wall fixings, adds to the sturdy, uncomplicated design of a wall-suspended shelf. The rustic appeal of this kind of design lends itself to a very natural-looking finish, such as waxing, a distressed paint effect, or a simple colour rub.

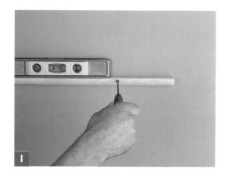

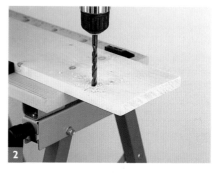

1 Cut a piece of 12.5-by-2.5-cm (5-by-1-in) planed softwood for your shelf, here 60 cm (2 ft). Cut a piece of 2 cm (¾ in) quadrant beading to the same length. Screw the quadrant into the wall at the required shelf height using a short level to make sure that it is level. Drill pilot holes and insert wall plugs, if necessary, for a good fixing.

2 Measure 2.5 cm (1 in) in from the edge of the shelf, and 7.5 cm (3 in) from its end, and make a pencil mark. Drill a hole at this mark, using a bit of a similar size to the rope being used to support the shelf—a diameter of 7.5 mm (¼ in) is ideal. Make another hole in the corresponding position at the other end of the shelf.

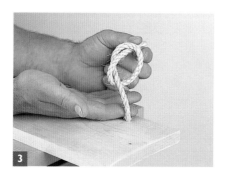

3 Cut two lengths of rope to about 45 cm (18 in) long. Thread one piece through each hole in the shelf and tie each piece with a knot on the underside, as shown.

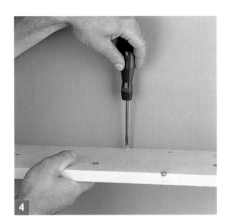

4 Position the shelf above the quadrant on the wall, making sure that the shelf edge is tight up against the wall/quadrant junction. Screw in three wood screws at equal distances along the back edge of the shelf, screwing through the shelf and into the quadrant below.

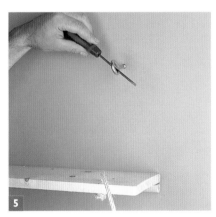

5 In a vertical line from the drilled rope holes, screw two large "eye" brackets into the wall about 25 cm (10 in) above the shelf. If necessary, drill a pilot hole before using a screwdriver as a lever to screw the "eye" into the wall. Once both "eyes" are in position, thread the two loose ends of the rope through their corresponding "eye," and tie them so that the rope is taut.

NATURAL LOOK
This shelf has been finished with a white liming, or pickling, wax to protect and decorate the wood, while maintaining its natural look.

CEILING-SUSPENDED SHELVES

S helving can be designed to hang from the ceiling, rather than using the wall as the main weight support. For this kind of shelving, it is essential to find a strong fixing point—a solid wooden joist—as the entire weight of the hanging shelf is taken by this one point. However, once this obstacle is overcome, suspended ceiling shelving creates an excellent effect, giving you secure shelving without any cumbersome supports. Three shelves are ideal for creating a balanced-looking shelving system.

1 Cut three 45-cm (18-in) lengths from 12.5-by-2.5-cm (5-by-1-in) planed softwood. At one end of each length, screw in two small "eyes," 12 mm (½ in) from the edge. Screw in two "eyes" at the other end of each shelf in the corresponding position.

2 Using wire cutters, cut four pieces of chain each measuring 90 cm (3 feet) in length.

3 Attach the bottom link of one chain to each of the four "eyes" on one of the shelves, using chain hooks. Measure 20 cm (8 in) up each chain and position another shelf, and finally measure the same distance again and position the final shelf. On the chain shown here, 20 cm (8 in) is the same as 20 links of the chain, which is an easy way of measuring between "eyes."

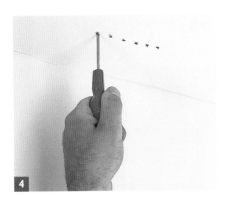

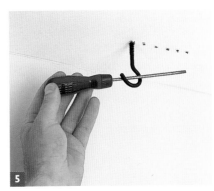

4 To find a firm fixing point in the ceiling, make a number of holes with an old screwdriver or bradawl until you find a solid wooden joist. Try and find a fixing position no more than 7.5 cm (3 in) away from the wall, so that the shelf will gain some small support from the wall to prevent it from spinning around.

5 Screw a large hook into the fixing hole. Use a screwdriver as leverage to make sure that the hook is solidly screwed into place. Fill in the other holes. Take the four loose ends of chain and position the final link of each four over the hook, adjusting the chains into the correct position, if necessary.

SUSPENDING SHELVES
Once in place, all the effort of suspending shelving is well worthwhile. A simple coloured stain is the ideal way of finishing the shelves to create a stunning suspended shelving system.

ADJUSTABLE SHELVES

A track shelving system is easy to install. It consists of two or more lengths of vertical metal track and a series of matching shelf brackets that fit into slots or channels in the tracks. They are available in white, bright primary colours, and metallic effects. The system can support shelves made of a variety of materials, including wood and MDF. You can use ready-made ones or cut and finish your own.

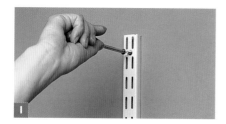

1 After you decide on the positioning and spacing of the tracks, hold the first end track against the wall and mark the position of its topmost screw with an awl. Drill the hole and plug it if you have a masonry wall. Drive in the screw partway.

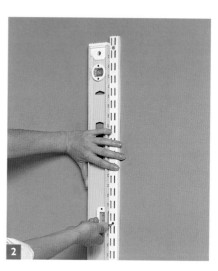

2 To position the track vertically, hold a level against it and adjust it until the bubble is centred in the appropriate tube of fluid. Then mark the positions for the other screws, swing the track aside so you can drill the holes (and install plugs, if necessary), then reposition the track and insert the remaining screws.

3 To position the other end track, slip a bracket into the same slot in both tracks. Standing a shelf on end on the bracket on the first track, with a level on top to keep it horizontal, set the other end track in place and mark the topmost screw. Then repeat steps 1 and 2 to secure the track to the wall. Repeat for any intermediary tracks.

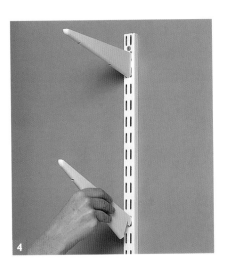

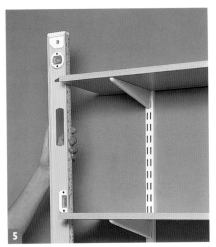

4 Slip the shelf brackets into place in the slots in the track, checking that they are level with each other—count the number of slots above or below the brackets. If necessary, cut the shelves to length—you can add strips of veneer to the ends to hide cut ends.

5 Some brackets have a bump on the end to prevent the shelf from slipping forward. If your shelf is wider than the bracket, mark the location of the bump on the bottom of the shelf, and drill a hole partway through so the shelf can rest level on the bracket. Position the shelves on the brackets; use a level or plumb line to align their ends.

6 Unless the shelves are in an alcove and, therefore, captive, it is best to screw the shelves to the brackets. Drive the screws up from the bottom of the brackets, supporting the top of the shelf with your other hand. Make sure the screws penetrate only about two-thirds of the shelf's thickness.

KIDS' STORAGE
Adjustable shelving is perfect for storing children's toys—the shelves can be moved up and down to accommodate new toys and other belongings as the children grow up.

REVAMPING SHELVING

S helving is probably the most common storage system found in our homes. Shelves benefit from a makeover just as much as any other household fixture. One way of revamping a shelving system is to give it a different look by creating the illusion of greater height. Other cosmetic changes include painting and using decorative moulding.

USING FLAT STRIPS

One of the easiest ways of giving shelving the illusion of greater height, or a more solid look in general, is to pin flat strips of beading along the front edge of the shelves. Calculate how much beading you require by simply measuring the combined lengths of the shelves you wish to remodel.

1 Cut the beading to size and hammer in some panel pins along its edge before positioning it against the shelf. It is much easier to start hammering pins into the beading while it is off the shelf, rather than trying to do it when it is in position.

2 Hold the beading against the edge of the shelf and hammer the pins into the shelf, making sure the top edge of the beading is flush with the surface of the shelf. Use a nail punch to ensure that the pin heads go in below the surface level.

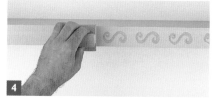

3 Use all-purpose filler to fill the pin-head holes. Leave it to dry before sanding the entire edge to a smooth finish.

4 Paint the shelf, then give the edge an added decorative effect by stamping a design along it—this will also enhance the more solid appearance the shelving now has.

Using A Decorative Moulding

A similar "height-increasing" effect can be achieved by using a more decorative moulding to act as the front edge to the shelf. This in itself provides greater opportunity for extravagant decorative paint effects, transforming the original simple shelving system into a more eye-catching and creative feature.

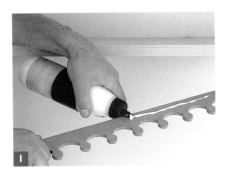

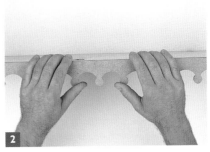

1 As an alternative to using pins to secure the moulding in place, it is possible to use wood glue. Glue is especially suitable if the moulding is lightweight and unlikely to slip once it has been positioned and the glue is drying.

2 Position the moulding, ensuring that its top edge is flush with the broad surface of the shelf.

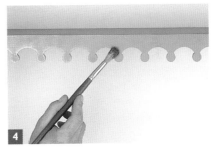

3 Once the glue has dried, paint the shelf and moulding to blend both components together and make them into a more solid-looking single shelf structure.

4 Gold highlighting is a good way to add decorative interest to the shelf front. Use a fine paint brush with very little gold paint on the bristles—ensure that the excess paint is removed after you have loaded the brush. Gently brush backward and forward across the edges of the moulding to produce a highlighting effect which gives an aged, antiqued appearance to the whole shelf.

INVENTIVE SHELVING OPTIONS

Shelving is usually confined to wide open areas of wall space, because that appears to be the most obvious or easiest position for it. However, if you want to be more inventive about shelving, you can produce all kinds of novel systems, all of which can add an extra dimension to the appearance and function of your shelving.

UTILIZING SPACE

The secret of utilizing space is to create shelving in areas that would otherwise be redundant. This has the effect of producing an interesting decorative feature, while satisfying practical needs. The following are a few examples of areas where shelving can be built to give this sort of effect.

- Fireplaces: disused fireplaces provide an ideal area for shelving in what would otherwise be wasted space.
- Picture rails: create a shelf at picture-rail height to make use of otherwise unused wall space.
- Dado trim: as with picture rails, the area directly above dado trim is often unused. In many cases this is because a shelf would stop furniture from being placed against the wall. However, where this is not the case, a dado-level shelf is a serious option for creating extra storage.
- Radiator shelf: positioning a shelf above a radiator can help to draw the eye away from the radiator itself. Always leave a gap between the radiator and the shelf to allow the air to circulate. Also, make sure that the shelf is made from a board such as medium-density fibreboard— softwood shelving is likely to warp with the heat from the radiator.
- Above doors: this is another under-

used area that can be enlivened by the addition of a single shelf.

- Pelmets: the frame of a window pelmet can often make a useful ornamental shelf as long as it is made from a material that is substantial enough to be load-bearing.
- Corners: building a shelving system across a corner can provide a useful storage area, as well as smoothing the angular appearance of a corner and giving a better decorative effect. See pages 152–155.
- Integral shelving: not all shelving has to be for display—there is often a lot of wasted space in the larger storage systems, such as cupboards and wardrobes. Adding shelves to the underutilized spaces in these areas can provide a great deal of hidden storage capacity.
- Bathrooms: because bathrooms are one of the smaller rooms in the home, space-saving ideas are essential. Rather than store toiletries outside a shower cubicle, have a storage facility in the shower for items that will not be affected by moisture. Manufacturers are very innovative in this area and they are producing lots of designs for shower shelving and hanging systems.

WINDOW SHELVING

This may appear to be an unlikely area to consider when thinking about shelving, but not all windows have a breathtaking view or let in a great deal of light. In such cases, it can be worthwhile using the window for a shelving system, creating an attractive and useful area in what was otherwise a rather bland and underused area of the room.

1 Draw a level pencil guideline in one side of the window recess at the height where you want the shelf to be positioned. Screw in two jointing blocks along the pencil guideline to act as the shelf supports.

2 Cut the shelf to size and rest one end on the jointing blocks. Pencil a guideline on the opposite side of the recess, using a level to ensure that it is straight. Secure two more jointing blocks and position the shelf.

ORIGINAL SHELVING SYSTEM
This pretty window shelf combines practicality with a very original look. The ornamental and display properties of this type of shelving are highly effective.

UNDERSTAIRS STORAGE

T he area under the stairs is often a much underused part of the home and one that is worthwhile considering for refurbishment. In some cases, it may be possible to turn the area into a downstairs bathroom, although some professional help will be required to carry out a project of this nature. More often, understairs areas can be turned into useful storage space.

Closed system: a neat, compact finish can be achieved by constructing a closed system that encloses the entire understairs area. This makes good use of the space while maintaining an understated look. The design of such systems will vary according to the available space and the general layout, but a simple construction is usually the best.

THE TRADITIONAL LOOK

For a traditional look, a panelled storage system with hinged doors is a good way of integrating it into the rest of the decorative scheme.

Sliding compartments: instead of using traditional cabinet doors, a more innovative approach is to create sliding compartments that bring the storage system out into the hallway when access is required. It makes access to the shelves much easier, but it does require more advanced skills to create such a storage facility.

Display system: in some situations, it may be better to use the area under the stairs as an open storage and display system. The actual size of the whole system and the depth of the shelves will depend on the design of the staircase.

Open system: rather than closing off the storage area below stairs, it can be just as practical—and very attractive—to keep it open and create a more visible storage system with easy access to all the things kept there.

WINDOW SEATS

W indow seats can be constructed to form an excellent storage system while providing an attractive feature in your home. They are best suited to windows with a relatively deep recess to give enough depth for a reasonable seating area.

SEAT CONSTRUCTION

The design, size, and depth of window recesses may vary dramatically, but there are a number of general principles that apply to the construction of all window seats. The most important consideration is to ensure that the seat is hinged so that it can be opened to provide valuable storage space.

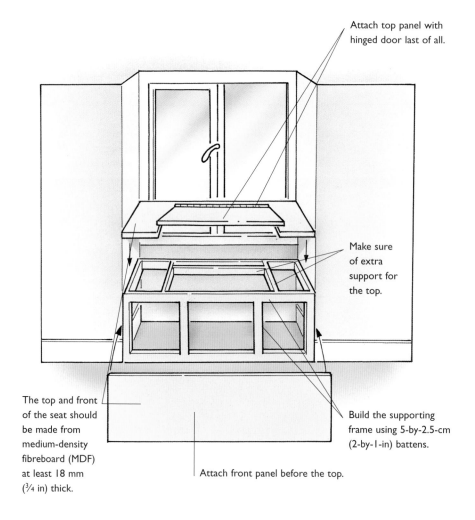

Attach top panel with hinged door last of all.

Make sure of extra support for the top.

The top and front of the seat should be made from medium-density fibreboard (MDF) at least 18 mm (¾ in) thick.

Attach front panel before the top.

Build the supporting frame using 5-by-2.5-cm (2-by-1-in) battens.

ATTACHING THE HINGE TO THE SEAT

The trickiest part of building a window seat is creating the hinged door to allow access to the storage area underneath the seat. The easiest method is to cut the actual door out of the top surface of the seat using a jigsaw. The cut-out portion can then be turned into a door by attaching a flush hinge all the way along its length before reattaching it to the main seat area.

1 Cut the flush hinge to the length of the medium-density-fibreboard door with a hacksaw. Position the hinge along the edge of the door, reverse side upward. Mark with a pencil the position of each screw point along the length of the hinge.

2 Remove the hinge. Then drill pilot holes at every pencil mark along the edge of the door.

3 Position the hinge the right side up and screw it in place, ensuring that it fits flush along the edge of the door. To fit the door to the main part of the seat, again drill pilot holes, then secure in place with screws.

A WINDOW SEAT

Window seats combine practicality and good looks to produce an excellent feature in any room. The tongue-and-groove panelling across the front of this seat is given a stylish look by the sumptuous cushions arranged along the top of the seat.

CUPBOARDS

C upboards provide an essential part of the storage capacity in most homes. They are an important area of concern when remodelling and improving your home. Making the best of cupboard capacity and its appearance is therefore important when considering storage.

Cupboard styles: the term "cupboard" is used to refer to all sorts of sectioned-off storage spaces around the house. Choosing the best system for a particular area is very important for creating the right balance between being functional and looking decorative in a room.

Wardrobes: these can be separate items of furniture or they can be fitted into the overall scheme of a room. The latter option saves space by making use of alcoves and other redundant areas. Decorating the wardrobes so that they become integrated into the room's colour scheme can also be very effective.

Cupboard combinations: storage facilities do not have to be confined to one system—one attractive option is to combine closed-off cupboards with more open storage areas, such as these shelves.

Display cabinets: one of the more decorative aspects of a storage system is the facility to combine the two functions of storing and displaying items at the same time. A glass-fronted cabinet, filled with pretty items like glass or china, can do this with impressive effect.

CHANGING A CUPBOARD'S APPEARANCE

Many cupboards can have their entire appearance transformed by changing the doors, or by simply altering the look of the existing ones. The method by which this is achieved will vary according to the design of the cupboard. The examples shown here demonstrate how a simple panel door can be dramatically changed using one of several decorative finishes.

Removing the middle: to change the look of a panel door, first remove the central area, so that an alternative decoration can be attached to the door. On some designs the panel will fall out with a few firm hammer knocks; in other cases, it may be necessary to cut out the middle panel using a jigsaw. Drill four holes, one at each corner of the central panel, to accommodate the jigsaw blade and allow for accurate cutting.

The mirror look: use mirror adhesive to stick a mirror to the back of the door frame. For a heavy mirror, use special mirror fixings. You can change a single door in this way, or a number of doors as part of an overall fitted wardrobe system—the effect can be quite dramatic. Ensure that the mirror you choose is appropriate for door use and is shatterproof.

The material look: attach wire mesh and fabric to the back of the door frame to give the front a rustic look. Pull the mesh and fabric taut and secure in place with a staple gun.

Using fretwork: cut a piece of fretwork the size of the door and paint it a contrasting colour to the door frame. Pin it in place on the back of the frame. This produces an attractive open display system for a cabinet.

MAKING GOOD USE OF CUPBOARDS

Even with the most ingenious use of space in the home, there comes a point where you can't fit in any more storage units. When you reach that stage, you'll have to make better use of your existing storage space. The kitchen and the bedroom are the main areas for storage, and there are many space-saving fittings available to make use of even the most inaccessible areas.

FITTING A CLOTHES POLE

1 To fit a clothes pole, measure and mark the position of the brackets on each side of the closet. They should be in the centre of the side uprights and equidistant from the top of the closet. Mark the screw hole positions, drill the holes, and screw the brackets in place.

2 Measure from the inside of one bracket to the inside of the other. Cut a solid wood pole or length of metal tubing to this length, using a hacksaw. Insert one end of the pole or tubing into one bracket, then bring the other end up and drop it down into the opposite bracket.

FITTING A SWIVEL HANGER

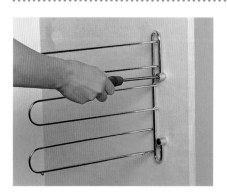

This hanger swivels outside of the closet, so when you decide on its position bear this in mind. Mark the position of the screw holes, drill the holes, then screw the swivel hanger to the side of the closet. You can buy a similar type of hanger designed to hold ties and scarves.

Fitting A Carousel Unit

In the kitchen, some useful ideas include carousels to increase storage in corner base units (see below), and wire baskets and racks in all shapes and sizes to fit in pull-out storage units and on door backs.

1 Start by deciding on the relative positions of the trays—this will depend on the height of the items that you want to store in them. Position the hinge bracket on the cabinet frame, mark the position of the screw holes, and drill pilot holes for the screws.

2 Screw the brackets into the frame, then continue with the other brackets until they have all been mounted.

3 Position the lower carousel tray on the appropriate bracket, making sure that the top flange on the tray goes on the top flange of the bracket. Insert the bracket pin and gently tap it down with a small hammer.

4 Fit a follower bracket to the door—it pulls the tray out when the door is opened. Pull the tray out so it meets the open door, position the follower bracket on the door with its hook over the tray, and mark the screw holes. Remove the bracket, drill the holes, then screw the bracket in place with the tray under the hook.

KITCHEN CAROUSEL
A carousel unit is the perfect storage device for corner units in a kitchen. It swings out or revolves to make items stored on it accessible.

DECIDING ON BATHROOM STORAGE

There are all sorts of factors to consider when choosing bathroom storage areas. You have to decide how practical these areas need to be and balance it with their decorative appeal. House size as a whole is important—in many cases the linen closet and storage space for toiletries must be included in the bathroom. Where these can be built in other parts of the house, storage in the bathroom becomes less vital, and decorative shelving and display areas can be more important.

Combining storage and style: open shelving allows for both storage and display; it is a very practical way of housing items vital to bathroom activities and combines this function with an ordered look, keeping things close at hand and easy to find.

Practical storage: well-designed shelving is an excellent space-saving facility, making use of otherwise wasted areas of the bathroom, and accommodating lots of items in a relatively small space.

The built-in approach: a neat, compact finish is easy to achieve if you have a number of built-in cupboards. These maximize storage while minimizing space wastage. Professional help may be required to produce a perfect custom-made finish, although many retailers do sell "flat-packed" cupboard and shelving systems that are relatively simple to assemble and install.

Maintaining ventilation: bathrooms are prone to high levels of moisture in the air, so it is essential to keep them well ventilated. This is an important consideration with the storage facilities—cabinet doors that allow air to circulate are very helpful, especially in smaller bathrooms.

STORAGE IDEAS

- Displaying and concealing: it is always a good idea to have some storage areas that can be used to show off attractive items, but it is equally important to have unobtrusive cabinets and shelving for storing items that do not necessarily warrant open viewing.
- Child-proofing: medicines are often kept in bathroom cabinets and these cabinets should be positioned out of the reach of children and, if possible, have a lock on them.
- Dual purpose: combining functions is the secret of clever storage. For example, a wall cabinet containing a mirror or a shelf with hooks on the underside are prime examples of maximizing space by having one item fulfil two jobs.

CORNER SHELVES

Corners are often wasted areas of a room, especially in bathrooms, where sinks and other fixtures prevent larger pieces of furniture from being positioned there. Corner storage systems tend to require securing into the walls, rather than having a fixed base. All kinds of corner units can be bought from retailers, but, using a few simple ideas, you can create clever designs of your own, such as tile shelving.

TILE SHELVING

Tiles are often used to form shelved areas in bathrooms, but this is normally confined to bath ledges or window sills. A more innovative use is to just use the tiles themselves, as single shelves in their own right. Large floor tiles are ideal for this purpose and can be used to create novel corner shelving.

1 Mark a diagonal line from corner to corner across a floor tile, using a piece of batten for a straight edge. Using a tile cutter, cut two identical triangular shapes.

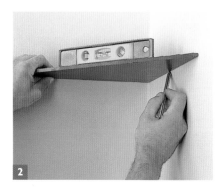

2 Hold the tile, wrong side down, at the approximate required level in the corner and adjust its position until it is level. Make a pencil mark on the wall along the underside of the tile.

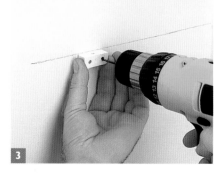

3 Hold a jointing block just below the pencil line and drill two pilot holes. Depending on the wall, you may need wall plugs in order to provide a firm fixing hole for the screws.

4 Screw in the jointing block, then position another close to it. Position two more blocks on the adjacent wall.

5 Position a tile on the blocks and apply a gloss or mat varnish to the cut edge of the tile, depending on the finish required. The shelves can be left so that they can be easily removed. Alternatively, to make the shelf more secure, some adhesive can be applied to the top of each jointing block before the tile is positioned.

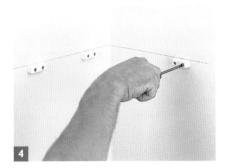

ADDING MORE SHELVES
Add more shelves to the corner as required. Since the jointing blocks are small enough to hide how the tiles are attached, they do not detract from the look of this "suspended" tile shelving.

PRACTICAL CORNER STORAGE

C orner spaces are ideal for use as practical storage areas. These will add to the decoration of the room while making maximum use of the space. They also give you the opportunity to test your skills by building across the corner and creating open storage systems. Precise measurements and accurate cutting are essential if you want to produce excellent results.

MAKING A TOWEL STACK

Bathrooms are always full of towels and these are often hidden away in closets. Displaying them gives you the chance to make an otherwise dull storage system far more attractive, and keeping them in the open means they are well ventilated and within easy reach.

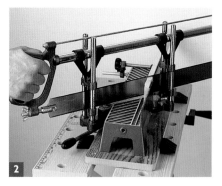

1 Measure out 45 cm (18 in) from the corner and draw a level line from this point back to the corner.

2 Cut a 45-cm (18-in) length of 5-by-1-cm (2-by-½-in) batten, mitring one end.

3 Attach the batten above the pencil line, using two masonry nails, with the mitred end pointing away from the corner. Attach a corresponding batten, 44 cm (17½ in) in length, on the adjacent wall. Measure the distance between the end point of the mitre on each wall, and cut another length of batten to this size, mitring the cuts so that the ends of the batten will fit snugly against the wall.

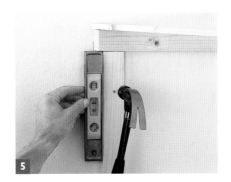

4 Nail the batten in place with brads. Continue to attach more battens along the top of the frame, measuring 2 cm (¾ in) along the wall toward the corner for each new length of wood.

5 Cut a 30-cm (12-in) length of batten and nail it vertically, set back slightly from the corner of the first horizontal batten. Continue to add three more battens at equal distances to the corner. Repeat these vertical lengths on the adjacent wall.

6 Repeat Steps 1–4 to produce another horizontal slatted platform below the vertical battens. Finish the wood with varnish or colour rub with an emulsion, as shown here. Leave the paint to dry then seal the wood with a coat of varnish. Allow it to dry before use.

COLOURFUL AND ELEGANT
A towel stack creates a colourful and elegant piece of practical shelving.

BATHROOM RACKS AND RAILS

S helves and traditional towel rails can be adapted to give them a more innovative appearance, while still maintaining their use as storage facilities.

TOOTHBRUSH-MUG RACK

The idea of a toothbrush-mug rack is by no means new, but some simple design changes, such as keeping the shelf very angular, and decorating it with something like metallic paint, can give it an ultramodern look. For the design below, the toothbrush mug must have a larger rim than the base.

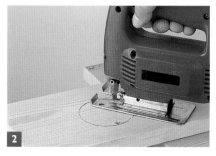

1 Cut a length of 12.5-by-2.5-cm (5-by-1-in) planed softwood to the required length, allowing for two triangular brackets to be cut from this length. Hold a toothbrush mug central to the shelf, but to one side of its width, and pencil a guideline.

2 Use a jigsaw to cut out both brackets. Drill a hole at the edge of the circular guideline to accommodate the jigsaw blade, and cut out the central area. Attach the brackets and the shelf to the wall.

SIMPLISTIC
This simplistic rack can be painted to match any colour scheme and will look perfectly at home in any modern bathroom.

Towel Rails

A novel towel rail can be produced from simple copper pipes of the type used for home plumbing. By combining straight lengths of pipe with right-angled joints and T-shaped connectors, it is possible to create all sorts of shapes and designs. Use a proprietary adhesive capable of securing two metal surfaces to stick the joints together.

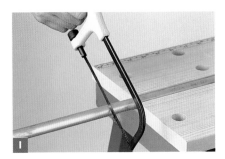

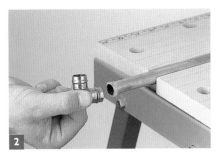

1 Decide on the dimensions of the towel rail you require, then cut lengths of pipe to size. Pipe cutters can be used, but a sharp hacksaw will do the job just as efficiently.

2 Glue elbow joints and T connectors to the pipe lengths, making sure that there is a strong bond. Wipe off any excess adhesive before it dries.

3 Drill holes through the T connectors that back onto the wall surface. Fix them in place on the wall before the rest of the framework is built up to give the finished rail no visible fixing points. Before using, coat the rail with a good-quality varnish to prevent damp towels from corroding the copper, and the towels themselves from becoming stained.

SLOPING FRAMEWORK
On this design, the two lower sets of the three pipes at the side of the framework become increasingly shorter as they go down the rack. When towels are hung on each level, they miss the towel below, which allows them to dry faster.

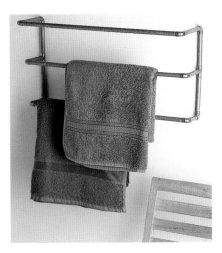

BATH HATCHES

There are sometimes areas at the foot or head of an inset bath that are underused and waste their space-saving capabilities. Instead of totally boxing in these areas, you can insert a door in the boxing and use the space as storage cupboards. Bath hatches need to be inserted according to the specific design of your bath (see opposite); however, there are certain points that must be considered before building any such storage system.

HINGED HATCHES

It is essential that hatch doors fit precisely and that their hinging mechanism ensures that the door sits flush. Use the aptly named "flush" hinges—these hinges are relatively easy to attach and run all the way along the hinged edge of the hatch, making a very precise finish to the door edge.

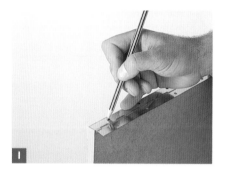

1 Cut the bath hatch to the right size and clamp it vertically onto a workbench. Cut the flush hinge to length, using a hacksaw, and hold the hinge along the appropriate edge of the hatch, marking the screw positions with a pencil.

2 Remove the hinge and drill pilot holes at the pencil marks on the hatch.

3 Hold the hinge along the edge, and fix it in place with the appropriate size screws. Holding the hinged hatch in place, mark the position for the corresponding hinge holes, drill the pilot holes, and screw it in position.

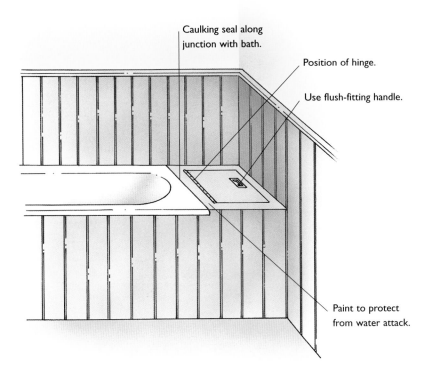

Caulking seal along junction with bath.

Position of hinge.

Use flush-fitting handle.

Paint to protect from water attack.

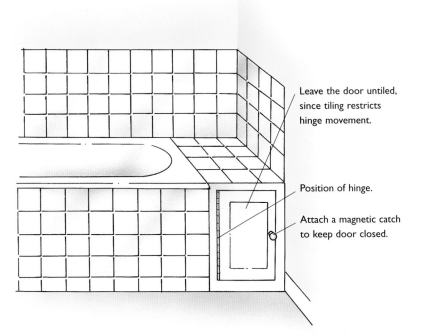

Leave the door untiled, since tiling restricts hinge movement.

Position of hinge.

Attach a magnetic catch to keep door closed.

USING THE KITCHEN CEILING

T he kitchen ceiling is often a neglected area when it comes to considering storage systems. Ceiling storage is usually a hanging system—a modern version of the old-fashioned clothes airing rack. This basic design is the ideal way of storing all manner of items, while keeping them easily accessible for everyday use, and it has become a popular way of storing cooking utensils in the kitchen. Such storage systems are ideal for a traditionally styled kitchen. For instructions on how to construct a ceiling rack, turn to page 134.

Integrating the scheme: painting a hanging rack the same colour as the kitchen cabinets helps to integrate the rack into the overall scheme and create a well-balanced and coordinated look.

Utilizing space: racks suspended from the ceiling are a perfect way of using space that would otherwise be wasted. They also avoid cramping any of the open, uncluttered areas in a kitchen.

PART TWO:
PAPERING AND PAINTING

DECORATING BASICS

Paper and paint are the primary adornments for home decorating, and creating colour schemes using these essential materials can be very rewarding—both conceiving the actual design ideas and the practical application of these ideas to rooms and surfaces within your home. Decorating is an ideal vehicle for self-indulgence since it allows you to express your personal tastes and preferences in a way that is beneficial to your lifestyle by making pleasant surroundings to live in, and beneficial in a practical way by improving the look of your home and adding to its financial value. Experienced decorators and novices alike will benefit from the techniques and advice in the following chapters, because there is always room for improvement, whatever the level of your ability. Trying different techniques and finishes, or experimenting with alternative products, is all part of the process. Painting and papering provide the finishing touches to your home, so enjoy the process and it will continue to give pleasure for many years.

CHOOSING COLOUR AND PATTERN

Style is very much a personal issue and the way you choose colours and patterns for your home is based on where you look for inspiration. Most of us have favourite colours and types of design, but moulding these into a finished product suitable for your particular room or rooms can be a daunting process. The best thing to do is to seek your inspiration from all areas of life. For example, using lifestyle magazines for ideas and fashion hints can be very helpful. Develop these external influences still further by noting the kind of things that attract you to certain rooms in other people's houses. Look at the variety of shapes and sizes that you come across in your everyday life, and consider how you could apply them to colour schemes and designs within your home. Devising a scheme can be as simple or as complicated a process as you wish to make it. By taking into account all the different influences open to you, choosing colour and pattern provides an open avenue to fulfilling your desire to create a well-decorated and attractive home.

THE PLANNING PROCESS

The most important part of any papering or painting job is the initial planning stage. The time spent choosing a scheme and preparing the surfaces will always pay dividends by helping to ensure a well-finished product. Chapter 1 provides all the information needed to deal with this stage of the decorating process, demonstrating the most efficient preparatory techniques to use on different surfaces.

ESSENTIAL PAINTING

Applying paint to walls and woodwork in the correct manner is an essential part of the decorating process. Different painting tools require different techniques, so choosing the tools that suit you, and are appropriate for the job at hand, is a matter of personal preference. Chapter 2 provides detailed instruction on using painting tools in the best way possible to ensure that your painted finish will live up to expectations. It also gives detailed instructions for painting problem areas such as doors and window frames in the most time-efficient and effective way.

CREATING PAINT EFFECTS

Paint effects are definitely the fun part of painting, as well as being the decoration that can produce the most dramatic finishes. The processes of producing these stunning effects have a learning curve, with some of the techniques being more difficult than others. Chapter 3 guides you through the various paint effects, plus some modern variations on the more traditional decorating themes, all of which combine to create an exciting, idea-provoking section of this book.

PAPERING PRINCIPLES

Chapter 4 explains the principles and basic methods involved in general paperhanging technique. The success of any papered finish is built on these firm foundations, and progress is dependent on a good grasp of these simple but effective methods. As well as providing instruction on paperhanging, this section also shows you how to solve all the common wallpapering problems experienced by most amateur home decorators.

AWKWARD AREAS

Most rooms are not completely square, and nearly all have some obstacles that need to be overcome during the paperhanging process. Chapter 5 deals with all these areas and provides clear instruction on the best methods to use, from how to deal with arches to building steady and secure platforms for decorating stairwells. A good understanding of these methods will help any decorator deal with the various problems and obstacles encountered on a wall surface.

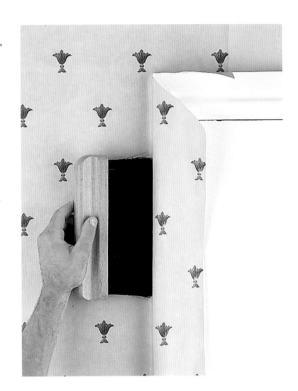

PAPERING EFFECTS

Although less flexible than paint, paper can be used in a surprising variety of ways. Patterned paper borders and frames can be used to add decorative interest to an otherwise monochromatic design scheme, or to add luxurious detail to a more elaborate look. Plain and patterned papers, or papers with complementary patterns, can also be effectively combined.

PAINT AND PAPER COMBINATIONS

Most decorative schemes can be enlivened by combining wallpaper and paint to create highly innovative finishes. Chapter 6 discusses the ways of using paper and paint in a scheme, as well as explaining how to apply paintable papers, which give further options to the home decorator. Combining these media can be a very rewarding process, leading to all sorts of highly original decorative finishes and designs.

MODERN INNOVATION

As well as perfecting both the simple and more advanced techniques involved in papering and painting your home, it is a good idea to investigate the innovations and developments in the area of home decoration. Manufacturers are constantly trying to produce new and better materials, which are often claimed to be revolutionary and essential for all enthusiasts. Usually the claims are exaggerated, but sometimes new products do make life much easier and it is worthwhile trying them out. For example, the introduction of rollers for painting was truly a groundbreaking event! Also, water-based paints are becoming by far the most popular paints to use because of their improved formula and ease of use. So, be aware of change and use it to your advantage—finding a new tool for a job, or even refining old techniques and improving them, can be a very enjoyable part of the paint and papering process.

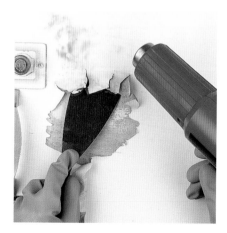

1
PREPARATION
AND PLANNING

*Good initial preparation will make the entire
process of decorating easier and help you to achieve
the best possible finish. As well as the physical
preparation required to make surfaces ready for
decoration, it is also essential to plan your
decoration. Choosing colour schemes and deciding
on finishes are the essential first steps of any
decorating job: take time to think over all the
options before making any final decisions. This
chapter covers all these aspects and provides a
firm base or starting point on which to build your
painting and paperhanging techniques—it discusses
the many different surfaces
in the home and the best
way to prepare them
for decoration.*

CHOOSING A COLOUR SCHEME

C hoosing the colour scheme for a room can be a difficult process because so many factors have to be taken into consideration. Personal taste should always be the main factor, but you also need to have some awareness of the effects of different colours and patterns and take these into account. Allow enough time at this essential planning stage and consider all the available options and alternatives before making a final decision.

THE COLOUR WHEEL

All colours are created from the three primary colours—red, yellow, and blue— with secondary and tertiary colours derived from these. The colour wheel below gives an indication of the way in which different colours relate to each other: how they can complement or contrast according to the effect you want.

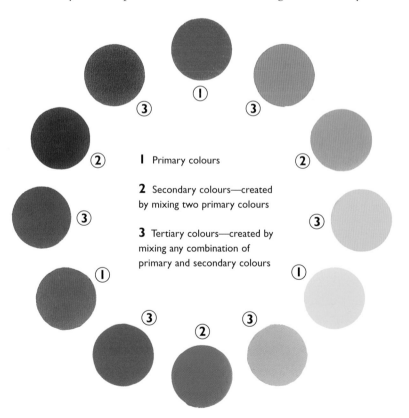

I Primary colours

2 Secondary colours—created by mixing two primary colours

3 Tertiary colours—created by mixing any combination of primary and secondary colours

LIGHT AND COLOUR
Colour choices should be
checked in both natural
daylight and artificial light
whenever possible, as light
can change some colours
very dramatically.

THE EFFECTS OF COLOUR

- There is no need to understand
  complicated colour chemistry
  when creating a scheme: simply
  use the colour wheel as a guide.
- Complementary colours: the
  colours that complement each
  other sit opposite each other on
  the colour wheel. Combined in a
  colour scheme, they produce a
  very balanced effect.
- Adjacent colours: using colours
  that appear next to each other
  on the colour wheel creates a
  very harmonious scheme with no
  strong clashes of colour.

NEUTRAL SCHEME
A neutral scheme can be very restful. In this
room, the creams, browns, and greys
complement each other.

PLANNING A SCHEME

- The actual planning of a scheme is
  affected by a number of factors, such
  as whether you are using paint or
  wallpaper. Wallpaper generally
  means that pattern will play a major
  role in the scheme, whereas paint on
  its own places more emphasis on
  large areas of a single colour.
- Focusing the scheme: choosing one
  color and building the rest of the
  decoration around it is a common
  method of producing a scheme.
- Practicality: busy areas of the home
  receive the most wear and tear—

make sure the scheme you choose
will stand up to the treatment it is
likely to receive. Expensive, delicate
wallpapers, for example, are not
ideal for bathrooms or kitchens.
- Furniture and surroundings: a colour
  scheme does not just involve walls,
  ceilings, and woodwork—flooring,
  furniture, and other accessories will
  all have to fit into the final plan.
  Consider the colour and design of
  all these items and check whether
  they will complement the ideas and
  colour changes you have in mind.

PROPERTIES OF PAINT AND PAPER

Once colours and designs have been chosen, it is essential to have some understanding of the actual makeup of decorating materials in order to judge whether a particular surface is suitable for the finish you want to achieve. Some wallpapers, for example, require specific treatment; whereas with paint, it is important to apply the correct type for the surface in question.

Types of paint: the majority of paints can be divided into two main types—the more traditional oil-based/solvent-based paints and the water-based/acrylic paints. Oil-based paints are much less user-friendly because of their longer drying times and unpleasant smell. They are also more harmful to the environment. For this reason, water-based paints have become increasingly popular and now dominate the marketplace. Oil-based paints used to be considered the most durable, but water-based paints have improved so much that they now match their oil-based counterparts. However, in certain cases, it is still better to use oil-based paints, and these situations are discussed in the following chapters.

PAINT AND ITS USES

- Primer: this type of paint is used to seal surfaces before applying more coats of paint. All bare wood, metal, and other untreated surfaces require priming, otherwise subsequent coats will not adhere properly.
- Undercoat: this is any coat of paint that comes between the primer and top coat on a new surface. It is also used on old painted surfaces before a top coat is applied.
- Eggshell: oil-based paint that provides a dull, almost matte finish. Ideal on wood and can be used on walls for a hard-wearing finish. Eggshell hybrids bridge the gap between a totally matte finish and a high-gloss one.

- High gloss: the hardest-wearing oil-based top-coat paint, providing a shiny finish. Ideal for wood.
- Emulsion: many different varieties are available. Some include vinyl, which produces a slightly shiny, wipeable finish. Various proprietary emulsions have specific properties, ranging from totally smooth finishes to textured ones. Easy to use and ideal for all large surface areas.
- Natural finishes: these translucent paints are used to highlight the natural grain of wood. Stains and varnishes are the best-known ones, although there are now many other different varieties of finish available.

WALLPAPER AND ITS USES

- Plain lining paper: off-white in colour, this paper is often used as an alternative to plastering walls that are uneven, because it creates a smooth, sound surface. It can be used as the base for some wallpaper finishes, by being applied to walls and then allowed to dry thoroughly before the final wallpaper is applied over the top; and it can also provide a good base for painting.
- Paintable papers: as well as lining papers, there are other types of textured wallpaper specifically designed to be painted. Woodchip paper is the most common example.
- Vinyl: this is a very popular wallpaper that is ideal in all areas of the home, providing an easily wipeable surface. The hard-wearing properties vary according to the grade of vinyl.
- Standard patterned wallpaper: again, very popular and manufactured in

many different varieties. Because it is not as durable as vinyl, it is best used in areas like the living room, rather than the kitchen.
- Handmade and hand-painted paper: this is only available in quantity from specialist stores. It is often extremely expensive, but can produce a breathtaking finish.
- Proprietary variations: there are various other papers that may require the use of a specific paste. Always follow the manufacturer's guidelines for these papers, especially if they contain natural fibres such as silk or burlap.

Types of wallpaper: the vast majority of wallpaper falls into two categories: vinyl and standard patterned paper. Vinyl is more hard-wearing because of its protective coating. Most wallpaper is hung on the wall using the same technique, though there are small refinements with some papers. The important difference between wallpapers is the method by which they are pasted (see Chapter 4). The main thing at this stage is choosing the correct paper for the purpose (see above), and understanding the effect that a finish may have on a room.

CAUTION

Decorating materials sometimes contain hazardous chemicals that can be damaging to health. Always obey the basic rules of decorating by ensuring good ventilation in the work area, and carefully follow the manufacturer's safety guidelines for whichever product you are using.

CHOICES FOR KITCHENS AND BATHROOMS

I n the areas of a kitchen or bathroom that are likely to be splashed or suffer badly from damp, tiling is the most practical option. But damp-resistant paint and paper are increasingly popular choices, either used in combination with tiles and wood panelling, or on their own.

Papering: wallpapering is the easiest way to create an instant pattern, as well as provide texture and warmth. Vinyl papers are best in bathrooms and kitchens as they are durable and can be wiped easily. It is doubly important in a bathroom to make sure that the paper is well stuck down, especially around the edges and along seams.

Painting the walls: the quickest way to change the look of a bathroom or kitchen is to paint the walls. In a bathroom, an alternative to tiling is tongue-and-groove panelling (see pages 42–43 and 104–107), which can be painted with the same colour of paint as the walls, or with a toning shade.

PAINT

Paint is the most readily available of all decorating materials and is very easy to use. However, it is important to use the right paint in the right place, especially where damp bathrooms and dirt-prone kitchens are concerned.

PAINT IN BATHROOMS AND KITCHENS

- Hard-wearing: the most hard-wearing paints used to be oil- or solvent-based, but improved-formula, water-based equivalents are now nearly, if not totally, as good as their oil-based counterparts. Many manufacturers produce specific kitchen and bathroom paints, which are damp-resistant and wipeable. Otherwise, paints that contain vinyl can also be wiped easily.
- Drying times: the other advantage of water-based paints is that they dry quickly, allowing for more than one coat to be applied in a day. Because bathrooms and kitchens are such busy areas, this means that the job can be completed quickly with little household upheaval.
- Around baths and splashbacks: although this is normally the domain of tiles, these areas can be painted to good effect. Tongue-and-groove panelling looks particularly impressive around baths (see pages 104–107). However, because of the constant water splashes, it is advisable to use a waterproof paint.
- Make sure that you follow the manufacturer's safety advice for ventilation during painting.

PAPER IN BATHROOMS AND KITCHENS

- Hard-wearing: use vinyl papers or, alternatively, varnish standard wallpapers after they have been applied.
- Avoiding damp: it is essential to keep paper away from areas prone to water splashes or excess moisture, such as around cooking areas, sinks, or baths. When first applied, wallpaper looks great, but in no time at all, the surface will deteriorate if it gets damp, whether it is vinyl-coated or protected with varnish.
- Extra adhesive: overlap adhesive can be used along the edges of all lengths of paper to ensure a better seal and make the paper less likely to lift.

WALLPAPER

There is no problem with using wallpaper in bathrooms and kitchens as long as you follow the guidelines (left) and use the correct type of paper.

PREPARING THE ROOM

T he first stage of the practical side of room decoration is preparing the room itself. Having plenty of space to work in, and ensuring that there are no obstacles in the way, is essential when carrying out any papering or painting task. As well as making it easier to carry out the work, a well-prepared room speeds up the job and ensures that it is completed with the least inconvenience in the quickest time possible.

CLEARING THE ROOM

Ideally, everything should be removed from the room you are planning to decorate. If this is not be possible, there are a number of compromises you can make.

- Carpets: if the carpet is going to be changed, this is the time to remove it. Otherwise, it can be taken up and relaid after decoration, or dust sheets can be put down to protect it during the work. If using dust sheets, stick masking tape around the skirting board–carpet junction, to protect the carpet from paint spray.

- Furniture: remove as much furniture as possible. A few heavy items can be moved into the centre of the room and covered, but always ensure that all wall surfaces are clear of obstructions.

- Ornaments: take as many as possible out of the room and store them elsewhere until the decorating is finished. Some larger items can be put underneath furniture in the centre of the room, but the majority of items should always be removed from the working area.

Covering furniture: use transparent plastic dust sheets for furniture. These protect totally from paint spray, but allow you to see what is under the dust sheet, which is important if any of the items are breakable.

Covering floors: always use good-quality, fabric dust sheets on the floor—cheaper ones let paint through—and make sure they are laid right up to the wall.

IDENTIFYING PROBLEMS

All surfaces require preparation before decoration; once the room is clear, it is much easier to identify the areas that require the most preparation.

Ceiling cracks that follow a relatively straight path are often caused by movement of the building boards used in the ceiling construction. Line ceilings where this occurs, as the cracks will quickly return if you only use filler.

Cracks along ceiling/wall junctions are generally due to settlement in new buildings. Most cracks are due to only slight movement and should be filled with a flexible filler. In older buildings, if the cracks widen, you may need professional advice to check for more serious movement.

Cracks at the corners of windows and doors are often due to slight movement when opening and closing them. Fill with all-purpose filler.

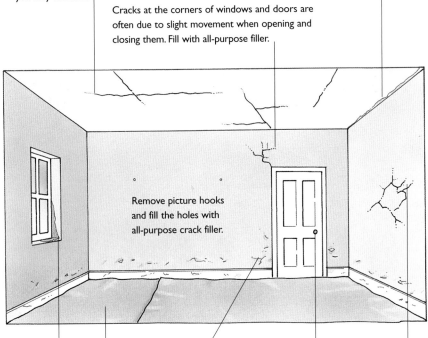

Remove picture hooks and fill the holes with all-purpose crack filler.

Look out for areas of damp, especially around windows. These may need exterior treatment before decoration begins. Alternatively, the damp could be due to condensation.

Scrapes and knocks are part of everyday life. Use all-purpose filler to make good.

Be sure to cover the entire floor with dust sheets.

If the door hardware is to be replaced, now is the time to remove it. Fill redundant screw holes in readiness for fitting the new door hardware.

Cracks that form irregular shapes such as this often suggest that the plaster on old lath-and-plaster walls may be separating from the wall. Tap it with your hand to see if it sounds hollow. If this is the case, the plaster in that area will need to be removed and patch plaster applied.

REMOVING FIXTURES AND FITTINGS

W hen stripping a room, the best way to work is to go around the room and systematically remove anything that can interfere with the decoration. Keep each fitting and its screws in a separate polythene bag. Always turn off the electricity to a fixture before working on it.

STRIPPING WALL FIXTURES

1 You may have shelves, towel racks, mirrors, curtain rods, and so on to remove. This will simply be a question of unscrewing their supports such as one or more brackets. You may want someone to help you handle large, cumbersome items such as curtain rods.

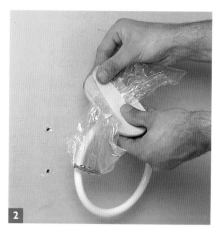

2 The best way to avoid losing the screws and other hardware that normally hold the items in place is to seal them in a plastic bag, then tape the bag to the item.

3 To avoid wiring and pipes buried in the walls, try using the original mounting holes to rehang the items once you finish the decoration. Because wallpaper will cover the holes, insert into them toothpicks or matchsticks trimmed to protrude slightly from the wall—they will poke through the wallpaper.

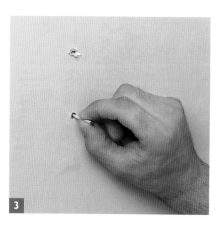

PULLING OUT A SWITCH OR SOCKET

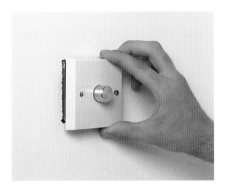

With the electricity turned off, release the mounting screws and pull the plate away from the wall. You can leave the switch or outlet in this position until the decoration has been completed. As further protection from paint, you should always apply masking tape to the edges of the switch.

PULLING OUT A DOWNLIGHT

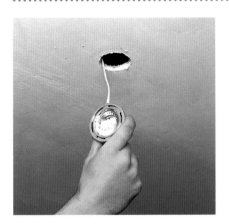

As always, first turn off the power. This light fixture simply drops down from its hole in the ceiling. If it isn't heavy and you're painting the ceiling, tape a polythene bag around the body. If you're covering the ceiling with lining paper or wallpaper, it may be necessary to detach the body from the wires. Do this only if you are completely sure of your electrical skills. If not, call an electrician. See "Electrical Safety."

ELECTRICAL SAFETY

The most important rule when working with electricity in the home is safety. It might be tempting to think that you can wallpaper around a switch by simply pulling the cover plate forward because you're unlikely to touch any wiring—but you could touch an exposed wire, with disastrous consequences.

It takes just a few seconds to go to the consumer unit and isolate the switch, socket, or light fixture by turning the power off at the fuse or circuit breaker for that circuit. Then use a circuit tester to check that the switch, socket, or light is "dead." This ensures you have isolated the correct fuse

Never disconnect a light fitting from its wires unless you have turned off the electricity and are completely sure of your electrical skills. It may seem simple enough to disconnect the fitting, but it is another thing altogether to replace it. If in any doubt, always call a qualified electrician.

PREPARING WALLS

M aking sure that wall surfaces are smooth before the application of paint or paper plays an important part in achieving a good finish. Lumps and bumps or depressions in the wall surface will be accentuated by the new decoration and spoil the overall look. The amount of preparation will depend on the wear and tear that the walls have received since the last time they were decorated. In many cases, lightly sanding, cleaning, and adding some filler in one or two places may be all that is required (see pages 16–17). If damage is more extensive, it may be necessary to replaster some areas. Remember that if your walls have old wallpaper coverings, these must be removed before further preparation can start (see pages 184–185).

PATCH PLASTERING

Plastering is a highly skilled trade and, as a rule, attempting to plaster entire rooms on your own should be avoided—it makes far more sense to employ professional help. However, small localized areas that require only slightly more than simple all-purpose filler can be patch plastered—a job well within the capability of the home decorator. Make sure you buy "one-coat plaster," which is easier to work with than the more traditional two-coat plastering systems. Mixed to the manufacturer's guidelines, it takes on the consistency of a stodgy, but easily workable, paste.

1 Dust away any loose debris from the sides of the hole, and dampen the area with a PVA solution (one part PVA to five parts water). Use a plastering float to press the plaster firmly into the hole while drawing the float across the face of the entire filled hole.

2 Smooth the surface of the plaster and allow it to dry slightly (for about 30 minutes). Then wet the face of the float with water and smooth the plaster surface again. Continue "polishing" the surface of the plaster with the float until a smooth and flush finish is produced.

REPAIRING A PLASTERBOARD WALL

Plasterboard or dry-lined walls require a different technique in order to fill any holes in the surface layer of the plasterboard. Because the wall is hollow, plaster or filler will simply fall inside the wall cavity if it is applied directly to the hole. For large holes, a section of plasterboard may need to be replaced; for smaller holes, the technique demonstrated here is the ideal solution.

1 Use a craft knife to cut away any loose material from around the edge of the hole.

2 Cut a new piece of plasterboard, slightly larger than the hole. Drill a hole in the centre of it and thread a piece of string through it, knotting it on one side. On the opposite side, spread all-purpose adhesive around the edge of the piece of plasterboard.

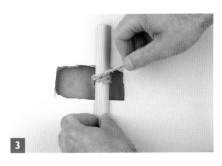

3 Holding the string, drop the piece through the hole and move it into place on the reverse side of the hole. Tie the string to a small piece of wood to hold the plasterboard in place.

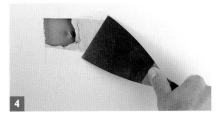

4 Leave the adhesive to dry, then cut the string away and fill the gap in the wall with plaster.

Minor hole filling: small depressions and holes can be filled with all-purpose filler applied with a filler knife. Where there are several small holes close to each other, a caulking blade can be used to sweep filler over the entire area, filling all the holes with maximum speed and minimum effort.

PREPARING WOOD

Wood tends to act as the frame to the wall decoration and plays an equal part in the overall look of the room. If a professional finish is to be achieved, wood preparation is as important as wall preparation. Wood surfaces can present more problems than walls, as moulded corners and edges can make filling and preparation a slightly more intricate task than the broader open surfaces of the walls.

BEFORE FILLING

Before filling the dents and holes in wooden surfaces, you need to deal with any protruding areas. This takes little time, but it helps to ensure a smooth finished product.

1 Knock in any nails that are sticking out of the wood surface, using a hammer and punch.

2 Paint-bumps on old surfaces can be removed by running a scraper along the face of the wood.

FILLING FLAT SURFACES

All-purpose filler can be used to fill the flatter wooden surfaces. Make sure that it is mixed into a smooth, creamy consistency, with no lumps.

1 Filler shrinks as it dries, so fill holes so that the filler sticks up slightly higher than the hole's edges.

2 Once it is dry, the filler can be sanded by hand, or with an electric sander as shown here.

FILLING JOINTS AND CRACKS

Cracks are commonly found at the junction between wood and walls, as well as in the jointing system of wooden items—such as the edges of panels in doors, or the point at which the casing joins onto the main part of the door frame. In all these cases, you need to use a flexible filler that can cope with the slight movement that most of these areas experience. Flexible filler, or caulking, is dispensed from a tube using a sealant gun.

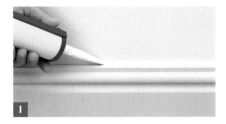

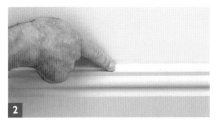

1 Cut the nozzle of the tube, and pull the sealant gun trigger to allow a thin bead of filler to run along the joint. Keep even pressure on the gun trigger while guiding the nozzle along the joint.

2 While the filler is still wet, use a wetted finger to smooth along the bead surface to give an even and neat finish, ready for painting.

UNPAINTED WOOD

After filling as necessary, previously unpainted wood must be sealed before coats of paint can be applied. This is a two-part process involving the use of a solution that seals wood knots and a primer.

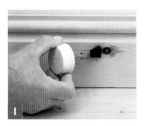

2 Once the knotting solution has dried, seal the entire wood surface with primer, making sure it is totally covered and that the primer is well brushed into the wood.

1 Brush knotting solution into all knots in the bare wood. This seals in any resin and prevents it from bleeding through the coats of paint, which would spoil the surface.

NATURAL WOOD ALTERNATIVES

For natural wood finishes, the wood must be sanded smooth as usual, but use stainable fillers to deal with holes—knotting solution and primer are not usually used on natural wood finishes. Alternative methods are demonstrated on pages 204–205.

PREPARING OTHER SURFACES

As well as walls and wood, there are other surfaces that require preparation before they can be decorated. The most common of these are metal surfaces and artificial surfaces such as plastic and melamine. With the correct preparation, nearly all of these can be painted to fit in with your chosen colour scheme.

METAL SURFACES

The preparation of a metal surface depends very much on the type of metal and whether it has been painted before. There are various all-purpose primers that can be used as a base on most metals, although in many cases it is better to use a primer designed for the specific metal.

PAINTING RADIATORS

Radiators are one of the more common metal surfaces in the home, and they can be painted to either complement or contrast with the rest of the decoration in the room. Because most modern radiators are supplied pre-coated, changing their colour is a simple process.

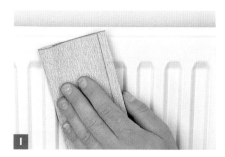

1 Use a fine grade abrasive paper to lightly sand the surface of the whole radiator.

PRIMING METALS

- Copper: there is no need to prime copper—undercoats and top coats can be applied directly to cleaned and sanded surfaces.
- Iron and steel: because these metals are ferrous, they are prone to corroding or rusting. On older surfaces, any old flaky material must be removed. Use a proprietary metal primer before applying more coats of paint.
- Aluminium: generally, proprietary aluminium primers can be used to secure a base coat that may then be painted with top coats.

2 Make sure that the radiator is turned off and cool before you paint it. Apply an undercoat and let it dry, then paint with a top coat.

MELAMINE

The surface of kitchen cabinet units is often melamine, which is designed not to be painted. However, with recent product developments, it is now possible to paint it, as long as the correct surface preparation is carried out.

1 Clean the melamine surface with a mild detergent solution, rinse with clean water, then leave it to dry completely.

2 Sand the entire melamine surface with a fine grade abrasive paper.

3 Apply a proprietary surface preparation solution to the melamine, wiping it onto all areas with a clean cotton rag.

4 Wipe off the excess solution with another rag and leave to dry. The melamine surface is now ready to accept an undercoat, followed by top coats of paint.

OTHER UNUSUAL SURFACES

Various other surfaces around the home can also be painted, though you should always check the manufacturer's guidelines to see if a particular paint is suitable for a specific surface.

- Tiles: clean and sand tiles, then apply a proprietary tile primer before painting them.
- Textured ceiling coatings: with a previously painted surface, apply latex paint in the usual way. For a new textured coating, seal the surface with diluted latex paint and leave to dry before applying more coats of paint.
- Glass: clean thoroughly, then use proprietary glass paints to create a decorative effect.
- Plastic: clean thoroughly, then apply top coats directly to the surface.

STRIPPING PAPER

It is always best to remove old layers of wallpaper before carrying out any redecoration. However secure the old paper may appear on the wall, once it is painted or wallpapered over, any defects will begin to show, and these will ruin the look of the newly decorated room.

REMOVING THE WORST

Begin by simply removing those layers of paper that come away from the wall surface with relative ease—starting with any loose seams.

1 The top layer of paper can often be pulled away from its backing, especially when it is vinyl paper.

2 Use the scraper to get behind the paper and remove areas that are no longer stuck to the wall surface.

SIMPLE STRIPPING

Using warm water is frequently the best method of stripping paper that is still stuck to the wall after the top layer has been removed. Do not use this method if vinyl paper is still on the wall, since the water will simply run off the surface.

1 Apply plenty of warm water to the paper. Let the water soak in and make the paper bubble.

2 Scrape away the damp, loosened paper, trying not to dig the edges of the scraper into the wall surface.

USING A STEAM STRIPPER

For stubborn areas of paper, a steam stripper is the best removal tool. The design of steam strippers varies, but in general they combine a large water heating reservoir that boils the water and pushes steam down a connecting pipe into a large plate held against the wallpaper surface.

1 Make sure that the steam stripper is turned off, then fill the reservoir with hot water up to the indicated level. Using hot water speeds up the time it takes for the water to boil. Fit the connecting pipe, then the stripper can be turned on.

2 To speed up the process, score the surface of the wallpaper. Use a scorer to make small holes in the top layer of the wallpaper surface so that steam can penetrate behind the paper and speed up its removal.

3 Once the steamer has boiled, hold the steaming plate flat on the wall surface, keeping it in position for several seconds.

4 Move the plate along and remove the previously steamed piece of paper with a scraper. The time this takes depends on the type of paper and how many layers there are.

CAUTION

Always wear protective equipment when using a steam stripper. Gloves and goggles should both be worn to protect from the steam.

STRIPPING WOOD

U nlike wallpaper stripping, which is usually a necessity before
    redecoration, stripping wood is not always essential. However, if
you are going to apply a natural wood finish to a previously painted
surface, or there are layers of old coatings, you need to strip the wood.

HOT-AIR GUNS

Hot-air guns remove paint by heating up the old paint on the surface. This
makes it bubble and loosen its grip so it is easy to scrape away.

Using a hot-air gun: hold the nozzle
of the gun close to, but not touching,
the painted surface. As soon as the
paint begins to lift, scrape it away
and move the nozzle to a new area,
so you do not scorch the wood.

CAUTION
Wear protective gloves and always read the manufacturer's guidelines before using a hot-air gun.

CHEMICAL STRIPPERS

Chemical strippers can be used on paint or natural wood finishes with equal
effect. Using this kind of stripper can be a messy business, but it is a very
effective way of removing old coatings.

1 Wearing protective gloves, apply
chemical stripper liberally to the
wood using an old paint brush.

2 Let the chemical stripper react
with the old coatings, then gently
scrape away the residue.

PASTE STRIPPERS

Paste strippers are a form of chemical stripper that is particularly suitable for intricate areas that require total coating removal. They take longer to react with the old coatings, but can remove a number of layers with one application. They are messy, so make sure that all areas are covered with drop cloths.

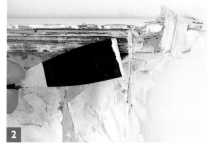

1 Apply the stripper to the surface using a scraper or filling knife. Cover the area to be stripped with an even layer of the paste and leave it on for up to 24 hours to allow it to react with the painted surface.

2 Use a scraper to peel away the paste and reveal the bare wooden surface below. The stripper works by both dissolving the paint and lifting layers away at the same time.

CLEANING WOOD

After any stripping process, wood will require a thorough clean before it can be redecorated. As well as washing with water, it may be necessary to use other solvents, depending on the type of stripper you are using. White vinegar is often used to neutralize the stripper residue, but always check the stripper manufacturer's guidelines on specific recommendations.

1 Wearing protective gloves, wash the entire surface to remove the remnants of previous coatings and any stripper residue.

2 Any ingrained areas of paint can be removed by rubbing a small ball of fine-grade steel wool across the affected area.

STRIPPING AND PREPARING METAL

P aintwork on metal that is in good condition—whether a cast iron fireplace surround, steel window frame, or a radiator—may need only a wash with sugar soap or detergent to clean grime and a sanding to provide a key for the new paint. Additional preparation may only be a matter of sanding down drips flush with the surrounding area, but a buildup of paint obscuring details needs stripping.

TREATING RUST

Sadly, cast iron fireplace surrounds and steel-frame windows are often neglected. Rust can form in iron and steel where paint is chipped away, and, if left alone, the rust can eventually eat away at the metal, causing pitting.

1 To remove a small patch of surface rust, or rust near a moulded area, fold a piece of emery cloth and rub the rust away.

2 Where there are large patches of chipped paint or rust, a handheld wire brush is a more efficient tool to use.

3 For large areas of loose, flaking paint and rust, you can use a powerful electric drill fitted with a wire brush attachment. A cup-shape brush is best for detailed moulded areas; a wheel-shape one allows you to hold the drill at an angle. Remember to wear safety goggles and a dust mask.

4 To sand down paint drips, use emery paper wrapped around a sanding block until the paint surface is flush with the surrounding area.

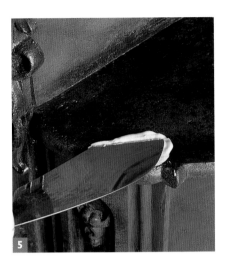

5 Fill in any pitted areas with a two-part epoxy or acrylic filler. (Removing old paint and rust will expose the pits.) Apply the filler with a putty knife; then use the blade of the knife to scrape off any excess until it is smooth with the surface, or leave it slightly protruding from the surface and rub it down with sandpaper once it is dry.

6 To remove paint in detailed areas, use an old paint brush to apply a thick layer of chemical stripper, and leave it in place the amount of time recommended by the manufacturer.

7 Once the paint has softened, it is ready to be removed. Use a small brush—an old toothbrush is ideal—to scrub away the paint from nooks and crannies. Some manufacturers suggest using soapy water.

8 Finish the work by cleaning the metal with water or white spirit (depending on the brand of stripper used) to neutralize any remaining traces of the chemical. Use steel wool in intricate areas.

SEALING SURFACES

O nce surfaces have been stripped and cleaned, you may need to seal them before they will accept paint or paper. In addition to the wood, metal, and miscellaneous surfaces discussed in this chapter, walls, ceilings, and the larger areas of the room as a whole need sealing to stabilize them before they are decorated.

SEALING CHECKLIST

- Previously wallpapered walls: once the paper has been stripped, the walls should be filled and prepared as usual. The surface should then be sealed with a PVA solution (one part PVA to five parts water). If wallpaper is going to be used on old, unsound walls, they can be lined first. Walls that are going to be painted, may also require lining first if they are very rough.
- Previously painted walls: after filling and preparing, walls can be painted immediately. If they are to be wallpapered, apply a PVA solution to the surface before proceeding.
- Previously paper-lined walls: ones that have been painted can be painted

again after general preparation. Wallpaper can be applied directly to a wall as long as the lining paper is stuck down. However, it is better to seal the walls with a PVA solution (one part PVA to five parts water) first.
- New plastered walls: they should be sealed with a diluted emulsion (10 parts paint to one part water) before more coats are applied. For wallpaper, walls should be prepared and sealed with a general-purpose sealant, or dilute wallpaper paste (mixed as per manufacturer's guidelines for size), before you proceed.
- New dry-lined walls: these should be treated like new plastered walls.

DEALING WITH STUBBORN STAINS

Standard primers and sealants cannot deal with all the stains that appear on walls and woodwork in the home. Sometimes a more robust form of sealant is required to deal with any areas that continue to bleed a stain through the decorated surface.

Using a stain blocker: apply two or three light coats of aerosol stain blocker to stubborn areas of staining that refuse to disappear even after the usual sealing or priming. Then decorate the surface as usual.

2
PAINTING
TECHNIQUES

When it comes to actually applying paint to the walls, painting techniques are often considered with a certain amount of indifference, and this attitude can lead to mistakes that are not easy to rectify. Having prepared surfaces thoroughly, the actual painting part of decorating can be very enjoyable as long as you take the time to ensure that paint is applied correctly. Modern tools make painting a relatively straightforward job, but there are lots of ways of applying paint and it is important to choose an appropriate method for the surface in question and the finish you are trying to achieve.

WHAT TOOLS TO USE WHERE

D ifferent painting tools are designed for particular surfaces, although some tools can be used for more than one type of surface. Most home decorators develop preferences for certain tools and tend to use their favourites as much as possible. However, there are some points that are worthwhile considering when choosing the tools for the job, since they can affect the speed and efficiency of the work.

CHOOSING TOOLS

The table below sets out the advantages and disadvantages of available painting equipment to help you select the right tools for the particular painting job.

PAINTING EQUIPMENT	
Brushes	These are the most versatile of all decorating tools, manufactured in all shapes and sizes, and designed for every possible need. Pure bristle brushes are still the best quality, although some of the modern synthetic-fibre brushes are constantly improving in their performance—especially for use with water-based paints. Brushes can be used successfully in all areas, although for large expanses of ceiling or walls other methods provide much quicker coverage.
Rollers	These are ideal for dealing with large open areas, covering surfaces quickly and with great efficiency. They are manufactured in sheepskin (the best quality) and synthetic materials. Sizes range from about 45 cm (18 inches) down to about 2.5 cm (1 inch), so it is possible to find the right size roller for any job.
Paint pads	These are the direct competition to rollers, as they have very similar properties—it's usually a matter of personal preference. Paint pads create far less mess than rollers, and there is some suggestion that they are much more efficient on paint use than rollers.
Sprayers	These are very successful at covering large surfaces quickly, but the mess created, and the amount of masking off that is required, often makes them too inconvenient. They are useful for large areas of uninterrupted wall space; otherwise they are more suited to industrial painting. However, aerosol spray-can paints are becoming increasingly popular—they are easily directed into inaccessible areas and require no cleaning as they are simply thrown away when empty.

AREAS OF USE

The illustration below shows the different areas of a standard room design and indicates which painting tools are most suitable to use.

Radiators can be painted with a brush or sprayed with an aerosol. A small, long-handled roller can be used for painting behind them.

Large rollers or large paint pads are ideal for ceilings and walls. Paint pads tend to cause less mess. However, it will still be necessary to cut in around the edges of walls and ceilings using a 5–7.5-cm (2–3-in) brush or small paint pad.

Doors can be painted with mini rollers, but the panel edges and frames need finishing with a 2.5–5-cm (1–2-in) brush.

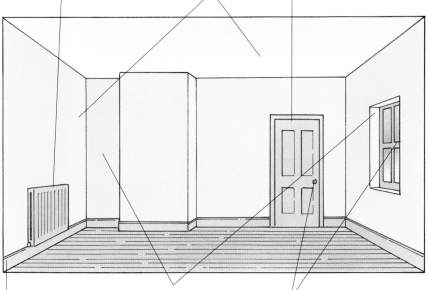

Skirting boards can be painted with a medium-size paint pad or a 2.5–5-cm (1–2-in) paint brush.

Wall alcoves and window recesses are usually too small to accommodate a roller and need to be painted with a 7.5-cm (3-in) paint brush or a medium-size paint pad.

Window and door fixtures that require painting should be removed and sprayed with aerosol paint. If you don't want to spray with an aerosol, use a fine paint brush.

KEEPING UP TO DATE

It is worthwhile being aware of new paint tools that come on the market since the manufacturers constantly vary shape and design of painting tools in an effort to improve their performance and, ultimately, the finish they produce. Be careful, though, because it is easy to fall into the trap of buying gimmicky tools, which sometimes promise more than they are capable of delivering.

PAINTING BASICS

O nce you have done all the necessary preparation work on the walls and ceilings and have chosen the paint and tools you need, your next task is to figure out how much paint you'll need and to plan the order of work.

ESTIMATING QUANTITIES

On previously painted surfaces, normal emulsion paint covers about 15 sq m (160 square feet) per litre (1 ¾ pt). On rough surfaces the coverage rate may be only half that amount. New plaster is more absorbent, so coat it first with a primer. The method of applying the paint—for example, by brush or spray gun—can also affect the paint coverage. To work out the area of the walls in a room, measure the wall height, add together the lengths of all the walls, then multiply the two sums. Similarly, work out the area of windows and doors in the room, then subtract this from the overall area. Measure the floor to find the dimensions for the ceiling.

ORDER OF WORK

The numbers in the diagram below indicate the order in which to paint. Start with the ceiling so that any splashes of paint that land on the walls can be painted over. On a ceiling, paint in rows 1 sq m (10 square feet) at a time. On walls, covering the same size areas, start at the top and work down. If you are right-handed, start at the right-hand corner; if you are left-handed, the left one. This allows you to rest your non-painting hand on an unpainted surface.

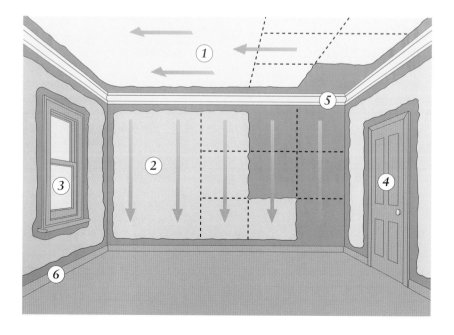

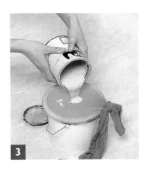

1 To protect adjacent surfaces, such as wood trim, that you don't want covered with paint, apply masking tape in short lengths—they are easier to handle and apply than longer ones. Firmly press down on the edge next to the surface you are painting to prevent paint from seeping underneath it.

2 Tape dust sheets to skirting boards to stop them from creeping and exposing floor coverings to splashes. Start with vertical strips to hold the cloth in place, then apply the tape horizontally so paint doesn't drip behind it. Use fabric dust sheets that absorb paint splashes, instead of polythene ones, which do not.

3 If the can of paint has already been partly used, strain the remaining paint through old nylon fabric such as a pair of tights stretched across the mouth of the bucket. If you are using a freshly opened can of paint, simply pour the paint directly into your bucket.

4 Be prepared for pauses in your painting by having plastic kitchen wrap, a polythene bag, or aluminium foil handy. Simply wrap the roller sleeves or brush bristles in the plastic or foil to stop the paint from drying out. A paint tray can be protected in the same way.

HELPFUL HINTS

It is never a good idea to use paint straight from the container it comes in, unless you plan to use the entire contents in one painting session. The main reason for this is that the paint may become contaminated by loose bristles from paint brushes and by dust, fluff, and other particles picked up by the brush during the painting session.

In any case, if you have purchased your paint in large, economical containers, they will be too heavy to hold comfortably. Instead, pour the paint into a paint bucket or roller tray, depending on which implement you'll be using to apply it.

BRUSHES

T he correct technique for using a brush varies slightly according to the surface being painted and the type of paint you are using. Make sure that the brush is in good condition with no loose bristles, which could moult and end up on the painted surface.

WALL TECHNIQUE

To save time, use a relatively large brush when painting walls. However, bear in mind that if your brush is too large, it will be heavy and make your wrist tired, and this may affect your efficiency.

1 Apply the paint in random strokes across the wall, allowing the bristles of the brush to spread the paint as evenly as possible.

2 Once a small area of wall has been painted, without reloading the brush, stroke the bristles lightly across the painted surface to blend in any visible brush marks in the paint. This process is known as "laying off."

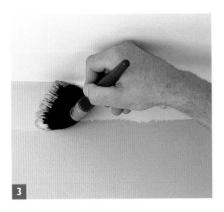

3 Use a smaller brush to cut in around the edges of walls, letting the extreme edge of the brush "bead" the paint precisely along the wall/ceiling junction.

CUTTING IN

Cutting in is a technique for finishing off around edges, such as those between a wall and ceiling, or the wall and a door frame.

WOOD TECHNIQUE

The same aim of producing a smooth finish applies to painting wood, but the technique varies slightly from that used for walls. If you are using an oil-based paint, make sure that you apply a few more strokes to each paint application so the paint is thoroughly "brushed out," otherwise it may run or drip.

1 Use a smaller brush for wood application since the work always tends to be more detailed. Working in small areas, apply vertical strips of paint, loading the brush separately for each strip. For the door shown here, three strips cover the width of the panel in the door. Without reloading the brush, blend the strips together by stroking horizontally across the painted area.

2 Finally, and without reloading the brush, make light vertical strokes over the painted area to remove any brush marks and provide a uniform appearance.

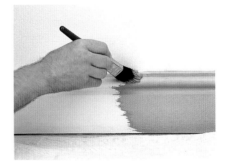

For the edges where wood meets walls, such as the skirting board, use a small brush to cut in along the top of the skirting and create a precise line dividing the two colours.

CLEANING AND STORING BRUSHES

- Temporary storage: wet brushes can be stored temporarily in clinging plastic wrap. Brushes covered with oil-based paint can be stored in a suitable solvent.
- Cleaning: water-based paint should be washed out of brushes with mild detergent, then the brushes should be rinsed thoroughly under cold water. Wash oil-based paint out of brushes with a suitable solvent, leave them to dry, then wash with a mild detergent and rinse with water.
- Storage: loosely bind the bristles of the brush with brown paper, secured in place with an elastic band.

ROLLERS

R ollers vary in texture and size, but all are extremely efficient at covering flat areas easily and evenly. They are most commonly used on walls and ceilings, although smaller ones and roller sleeves with a very smooth pile can be used on some wooden surfaces.

WALL TECHNIQUE

Large rollers can cover wall surfaces very quickly. Choose a roller sleeve according to the amount of texture you want on the wall—a roller with a thick pile is particularly good if the surface is undulating or uneven. Always load paint evenly onto the roller, being careful not to overload it.

1 Load paint evenly onto the roller, then glide the roller over the wall surface in a zigzag pattern.

2 Reload the roller and fill in the gaps. Glide the unloaded roller gently over the painted area to even up the finish.

EASY ACCESS

Ingenious designs mean that rollers can get into a variety of different areas with relative ease. This easy accessibility makes the roller a very versatile painting tool, which is not confined to straightforward wall spaces.

Gaining height: an extension pole attached to the roller makes it possible to paint the higher areas of a wall without the need for a stepladder. It is also useful for ceilings.

Getting behind: a small, long-handled roller makes it possible to paint behind radiators, or similar obstructions, without removing them from the wall.

WOOD TECHNIQUE

Very similar painting techniques apply to wood and to walls, and rollers are becoming increasingly popular for use on many wooden surfaces in the home, with doors at the top of the list. The main reason for this popularity is the speed at which a roller can paint a door compared to the more traditional methods of paint application.

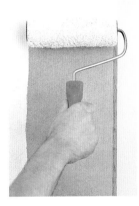

1 For panel doors, mini rollers are ideal for painting all the flat areas on the door surface.

2 Use a paint brush for the more intricate mouldings of the panel edge.

Painting flush doors: a roller is ideal for painting these as there are no intricate areas to interrupt the progress of the roller across the door's surface.

CLEANING AND STORING ROLLERS

- Water-based paints: rollers are designed to be used with water-based paints and can be cleaned with a mild detergent solution before rinsing thoroughly with clean water. This can be a lengthy process, especially with long-pile roller heads, but it is essential to make sure all traces of paint are removed from the roller so that it can be used in the future to apply different colours. Although sheepskin roller heads are more expensive than synthetic equivalents, they tend to wash out more quickly.

- Temporary storage: rollers can be temporarily stored in plastic wrap for a few days, but should be washed out before this extends to a week.

- Oil-based paint: on the rare occasion that oil-based paint might be used with a roller, it is virtually impossible to clean, and would take far too much solvent. In this case, it is more sensible to use a cheap roller head and throw it away afterward.

PAINT PADS

Paint pads are similar to rollers in that they are designed for covering large surface areas quickly, with relatively little effort and maximum efficiency. Paint pads are flat and rectangular with a large number of tightly packed small fibers, which makes them similar to brushes in the way they convey paint to surfaces. However, paint pads manage to apply the paint very evenly with one sweep of the pad, rather than a number of different strokes. They come in a range of sizes, with large pads designed for painting walls. The precise nature of pad design often means that relatively large pads can also be used for cutting in around edges.

1 Dip the face of the pad in the paint and use the ribbed part of the paint pan to distribute the paint across the pad surface.

2 Remove excess paint from the pad by drawing it across the back edge of the paint pan.

3 Apply paint to the wall using uniform, slightly overlapping strokes across the surface.

4 Cut in around the wall edges by running the extreme edge of the paint pad precisely along the wall/ceiling junction.

WOOD TECHNIQUE

There is very little difference between the technique used for walls and that used for wood, except that the size of the paint pad needs to be reduced for painting wood. Small paint pads are far more versatile than mini rollers for getting into the detailed parts of wooden surfaces, and they are capable of painting all but the most intricate of areas.

I A small pad is ideal for cutting in along the window-frame trim next to the glass surface. The frame of the pad can be used to guide the fibres precisely along the wood/glass junction.

2 The same-size pad can be used to continue around the outer edge of the window frame, and to cut in along the wall edge.

3 Medium-size pads are ideal for painting a skirting board, but make sure that the profile of the skirting is not too detailed for the pad surface to mould into.

CLEANING AND STORING PAINT PADS

Paint pad fibres are very small and this means the pad itself retains little paint once unloaded. Because the fibres dry very quickly, they must be cleaned immediately after use.
- For water-based paints: remove the pad from its frame and wash it out with mild detergent, then rinse with clean water.
- For oil-based paints: it is nearly impossible to remove all traces of

paint with solvent, so the pad is best discarded after use.
- Temporary storage: paint pads can be stored temporarily in plastic wrap, but this can damage the fibres unless they are wrapped up very carefully. Because they are easily washed out (when using water-based paints), it is better to clean the pads during any breaks in the work or at the end of the job, as required.

SPRAY GUNS

S mall, electrically powered, airless spray guns are worth considering for painting walls if you have several completely empty rooms that require painting—for example, when moving into a new house. However, they are not suitable for spraying ceilings.

Although a spray gun can apply paint quickly, the fine overspray it produces means you must completely mask all doors, windows, wood trim, and floor coverings before using one. Spray guns are also difficult—as well as time-consuming—to clean, so you should carefully consider if using one is the right choice for you.

Runny types of paint generally work better in a spray gun than nondrip formulas. In fact, the paint may require thinning before you can use it; follow the manufacturer's recommendations. Make sure you strain the paint (see p.195), which will avoid blocking the nozzle on the gun.

You must wear a respirator and safety goggles to avoid inhaling the paint mist or getting it in your eyes while you work. You must also make sure that the room is well ventilated. However, avoid painting on windy days when open windows can create drafts crossing the room.

1 Airless spray guns all have slightly different performance characteristics, so it is a good idea to first practise on an out-of-the-way surface in order to establish your gun's spray pattern and optimum spraying distance.

2 On flat surfaces, you must keep the gun nozzle the same distance from and at right angles to the wall as you move it from side to side. Do this by flexing your wrist as you complete each side-to-side pass. Make sure you do not spray in an arc.

3 At an external corner, spray the flanking wall to within about 15 cm (6 in) of the angle. Then stand in front of the end of the wall and paint across it, using short side-to-side passes of the gun as you work your way down. Repeat for the adjacent wall.

4 When painting an internal corner, spray each flanking wall first, again to within about 15 cm (6 in) of the angle. Then fill in the corner by pointing the gun into the angle and moving it from top to bottom in one pass.

LADDER SAFETY

Whether painting your ceiling or walls, you'll need a ladder for areas above your reach. Always make sure the feet of the ladder are steady on the floor and the braces are securely locked down before getting on a ladder.

When standing on a ladder, always lean toward it. Never extend beyond a comfortable reach, which could cause the ladder to tip over.

NATURAL WOOD FINISHES

Brushes are the ideal tool for most finishes that are applied to natural wood. Wood stain, especially, requires brushing into the grain, a process that other decorating tools are unable to perform efficiently. Natural wood finishes differ slightly from paint ones in that there is no need for priming the wood or sealing knots before applying the desired finish, although it may take a number of coats of the finish to produce the required look.

WOOD STAIN

Wood stain is used to give wood a colour different from its natural shade. Stain is best used on untreated surfaces because it penetrates deep into the wood, adding colour and bringing out the natural grain. Dark wood cannot be made lighter, so the wood to be stained must be a fairly light colour to begin with.

1 Always apply stain following the natural grain of the wood. Make sure that the stain is applied evenly because any drips or areas of over-application will stand out when dry.

2 Treat different sections of the wood as separate entities, being careful to cut in precisely along all the divisions—any overlaps of stain will show through the finish.

Filling holes: use stainable fillers when dealing with holes in natural wood. Alternatively, mix a little of the stain you are using with some all-purpose filler to provide a precise match.

VARNISHING

Varnish is a decorative as well as protective finish, and can be bought in anything from matte to high-gloss varieties. It can be applied directly to bare wood or over some stains to act as an extra protective layer. Traditionally, varnish was transparent; nowadays, coloured varieties are readily available.

1 Varnish should be applied with the grain, in the same way as wood stain, and brushed well into the wood's surface.

2 Bare wood should be given at least three coats of varnish. Give the wood a light sanding between each coat of varnish.

OTHER TREATMENTS

Although stain and varnish are by far the most popular methods of treating bare wood, there are other alternatives that provide equally impressive finishes.

- Stain/Varnish: this all-purpose finish combines both stain and varnish finishes in one product. Apply in the usual way with a paint brush.
- Scandinavian oil: this is ideal for hardwoods since it penetrates deep into the wood and nourishes it. Apply with a brush and buff with clean cotton rags.
- Wax: the most traditional of all natural wood finishes. Apply the wax with a cotton rag and buff when dry to reveal the natural beauty of the wood. The one drawback is that waxed surfaces need to be recoated regularly to maintain their sheen.

Combining stain and varnish: you can extend the life of a stained surface, and increase the depth of the finish, by giving it a coat of varnish once the stain has dried.

PAINTING WINDOWS

B efore painting a window, especially one made of wood, carry out any needed repairs, replace damaged glass (let new putty harden for a week before painting), and remove flaking paint. Sand down the surfaces with fine sandpaper and thoroughly clean them, and apply primer to any bare wood. If a window has been painted too often, it can bind on its frame. To avoid this, plane or sand the edges before priming and painting. If you have removed a window to repair joints or replace sash cords, it will be easier to paint it before putting it back in its frame.

PAINTING A CASEMENT WINDOW

1 To paint the inside of a casement window, wedge the window slightly open. If you prefer, stick lengths of painter's masking tape onto the glass; leave a 2 mm ($\frac{1}{12}$ in) gap between the glass and frame so the paint can seal the joint between the two—this helps to block moisture.

2 Using a cutting-in brush, paint the glazing bars (including the rebates). Use the brush with a dabbing motion to get paint into the corners. It doesn't matter if the paint goes onto the tape, but try to avoid getting any paint on the glass.

3 Adjust the window to open it slightly more. Paint the top and bottom horizontal rails, then paint the vertical stiles of the window.

4 Open the window fully and paint the inside closing edge of the window, brushing down from the top. With the window still fully open, paint the frame. Just before the paint has dried completely, carefully pull the tape back on itself and away from the window—if allowed to dry, the tape can pull off paint as it is peeled away.

PAINTING A SASH WINDOW

1 To paint the inside of a sash window, push the inner sash to the top and pull the outer sash to the bottom. Using a narrow brush on the upper sash, paint the bottom rail, followed by the vertical stiles as far as you can reach. Paint the inside of the frame at the bottom.

2 Paint the lower rail of the inner sash, using the narrow trim brush to paint up to the glass; then paint the sections of the vertical stiles that are within reach.

3 Put the sashes back in their correct positions to reveal the parts that you haven't painted. Paint the top rail of the inner sash, followed by the remainder of the vertical stiles.

4 Slide the outer sash down, and paint its top rail and the unpainted areas of the vertical stiles. Paint the remainder of the inside of the frame and, finally, paint the window frame casing.

BEST RESULTS
The neatest results can be achieved by removing all the window hardware before painting.

PAINTING DOORS

When painting or varnishing a door, choose an appropriate finish. Inside, try a low-odor, quick-drying water-based paint. Outside, use a weather-resistant paint: either a two-coat system (primer and top coat) or a "micro-porous" paint, which may also act as a primer. With hardwood or pine doors, you can allow the beauty of the wood to show through. Use ordinary varnish for interior doors. Exterior doors need a durable yacht varnish with a UV prohibitor; a preservative stain is also an option. Before you start, remove the door hardware and make any repairs. With a new door, sand down all its surfaces; with an existing door, remove all loose and flaky paint.

PAINTING A FLUSH DOOR

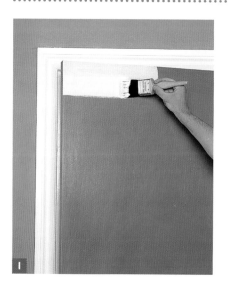

1 To ensure that the paint "edge" never dries out (this will leave a line that is difficult to remove), paint the door in blocks. Start in the top left-hand corner. Apply the paint horizontally until the brush is empty. Continue painting horizontally until the first block is filled.

2 To remove the horizontal brush strokes in this first block, lightly load the brush with paint and, starting at the top, brush down in vertical strokes until the block is complete. Now quickly move on to block two—alongside the first block.

3 Start block three by painting upward into the bottom edge of block one, using short vertical strokes. Then turn the brush around to create horizontal strokes to fill up the block. Eliminate brush strokes from this block with vertical strokes as before. Continue painting each block in this manner until the door is painted.

4 Paint the opening edge of the door. Using a narrow trim brush, start at the top and paint to the bottom of the door. Paint the top and bottom edges of an exterior door. For an interior door, if the top of the door can be seen from the stairs, paint that edge. Finish off by painting the frame, working from the top down.

PAINTING A PANELLED DOOR

1 If the door is glazed, start at the top, and use a narrow trim brush to paint the glazing bars. Do not overload the brush with paint, and avoid getting more than a thin band of paint on the glass.

2 Move to the topmost panel, and paint the mouldings that surround the panel before painting the panel itself. Repeat on the other panels of the door, working from top to bottom.

3 When all the panels are complete, paint the horizontal cross rails, starting at the top. Work down the door, painting each cross rail in turn.

4 Paint the vertical stiles on each side of the door (and in the centre, if there is one), from top to bottom. Paint the opening edge of the door, as well as the top and bottom edges if it is an exterior door or the top edge if it can be viewed from stairs above. Finally, paint the door frame: start at the top and work your way down.

FINISHING TOUCHES

O nce all the major areas in a room have been painted, it is important to pay attention to the more detailed places that may not initially appear to require any decoration. Adding finishing touches is highly beneficial to the end result, ensuring that the decoration is as good as possible.

PAINTING DETAIL

Painting the smaller features in a room requires some variation from the standard techniques already demonstrated in this chapter. As detailed areas have a smaller surface, the tools used to paint them need to be scaled down.

Using aerosols: ideal for getting into intricate areas, aerosol paints can be used on such items as window fixtures. Remove them from the window and spray them on an old board. They may require two or three coats to provide an even finish and, as with all spray painting, it is better to apply several thin coats rather than a few thick ones which will make the paint run.

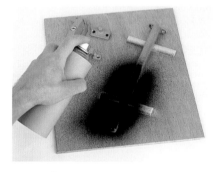

Painting in situ: some older window or door fixtures may be very difficult to remove from their position. In such cases, it is best to use a fine brush to paint them while they are in place.

Touching up scrapes: small knocks or imperfections on a newly painted surface should be touched up using a fine brush; painting the area with a large brush can sometimes create a rather shadowy finish. Since coats of paint should always be applied to complete surface areas rather than just small details, a detailed dab with a small brush will be less visible.

CLEANING DETAIL

Ensuring that all surfaces are clean after painting will add to the finished look. As well as general cleaning, it may be necessary to remove small paint spills.

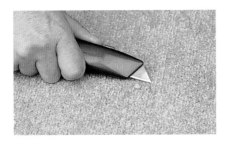

Carpet spills: paint drops can often find their way through dust sheets to the carpet below. Small splashes can be removed by scraping the edge of a craft knife blade across the surface of the paint once it is dry.

Cleaning handles: unpainted window and door hardware may need to have paint splashes removed from their surface. Polishing with a cotton rag will remove most paint spots; or, use a plastic non-scratch scourer.

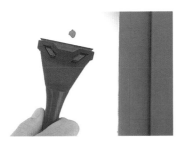

Glass overspray: paint splashes on glass are usually unavoidable when painting windows. Use a window scraper to remove them.

Electrical sockets: a window scraper is ideal for removing unwanted paint from the surface of electrical sockets. Be careful not to scratch the socket.

CLEANING CHECKLIST

Once the painting is finished, it is a good idea to spring-clean the room to show off the new-look interior.

- Curtains: this is the ideal time to get curtains dry-cleaned, along with cushion covers and any other soft furnishings in the room.
- Windows: clean all windows and other glass.
- Carpets: hire a carpet cleaner to revive older floorcoverings.
- Ornaments and accessories: polish all the odds and ends in the room to add to its new look.

PROBLEM-SOLVING

However proficient your painting technique, it is inevitable that you will experience some problems from time to time. Most are easily rectifiable and just require simple preparational work before recoating. Some of the most common problems are outlined below.

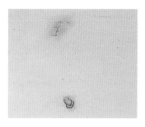

Drips: these are mainly experienced with oil-based paints, although poor application of water-based paints can also lead to drips or runs. Use a scraper to remove the run, sand the area, and recoat.

Bubbling: this is usually caused by impurities on the bare surface before paint was applied. Sand the area back and seal or prime as required, before recoating.

Bleeding knots: staining on painted woodwork is often caused by a knot that is bleeding sap through the painted surface. Scrape the sap away and sand back to the knot in question. Apply knotting solution, then prime and recoat, as required.

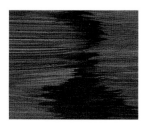

Blotchy stain: overlapping brush strokes on a stained surface can lead to a blotchy, unsightly finish. Sand the entire section of wood right back to bare wood before recoating.

Overlapping: on natural wood finishes, do not overlap wet brush strokes onto a dry area, or the joint will be very noticeable. Maintain a "wet" edge during application. Sand the area back and recoat.

Dust and dirt: a rough or gritty painted surface can be caused by poor preparation (lack of sanding) or a buildup of dirt on the brush that is then transferred to the surface. Sand the area and recoat.

3
SPECIAL PAINT EFFECTS

Special paint effects are a way of adding extra interest and texture to a wall or wooden surface by applying standard decorating paints or transparent glaze in slightly different ways. All these techniques are aimed at producing a finish that is far removed from a smooth, opaque painted surface. Paint and glaze applied in the ways outlined in this chapter add a totally new dimension to traditional decorating, giving you highly individual, dramatic finishes. Apart from their obvious impact, producing special effects is an incredibly enjoyable and satisfying process, and however proficient you become in a particular technique, every piece of decorative work you produce will be unique and add a personal touch to your home decoration.

WHAT PAINT EFFECTS TO USE WHERE

L ike paint in general, paint effects can be applied to most surfaces. However, some effects are more suited to particular areas than others; the box below will help you plan your effects.

WHERE TO USE PAINT EFFECTS

PAINT EFFECT	IDEAL AREA	COMMENTS
Sponging	Suited to large surfaces.	Avoid use on moulded wood.
Ragging	Similar to sponging, it is ideal for large surfaces.	Avoid rooms with too many intricate edges or corners.
Rag-rolling	Ideal for walls and panels; difficult around the edges.	If possible, fit skirting after the paint effect is applied.
Dragging and graining	Well suited to woodwork, intricate or plain.	Can be used on walls, but difficult to keep an even finish.
Colour-washing	One of the simplest effects to create on walls.	Effect is called timber rubbing when done on wood.
Liming	Ideal on light-coloured, bare wood surfaces.	Similar to timber rubbing, except a lime wax is used.
Marbling	Ideal way of breaking up a wall with "marble" panels.	Difficult effect to achieve, but produces impressive finish.
Aging effects	Excellent way of giving any surface a well-lived-in look.	Includes distressing and crackle varnishing processes.
Stippling	Ideal for walls and woodwork.	Provides a wonderful textured-looking finish, but takes time.
Combing	Good on walls as well as panels and woodwork.	Provides a coarser look than dragging and graining.
Stamping	Good on walls.	Good for repeating a design.
Stencilling	Reproduces painted designs on any surface.	Good for creating borders, frames, and other designs.

SPECIALIST EQUIPMENT

Producing paint effects requires a few extra tools. Always buy quality tools, since the extra expense will pay dividends in the work produced.

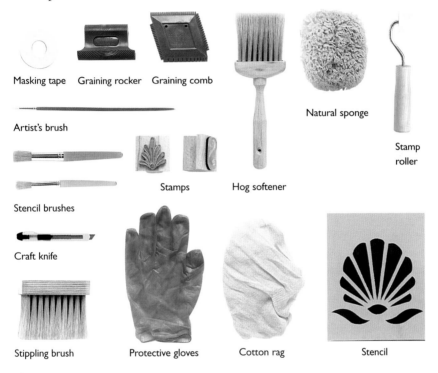

Masking tape   Graining rocker   Graining comb

Natural sponge

Artist's brush

Stamp roller

Stencil brushes

Stamps   Hog softener

Craft knife

Stippling brush   Protective gloves   Cotton rag   Stencil

GLAZES

Some paint effects, such as sponging, can be produced with standard emulsion paint, but in general most effects are produced by using transparent glaze. Adding colour to glaze creates the translucent, broken colour finish that is characteristic of most paint effects. Traditionally, glazes were oil-based, but now the vast majority available in the marketplace are water-based/acrylic. Water-based glazes tend to be much easier to work with and far more environmentally friendly. All the glazes used in this chapter are water-based, and demonstrate that they are quite capable of producing any effect you require. Mixing the glaze varies according to the manufacturer's guidelines: generally it is a simple case of mixing colourizers with the base glaze until you have the desired colour. It is vital to remember that all glazes—and therefore all paint effects—must be applied over a base coat of some description. Some water-based and some oil-based paints can be used, although a vinyl latex paint is often the manufacturer's choice. A light colour always works best as the base coat, so that subsequent glaze layers show to best effect.

SPONGING

S ponging is one of the simplest paint effects to produce, while achieving one of the most dramatic finishes. A natural sponge is used to make imprints on the wall surface, creating a finish that combines colour, texture, and depth to great effect.

SPONGING ON

Emulsion or glaze can be used for this technique, although glaze will create a far more translucent finish, which is often more appealing. As the name of the technique suggests, the sponge is actually used to apply the glaze to the wall.

1 Place a little glaze on an old paint-container lid. Dip the sponge into the glaze and remove any excess on the rim of the lid or on a piece of scrap paper.

2 Make a number of impressions on the wall before reloading the sponge with more glaze. Alter the angle of the sponge slightly with each new impression.

3 Reload the sponge and begin to fill in the bare areas of wall, gradually building up an even coverage across the wall surface.

4 Once one colour is complete, use a second colour to build up depth in the design.

SPONGING OFF

This technique differs slightly from "sponging on" in that the glaze is applied directly to the wall first and then a sponge is used to create impressions in the glazed surface. The finish tends to be slightly more subtle than "sponging on," but equally effective in producing depth and texture.

1 Use a brush to apply the glaze to the wall, making brush strokes in random directions and applying even coverage. Only cover an area of up to one square metre (yard) at a time, otherwise the glaze will start to dry in some places before you have the chance to produce the effect.

2 Press a dampened sponge onto the glazed surface, creating a mottled broken colour effect. As with sponging on, keep changing the angle at which the sponge comes in contact with the wall, to give a random but even finish.

REFLECTING TEXTURE
A sponged-off finish produces a wonderful overall effect, which changes its appearance according to different light intensity.

SPONGING IDEAS

In addition to the standard sponging instructions, the following ideas can be added to the general technique.
- Using different sides: most natural sponges have one side that has a much finer texture than the other. Choose whichever side creates the effect you want, or combine both.
- Creating shadows: vary the intensity of the pattern by making more impressions near any corners or alcoves—this will produce a very interesting shadowy effect.
- Dealing with corners: cut a small section off a sponge, tape it to the end of a pencil and use this to gain access to internal corners.
- Keeping clean: while producing sponging effects, wash the sponge frequently in plenty of clean water.

RAGGING AND RAG-ROLLING

Cotton rags are used in a similar way to sponges to create texture impressions on the wall surface with glaze. Although the technique is similar, the finished effect is very different.

RAGGING ON

Ragging on is similar to "sponging on" in that the rag is used to apply the glaze to the wall. You need to have a plentiful supply of rags at hand, since they soon become too ingrained with glaze to be used effectively.

1 Pour some glaze onto an old plate or paint-tub lid. Crumple the rag in your hand and dip it into the glaze. Remove any excess on the rim of the lid or on a scrap of paper.

2 In a similar fashion to sponging, press the rag onto the wall to create rag impressions. Keep altering the angle at which you apply the rag in order to create a random effect.

RAGGING OFF

This method is used to create a textured impression in wet glaze. Only apply glaze to areas of up to one square metre (yard)—it has a limited working time.

1 Apply the glaze randomly. For a more even finish, you can lay off the glaze in a vertical direction.

2 Press a damp, crumpled rag into the wet glaze, altering wrist and hand angle as you move across it.

RAG-ROLLING

Rag-rolling extends the principle of using rags by making the impressions that they create much more directional. Rag-rolling can be carried out in any direction, but by far the most common method is to use the rags to create vertical, relatively uniform striped patterns. Rag-rolling is much more effective using the "ragging off" method, rather than the "ragging on" one.

1 Screw up a number of pieces of rag and twist each one into an irregular sausage or finger shape. Make all the sausage shapes roughly the same size.

2 Apply the glaze to the wall, then roll a sausage-shaped rag down the wall surface, creating a tumbling, relatively uniform ragged effect. Make sure that you keep the rag in contact with the wall surface at all times, using a continuous rolling motion as it progresses down the wall. Use a washed-out rag for each subsequent roll down the wall.

RAGGING VARIATIONS

The name "ragging" is used as an all-encompassing term when referring to the technique demonstrated above. In reality, cotton rags are not the only fabrics that can be used to create this paint effect. Try experimenting with any of the items in the following list—each one creates a slightly different, very distinctive variation on the traditional ragged effect:

- plastic bags
- denim
- burlap
- lace
- muslin
- net
- velvet
- corduroy

THE FABRIC LOOK
Rag-rolling produces a highly textured fabric look on any wall surface. Although relatively simple to create, it gives the appearance of being extremely complicated.

DRAGGING AND GRAINING

Dragging and graining are both effects that are used to produce a highly textured and directional finish. They can either be applied on a wooden surface to accentuate its texture, or on other surfaces to mimic the grain of wood. Both techniques require practice but, once mastered, the effects you can produce are extremely gratifying.

DRAGGING

Dragging is a good effect to apply to any woodwork—especially panel doors. Special dragging brushes can be used, although good effects can be created with a flogger or softening brush, or even a paint brush with coarse bristles.

1 Apply the glaze to the door, treating different sections of the door as separate items.

2 Drag the brush through the glaze in the direction of the natural grain of the wood. Make sure that the bristles are at a very acute angle with the surface of the door. The coarseness in texture can be varied with the bristle angle.

3 After each sweep with the brush, remove excess glaze from the bristles with a clean cotton rag.

4 Treat each section of the door as a separate item, creating precise dividing lines between each one.

GRAINING

Graining bears some similarities to dragging, except that a specially designed tool—a graining rocker—must be used to create the desired effect. Graining can be carried out on wooden surfaces or, as in this case, the lower level of a wall can be grained to reproduce a wooden panel effect.

1 Apply the glaze to the wall surface, being careful to lightly smooth it out with vertical strokes of the brush.

2 Starting on the extreme edge of the wall, hold or fix a wooden batten so that it is precisely vertical. Then pull the graining rocker down through the glaze, using the edge of the batten as a guide.

3 The rest of the rocker strokes must now be made by eye—the wooden batten would damage the effect as you move across the surface. Make slight rolling motions with the rocker as you drag it through the wet glaze. This technique has the effect of mimicking the wooden knots and variations found in wood grain on the wall surface.

THE PANEL EFFECT
Graining is an extremely effective way of producing a mock panelled look on an otherwise flat, characterless wall surface.

COLOUR-WASHING AND LIMING

Both these effects are aimed at highlighting the features of the base surface below. Whether on walls or wood, the idea is to produce a translucent finish, with the use of colour and/or glaze, that accentuates features in that surface.

COLOUR-WASHING

A colour-wash uses glaze to create a translucent layer over a base coat of an emulsion or undercoat. Matt emulsion provides an absorbent base that soaks up the colour-wash; a vinyl base coat will produce a more subtle look.

Wiping away: the wash is brushed on and immediately wiped away. This creates a translucent finish with varying degrees of colour intensity.

Leaving alone: alternatively, the wash can be applied with random brush strokes and left as the finished effect, creating a colour-dominant finish.

TIMBER RUBBING

Timber rubbing can be considered as colour-washing on wood. The wood should have no base coat—glaze is applied directly to the untreated surface.

1 As with dragging, treat separate areas of the door as separate items, applying the glaze generously.

2 Use a damp rag to wipe away excess glaze to highlight the grain of the wood with a little glaze colour.

LIMING

Liming (or pickling) acts in a similar way to timber rubbing, except that white is the characteristic colour produced with the finish, and the actual product used to create the finish is a purpose-designed wax rather than a glaze. It is essential that the wood is untreated before this effect is applied.

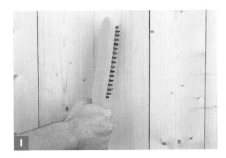

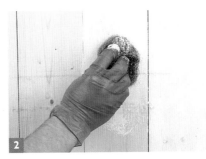

1 Open up the grain of the wood by scrubbing it lightly with a wire brush, working in the direction of the grain.

2 Apply generous amounts of the liming wax to the wooden surface using a ball of fine-grade steel wool. Make sure that the wax gets into all areas.

3 Wipe off the excess wax with a cotton rag. It is possible to buff the surface to give it a slight sheen, characteristic of all waxed surfaces.

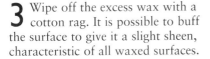

THE LIMED LOOK

Liming produces a very traditional rustic finish on wood, and limed panelling such as this creates a very restful, comfortable atmosphere. Liming is especially effective when it is combined with natural materials and other aged or distressed paint effects in a room.

MARBLING

Marbling is one of the most difficult paint effects to master: it is an attempt to reproduce the look of a natural substance. It takes a great deal of practice to achieve a really good marble effect, but it is possible to create this most luxurious-looking of all paint finishes. Naturally occurring marble differs hugely in colour and appearance, but the marbling method shown here provides an attractive two-colour marble effect for the walls in your home.

1 Paint the wall with a white vinyl base coat and let dry. Mix two glazes, one a light gray and one with raw umber as the only colourizer. Apply random patches of each glaze with a fine, flat-bristled brush; leave some white areas uncovered.

2 While both the glazes are still wet, use a stippling brush across the entire wall surface to apply a textured effect and blend the two glazes into each other.

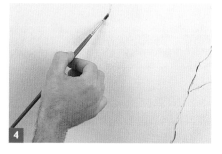

3 Use a softening brush or flogger to stroke gently across the glaze, blending both glazes still further and taking some of the harshness out of the stippled effect. First brush in the direction of the glaze, then across its grain, and then with the flow again.

4 Dip an artist's brush into some raw umber and then into each of the two glazes. Draw the brush across the wall surface while slowly rotating it between thumb and index finger. Keep the veins running in one direction to mimic natural marble.

5 Soften the veins by first brushing in the direction they are running, then across their "grain," and finally with their direction again.

6 Leave the wall to dry completely before applying two or three coats of lacquer.

7 Use a fine-grade abrasive paper to gently sand over the entire surface. Finally, polish the finish using a soft cotton rag.

LUXURIOUS FINISH
A marbled paint effect is a luxurious finish in its own right—it also makes the wall a dramatic backdrop for ornaments and other display items.

AGING

There are many different ways of aging a decorated surface in order to produce the comfortable, lived-in feel of years of wear and tear. The methods shown here are not the only ones, but they are extremely effective ways of creating this particular look.

DISTRESSING

This technique is particularly effective on wooden paneled surfaces, as a large area displays the finish to best effect. Choose colours carefully when creating a distressed look—it always works best if you have a base colour that is a lighter shade than the one used as the top coat.

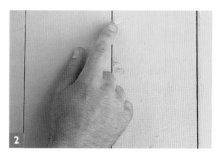

1 Apply the light base coat directly onto the untreated wood surface, and leave it to dry.

2 Where you want the colour to show through the top surface, apply random streaks of petroleum jelly, paying particular attention to the edges of the boards with just the odd streak along their central areas.

3 Apply the darker top coat over the entire paneled surface, being careful to cover it totally. Leave the top coat to dry.

4 Sand the panels with fine-grade abrasive paper. Where petroleum jelly was applied, the top coat will not stick; it rubs away to reveal the base colour. The degree of distressing depends on the amount of sanding.

CRACKLE GLAZE

There are a number of different crackle finishes, but crackle glaze is one of the most effective ways of producing this aged, antique look. Application methods vary slightly between manufacturers, but the method shown here demonstrates the most commonly used technique for producing a crackle-glaze finish.

1 Apply a base coat to the wall surface. Vivid bright colours work particularly well with this effect; even the base coat should be a strong colour, so it emphasizes the finish as clearly as possible.

2 Apply the crackle glaze with a generously loaded brush. It is essential to keep the brush strokes going in the same direction.

3 Thin the top coat of emulsion with one part water to 10 parts paint. Apply it using brush strokes at right angles to each other, never returning to an area once the paint is applied. Slowly but surely the crackle effect will begin to appear.

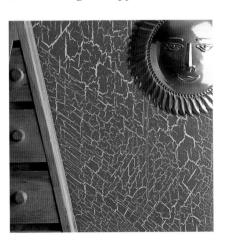

NATURAL CRACKLE
Crackle glaze produces a fascinating "crazed" surface, combining both colour and texture to great effect.

STIPPLING

S tippling produces a fine textured effect, and it can be built up in layers to produce greater depth. Flat, open surfaces are best suited to stippling, since it is easier to maintain a consistency of texture on them.

1 Apply the glaze to the wall with slightly swirling brush strokes, in all directions. Total coverage is not necessary, as small patches of base coat will be covered with glaze once stippling begins.

2 Once an area of one square metre (yard) has been covered with glaze, use the stippling brush to make small impressions on the surface. Make short dabbing motions, letting only the very tips of the bristles come in contact with the wall. Vary your hand angle as you gradually progress across the wall. Once one area is complete, apply more glaze to the wall and continue to stipple as before. Remove excess glaze from the bristles with a clean cotton rag after each glazed area is complete.

3 Use a stencil brush to complete the effect in the corner junction of the wall—it is difficult to gain access to internal corners with a stippling brush.

STIPPLING EFFECT
Stippling creates a wonderful warm glow across a wall surface. Light is refracted from it with different intensities, producing a truly three-dimensional finish.

COMBING

A special tool called a graining comb is used on a stippled surface to create this highly textured decorative effect. Combs vary in design, but all produce a directional flow of glaze that combines the base and glaze colour to produce a two-tone effect. The comb shown here has differing gaps and sizes of teeth, which can be used to create different grades of effect.

1 Apply glaze in random directions across the wall surface in areas of up to one square metre (yard) at a time, as the glaze has a limited workable time before it dries. Be careful to cover the area totally.

2 For a more even effect, stipple the glaze to give a uniform textured finish. See opposite for the technique of using a stippling brush.

3 Draw the comb down through the glaze to create a grooved effect, removing any excess glaze from the teeth of the comb with a dry rag after each sweep.

VARYING TEXTURE
By combining two sizes of combs, it is possible to create an interesting striped effect such as this one.

COMBINING EFFECTS

S ome paint effects complement each other really well and can be used together on a surface to create unusual and highly individual looks. Once you have the correct tools and have mastered the techniques on the previous pages, you can experiment with nearly any combination to create texture on a variety of surfaces. Combing and dragging combine particularly well together.

COMBING AND DRAGGING

Combing and dragging combine well as both have a pronounced texture that creates a very definite pattern on the wall surface. Both are suited to small areas—they can be overwhelming on large open surfaces. The panelled design shown here is an excellent compromise, reducing the amount of wall coverage of each effect while still producing a finish of considerable impact.

1 Mask off some equal-size panels on the wall, using floor tiles as a template. Measure a second panel inside the first, and mask off along its edges before glazing inside the panel with an ordinary paint brush.

2 Starting at the top left-hand corner of the panel, make vertical sweeps down through the glaze using a graining comb.

3 After every second or third sweep with the comb, wipe the excess glaze from the comb with a dry cotton rag. Once the vertical sweeps have been completed, use the same technique to create horizontal sweeps across the entire panel.

4 Allow the glaze to dry, remove the masking tape, and apply more tape around the outside of the outer panel. Although it would be easier to mask off the internal combed panel, the tape can pull away the glazed surface when removed and a glazed surface can be difficult to touch-in. Apply glaze to the outer "frame," taking care not to get any on the internal combed area.

5 Use a fairly coarse-bristled brush to drag through the glaze along each side of the "frame." A dragging brush could be used, but they are generally much wider than the area allows. Angle the brush so that it is at a very acute angle with the wall surface, and make smooth, even sweeps in the glaze.

6 Make sure you create a definite "square" joint between each side of the frame, since precise finishing at corners adds to the effect. When the frame is complete, remove the masking tape. Continue with other panels, repeating Steps 1–6.

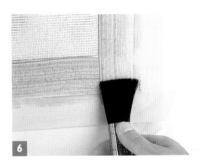

TEXTURED PANELLING
This panelled effect is impressive in any room, but in a bathroom the matching shape of the tiles and the panels produces a very smart and well-integrated decorative scheme.

STAMPING

S tamping is a quick and easy way of applying and repeating painted images across a wall or wooden surface. The images can be applied singly or in groups, and may be used to create single feature designs or mixed with other stamps to produce a collage effect. Stamps can either be bought or made—the application method remains the same.

HOUSEHOLD OBJECTS

Stamps can be made out of any number of objects found around the home, as long as the item chosen can absorb paint. A small brush can be used to apply paint to a stamp, or you can use a custom-made roller as shown opposite.

Sponges: draw an animal design on a sponge and cut it out using a craft knife. Reloading the sponge after each stamp is not necessary because it is so absorbent.

Corks: bind three corks together with tape to create a cloverleaf design. Reload the corks with paint after each stamp. Make the stem of the leaf with a small, fine brush or by rotating the painted edge of a single cork below the cloverleaf design.

Potatoes: draw a picture on the flat cut half of a potato, then cut out the design with a craft knife. Make sure that the entire surface area of the design is placed in full contact with the wall, then remove it to reveal the impression.

CUSTOM-MADE STAMPS

Although making your own stamps is great fun, manufactured stamps tend to be easier to use and create more defined impressions when applied to the wall. Choose a design that fits in with the particular theme and effect you are trying to create in your room.

1 Load a small foam roller with the chosen paint colour. Apply it to the stamp, ensuring that the entire design is covered. Before applying it to the wall, test the stamp on a piece of scrap paper to check whether you need to remove excess paint from its face before applying it to the wall.

2 Apply the stamp to the wall, making sure that there is full contact between the design and wall surface. Press down firmly.

3 Pull the stamp away from the wall, being careful not to smear the design, and continue to apply more stamps to build up your overall picture. Reload the stamp with paint as required.

CREATING A THEME
Stamps are ideal for creating a decorative theme in a room—they can be used for a subtle design or a dramatic effect.

STRAIGHTFORWARD STENCILLING

S tencils are similar to stamps in that they provide a technique for producing a design motif on a wall or wooden surface. However, the way in which stencils achieve this effect is completely different than the method for stamping. Stencils can be bought or made—making your own gives greater opportunity for personal expression.

MAKING A STENCIL

Stencils can be made out of custom-made cardboard or plastic. Stencil plastic is the most practical choice, since it is easily washed and can be used time and time again with equal accuracy. Stencil designs can either be drawn by hand or traced, and you can use various natural products as the basis for your design.

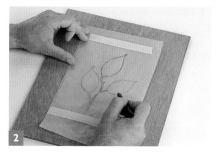

1 Choose a leaf cluster that demonstrates a strong shape as well as a balanced overall design. Place it on a board, using some tape to hold it in place, if required. Hold some tracing paper over the top of it and use a pencil to trace around the edge of the design.

2 Remove the leaves, and stick the traced image to the board with some masking tape. Hold a sheet of thin stencil plastic over the tracing paper, and use a fibre-tip pen to draw the traced design on the plastic.

3 Remove the tracing paper and stick the stencil plastic to the board with masking tape. Follow the fibre-tip pen guideline to cut out the leaves, stem, and stalk of the stencil design, using a sharp craft knife on a cutting board. The stencil is then ready to use.

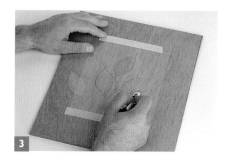

USING A STENCIL

The design below can be used as a border around doors or windows, or as a more overall wall pattern as demonstrated here. Custom-made acrylic stencil paints are the ideal materials to use for filling in the design. For a more imaginative finish, try mixing colour with emulsion and colourizers.

1 Use some masking tape to hold the stencil securely in position on the wall surface.

2 When using a stencil brush, load the brush with paint so that the bristles remain relatively dry—the excess paint can be removed by dabbing the brush a few times on a piece of scrap paper to leave just a trace of colour on the brush. Brush on the colour, using light dabbing motions perpendicular to the wall surface. Vary the colour within the design to make it look lifelike.

3 Once complete, remove the stencil carefully to reveal the finished design. Move along to the next area and repeat Steps 1 and 2.

COLOURFUL STENCILLING
Stencils can produce well-defined images on all manner of surfaces, creating a definite picture or scene that can be kept small or expanded to produce a much larger effect.

STENCILLING AND STAMPING FOR MURALS

H and-painted scenes and expansive murals are difficult projects because they require considerable artistic talent. However, it is possible for anybody to use stencils and stamps to produce designs for small localized wall areas or for parts of a big picture.

CHOOSE YOUR DESIGN

When choosing your mural, you may be limited by what stencils and stamps your local home decorating stores supply, unless you feel confident enough to make your own materials.

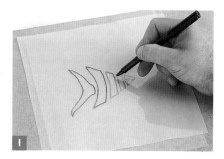

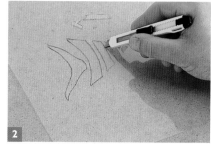

1 You may find it easier to make your own stencils than to make your own stamps. Once you have chosen your scheme and decided which motifs you can produce by which method, use a fibre-tip pen and acetate to trace your design, as shown on page 234.

2 As before, use a craft knife to cut out the required sections of the design.

STENCILLING TIPS

- Paint the design with rhythmic dabbing motions of your paint brush.
- Choose the colour scheme for your stencils carefully. It is often more effective to limit yourself to a narrow colour palette.

---

3 Secure the stencil with masking tape, then paint the design. Remove excess paint from the brush before each application and keep it perpendicular to the wall surface.

MIXING IN STAMPS

Single-colour stamps combine well with the multicoloured effect of stencils and are an easy way of applying specific images to a wall surface. For how to make your own stamps, see page 232. However, due to the popularity of stamping, your local home decorating store may now sell an inspiring range.

1 Spread paint evenly on the stamp with a brush or a custom-made foam roller. Apply the stamp to the wall surface, pressing down firmly to make sure all areas of the stamp are in full contact with the wall.

2 Lift the stamp carefully to avoid it sliding across the wall surface and smudging the paint. Vary the intensity of the image according to your personal taste by adjusting the amount of paint applied to the stamp and by removing excess paint from the stamp before applying it to the wall surface.

COMBINING EFFECTS

Stamps and stencils are ideal paint effects to combine on a wall, as each brings its own character to a painted scene. They can be used to make a variety of different scenes in children's bedrooms or the bathroom.

MULTICOLOURED EFFECTS
The single colour of stamps, mixed with the more broken, multicoloured effect of stencils, creates a wonderful combination of colour and design on this bathroom wall.

CREATING STENCIL EFFECTS

As your technique improves, it is possible to create more specialized effects with stencils. The increased use of colour, shading different areas with more paint, or highlighting parts of a stencil more than others, can create a shadow effect that hints at a specific light source and produces a more three-dimensional appearance. Shading more on one side of a stencil gives the effect of direct sunlight and the direction from which it is coming. Alternatively, making the edges of a flower design more pronounced, as shown here, gives a very vibrant lifelike finish to the stencil.

1 Attach the stencil to the wall with masking tape. Increase the colour intensity on the extreme edges of the design, while leaving central areas more sparsely coloured.

2 Carefully remove the stencil to reveal a textured effect that demonstrates more depth than the more simple stencil techniques.

ALTERNATIVE STENCILLING MATERIALS

In addition to standard stencil brushes, it is possible to use various other tools to apply paint to a stencil.
- Sponges: natural sea sponges have a pronounced texture, which makes them ideal for use on large stencils; always make sure you remove the excess paint before applying it.
- Aerosols: as the spray cannot be pinpointed on a small area, aerosol

paints are best used for stencil designs that do not require close colour changes. They are very quick to use.
- Crayons: stencil crayons are a good alternative to traditional paints. The sticks can be rubbed on a piece of stencil plastic that can then be used as a palette for transferring paint to the stencil with a stencil brush.

4
PAPERING TECHNIQUES

Wallpaper varies in design, pattern, and size, but the actual techniques for applying the different types changes very little. Once you have established a sound basic papering technique, you can hang nearly all types of paper with equal success. This chapter outlines the simple rules and correct techniques for carrying out straightforward wallpapering. Once this stage is mastered, it is simply a matter of refining these techniques for more complicated wallpapering situations. Follow all the necessary preparations outlined in Chapter 1, "Preparation and Planning," before beginning to hang the wallpaper, and don't try to hurry the papering process because speed will develop naturally with experience.

WHAT PAPER TO USE WHERE

Most paper can be applied in any area of the home, although some types of wallpaper are more suited to particular rooms than others (see page 171 for the properties of each type of paper). However, it is worthwhile considering the effects of different designs and patterns in conjunction with the use of the room and the style you are trying to achieve.

The formal choice: dining rooms and reception areas are the ideal places to use traditional designs, which can be linked to the period of the property or simply to add a touch of grandeur and style to the room as a whole. You can also use wallpaper to create an illusion of space. Stripes can provide a feeling of height and spaciousness in a small room.

Fun florals: floral wallpaper has a rustic and old-fashioned charm, but it can be used to great effect in a modern interior when teamed with contemporary furniture and accessories. This feature wall is decorated in a bold but pretty floral print.

THE EFFECTS OF DESIGN

Different designs on wallpapers can create completely different effects. In much the same way that colour can produce a particular feeling within a room, the pattern of the wallpaper can completely alter the atmosphere and mood; when choosing a design always take into consideration the effect that the design in question will have on the room as a whole.

Stripes

Vertical striped wallpapers always create a feeling of height and are therefore ideal for rooms in which you want to give the impression of "raising" the ceiling. Don't use striped wallpaper on uneven walls, as any slight undulations will be accentuated by the clear, sharp lines of the stripes.

All-over effects

Recent fashion has meant that there are a number of papers available that have an all-over, almost paint effect design, such as a colour-wash or stippled effect. These wallpapers tend to be easy to hang, but it can be difficult to hide seams since there is no precise pattern to draw your eye away from them. This happens with darker colours in particular, and it is worthwhile considering hanging and painting a lining paper a similar base colour to the wallpaper before hanging the wallpaper, so that any slightly open seams will have the appropriate background colour.

Floral papers

These are generally easy to hang since they tend to have a fairly busy design that hides the seams easily. Big floral patterns should be hung in large rooms, otherwise the pattern can look cramped and make the room seem smaller than it actually is. Small floral patterns tend to create a country cottage effect, and they are ideal for uneven or slightly rough walls because the busy pattern on the paper draws your eye away from any imperfections in the wall surface.

Singular designs

Wallpapers with one or two motifs repeated time and time again need precise matching—if the paper is not hung exactly vertical, any discrepancies will be very obvious on the wall. While they produce an excellent effect, these papers are not the easiest ones for a beginner to hang.

Papered scenes

Some manufacturers produce papers with landscape designs. The rolls of paper have to be applied to the wall surface in a particular sequence in order to build up a precise picture. This unusual effect can produce an impressive finish in any room as long as the size of the design can be fitted into the available wall space. Similar to these papers are trompe l'oeil paper panels, which can be used to create another faux effect on a wallpapered surface in a room.

Period papers

Some paper designs have a classical appeal that never seems to age over the generations or go out of fashion—the fleur-de-lys design, for example, has been copied for many years and still maintains its popular appeal. Many of these classic designs produce quite a formal decorative effect in a room and this factor should always be taken into consideration when choosing this type of wallpaper.

MEASURING, CUTTING AND PASTING

E nsuring that you have the right number of rolls for the job is obviously an important factor when papering. The way in which these rolls are prepared, cut and pasted, and ready for wall application is also essential in producing the required finish. Whatever type of paper is being used, the dimensions of the room must be measured accurately.

CALCULATING THE NUMBER OF ROLLS

A simple way of calculating the number of rolls required for a room is shown below. Manufacturers usually state the size of the pattern repeat on the roll label, but it is worthwhile checking it yourself.

$$\frac{\text{Height of room} + \text{Wallpaper repeat size} \times \text{Distance around skirting board}}{\text{Area of one roll}} = \frac{\text{Number of}}{\text{rolls required}}$$

AREA OF ONE ROLL

Most wallpapers are about 10 m (11 yd) long by 52 cm (20½ in) wide. However, there are variations, so work out the surface area of one roll of paper by multiplying the two dimensions together.

Adjust your calculations if entire walls are taken up by picture windows or fitted cupboards. However, doors and other smaller areas that do not need wallpapering should be included, since you will need to make allowances for trimming the paper while fitting around them.

MEASURING TO CUT

Measuring wallpaper to fit is a simple process as long as a few rules are followed. First, measure the height of a required length by measuring the exact distance between the ceiling and the top of the skirting. Next, the size of the pattern repeat must be added to this measurement and finally an extra 2.5 cm (1 in) must be added at the top and bottom of the length to allow for trimming. With particularly large repeats, this method can produce a lot of wastage. It is often better to hold up a roll of dry paper next to the previously hung length and match it, so that it can be cut precisely and then pasted before it is applied to the wall. For patterns with no repeat, such as stripes, only the allowance for trimming needs to be added to the standard height measurement. This means that with patterns that have little or no repeat, it is easier to cut a number of lengths in readiness for hanging, whereas with larger repeat patterns, it is often easier to cut one length to size at a time.

PASTING PAPER

Wallpapers are divided into two categories: pre-pasted paper with dry paste attached to its backing, which is reactivated by submerging in cold water, and paste-the-back paper, which requires traditional paste to stick it to the wall.

PRE-PASTED PAPER

1 Fill a water trough at the end of the pasting table two-thirds full. Roll up a length of wallpaper, pattern inward, and submerge it for the recommended soaking time.

2 Pull the paper onto the table, folding so that pasted surface meets pasted surface. Repeat this step at the other end of the length. Leave it to soak for the required time.

PASTE-THE-BACK PAPER

1 Roll out the wallpaper along the pasting table. Make sure that the paste is mixed according to the manufacturer's instructions for the type of paper you are using. Apply paste from the centre of the paper out toward its edges, ensuring total and even coverage.

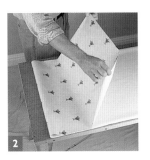

2 When the paper is covered with paste, pick up the end of the length and lift and slide it along the pasting table, folding as you progress along the length of it.

3 Continue the folding along the length of pasted paper. Remove the folded length from the table and leave it to soak for the required time before applying to the wall.

LINING

L ining paper can be applied to walls (especially old, unsound ones) in order to create the best possible surface for the wallpaper. It acts in a similar way to an undercoat before the top coat of paint. Although it is not essential, a lining paper greatly improves a wallpapered finish, and in many cases, manufacturer's guidelines state that lining is vital before applying their wallpaper. Paste is applied to lining paper in the same way as for wallpaper (see page 243).

CEILINGS

Although ceilings are not often wallpapered, they can benefit from being lined. Whether lining a ceiling for wallpapering or painting purposes, make sure that the surface is thoroughly prepared before applying the lining paper and check that the correct sealer or size has been applied.

Using the wall/ceiling junction as the starting point, begin lining. Alternatively, begin in the centre of the room in order to bisect a hanging light (see opposite).

Support the paper with one hand while brushing out with the other hand.

Line away from the natural light source in order to make seams less visible.

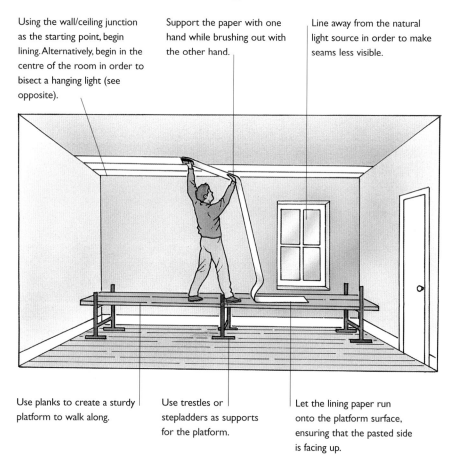

Use planks to create a sturdy platform to walk along.

Use trestles or stepladders as supports for the platform.

Let the lining paper run onto the platform surface, ensuring that the pasted side is facing up.

HANGING GUIDELINES

Ceilings may appear awkward to paper, but they can be easier than walls since they have far fewer obstacles. Beginning each length from a secure starting point is essential for papering ceilings successfully.

1 Brush the start of the length securely into the ceiling/wall junction, allowing a small overlap for trimming. Progress along the length, brushing out air bubbles and joining precisely with the previous length.

2 At each wall/ceiling junction, pull back the paper and cut along the creased guideline. To make the guideline more visible, you can mark the crease with a pencil before pulling the paper back.

3 Brush the trimmed paper back into position, to create a perfect cut edge.

DEALING WITH LIGHT FIXTURES

Hanging light fixtures can be dealt with in two different ways, as shown below. Whenever papering around electrical fixtures, ensure that the power is turned off at the electical distribution box before work commences.

Coinciding seams: if the paper will bisect the light, loosen its backing plate and brush the paper behind it.

Threading light: where it meets the light centrally, cut a hole in the paper. Thread the light through; trim.

LINING WALLS

Traditionally, lining paper is applied to walls horizontally, though this is not essential. It is best to apply lining paper so that the fewest possible lengths are used on any particular wall, whether this is vertically or horizontally. This means that large walls are best lined horizontally and small alcoves are best lined vertically. When lining vertically, the one consideration is to make sure that when it comes to wallpapering, the lining paper seams and the wallpaper seams do not coincide. The examples below show how to line walls horizontally; the vertical method can be achieved using the wallpapering guidelines shown later in this chapter.

1 Join lengths of paper at the corner junction, allowing for a small overlap for trimming purposes. Hold the folded paper in one hand while positioning with the other hand.

2 Using a paperhanging brush, smooth out the length, gradually unrolling the folds and joining the paper with the previous length. Always butt-join the lengths and avoid any overlaps.

3 Trim the paper into the corners, using scissors, or a craft knife as shown here.

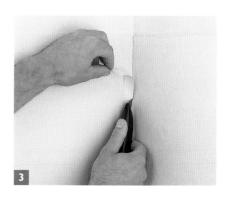

CORNERS

For internal corners, the lining paper should always be trimmed along the corner junction, as shown opposite. External corners require the paper to be moulded around the edge of the corner in order to maintain the continuity of a single length. The method demonstrated here will only work if the external corner is square. Where this is not the case, it may be necessary to use the method for dealing with external corners when wallpapering (see page 256).

1 Unroll the paper folds, letting the paper bend around the edge of the external corner and onto the adjacent wall.

2 Before brushing the paper out on the adjacent wall, use your fingers to crease along the edge of the corner, smoothing out and removing any air bubbles.

FINISHING OFF

Once the room is lined and the paper has dried, fill any seam gaps with filler to make a perfectly smooth surface for wallpapering. Apply some "size" (diluted wallpaper paste) to the lining paper and leave it to dry—this will make it much easier to hang the wallpaper because it lets the paper slip across the lined surface when you are positioning it.

Filling gaps: if there are gaps between seams in the lined surface, apply some fine filler to these areas to make a smooth surface. Sand the area lightly once the filler is dry.

Finishing corners: decorator's sealant around internal corner junctions and joints between lining paper and wood provides an even finish and stops the paper from lifting.

WHERE TO START WALLPAPERING

There are a number of factors to consider when deciding on the best place to begin wallpapering. In order to make sure that the wallpaper will create the best possible effect, you need to take a little time to decide on the most appropriate starting point as well as the best place to finish and join up the pattern as a whole. As room designs and layouts vary dramatically, it is difficult to cover every eventuality here. However, there are a number of points that can be considered as general guidelines when deciding where to begin.

Centralizing: bold patterned papers with large repeats may require the main design in the paper to be centralized on a particular wall in order to create a balanced overall effect. The obvious place would be on a chimney-breast or centrally between two windows on the same wall. With smaller patterns, this process is not as essential as the balance of the design will not be dependent on central positioning.

A complete start: always try to make sure that the first length you hang is a complete uninterrupted drop that requires no intricate trimming. Never trust an internal corner as a vertical starting point—it is best to use a spirit level to ensure that you are starting from a precisely vertical position.

Avoiding finishing with a seam match: where a room does not have a continuous wall surface around the entire circumference of the room, avoid having to join the paper at the end of the job. This avoids the need for what can often be a tricky pattern match in order to finish the room.

Marking the position: work out where subsequent lengths of paper will hang by measuring around the circumference of the room with a roll of wallpaper. Mark positions on the wall and adjust accordingly for the most suitable positions for lengths to hang.

THE STARTING POINTS

Centralizing

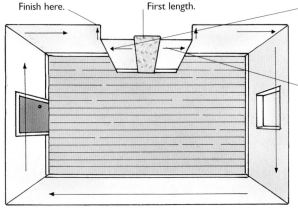

Finish here.

First length.

After the first length, paper around this corner of the chimney-breast.

Continue around the other corner of the chimney-breast and on around the rest of the room.

A complete start

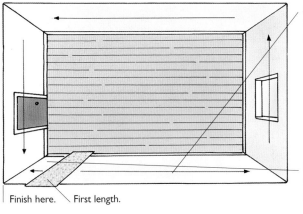

After the first length, continue around the rest of the room.

Final length may need to overlap in the corner to create a joint.

Finish here.   First length.

Avoiding finishing with a seam match

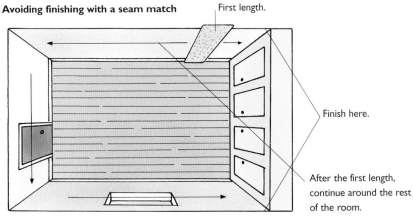

First length.

Finish here.

After the first length, continue around the rest of the room.

HANGING THE FIRST LENGTH

H anging the first length correctly is the most important part of creating any wallpaper design, as this initial application forms the base on which the rest of the pattern is built. If the first length is not vertical, this slant will be repeated throughout the entire room, so it is essential to take time to make sure that the first length is straight.

1 At your starting position, draw a pencil line from ceiling to floor, using a level to ensure that it is precisely vertical.

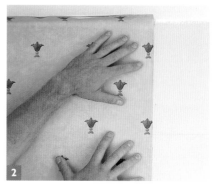

2 Position the first length at the top of the wall, and slide it into place so the edge of the paper runs along the pencil guideline. Allow a small overlap onto the ceiling.

3 Crease the top of the paper into the wall/ceiling junction, then brush the paper with a paperhanging brush to remove air bubbles and ensure that the paper is firmly stuck to the wall. Work the bristles of the brush from the centre of the length outward and downward.

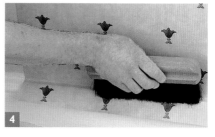

4 When you reach the bottom of the length, use the paperhanging brush to crease the paper securely into the skirting board junction.

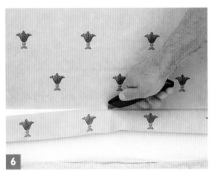

5 Return to the top of the length, then cut along the wall/ceiling junction with a craft knife. Cut slightly above the junction as this tends to give a much neater finish.

6 Brush back down to the bottom of the length and trim the paper with a craft knife, cutting slightly onto the top of the skirting board to produce a clean dividing line.

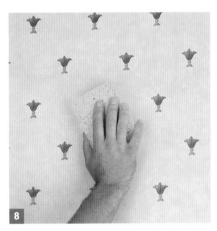

7 Return to the top of the length, then brush all the way down to the bottom again, removing any air bubbles that may have been missed during the initial sweep.

8 Finally, use a sponge rinsed in clean water to wipe over the surface of the entire length of paper to remove any paste residue. Wipe over the adjacent areas of wall and skirting board as well, to ensure that they are paste-free.

JOINING LENGTHS

Whether a wallpaper has a pattern that requires matching or not, adjacent lengths of paper need to be joined very accurately to produce a good finish. The aim should be to butt-join the lengths so that the two pieces form a seam where they meet, without overlapping.

MAKING THE SEAM JOINT

Where the pattern requires precise matching, it is obviously important to make the match between papers as precise as possible. However, some papers are prone to stretching, and some may even have slight variations within a roll, which makes pattern matching difficult. Always try to make the first point of matching at normal eye level in the room; if there are cases where the pattern drops, these inconsistencies will be positioned lower down the wall where they will be far less visible.

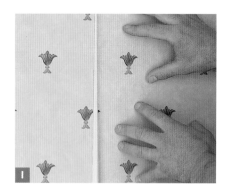

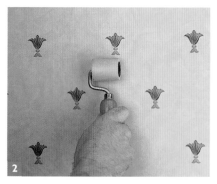

1 Slide the new length up to the previous one, matching the pattern first at eye level and then down the rest of the length. Brush out and trim the length in the usual way.

2 Most papers will join easily, but it may be necessary to run a seam roller lightly down the seams to ensure a good finish.

3 Where the edges dry out too quickly, apply some more paste with a fine paint brush, then stick the paper down again, as required.

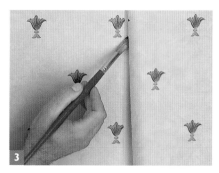

TYPES OF MATCH

Wallpaper patterns are matched between lengths using more than one method. It is important to be aware of the subtle differences between the designs as these can affect the way in which pattern matching is achieved. Use the best method for the particular paper you are trying to hang.

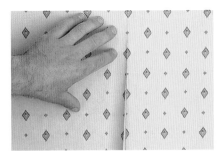

Straight match: the seam for a straight-match pattern is made very simple by having the match bisect a main feature in the design itself—when two pieces of paper are being joined, it is perfectly clear where the second paper should be positioned in order to reunite the pattern.

MISCELLANEOUS MATCHES

Some designers produce papers that have variations on the matches demonstrated here, but in such cases, instructions are usually supplied with the paper. Sometimes, straight-match paper design is slightly "offset" so that joining is not as clear as in most cases. Also, some free-match papers are in fact straight match, which may only become apparent once the paper is hung. Always read the manufacturer's guidelines before hanging a wallpaper, especially when the design is not straightforward.

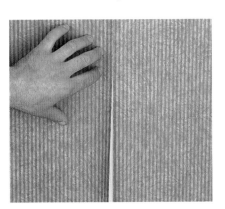

Free match: these are often the easiest papers to join as you don't need to worry about matching the pattern at specific points—it is butt-joined at any point. However, manufacturers often suggest that for papers with a strong overall pattern, every second length should be inverted.

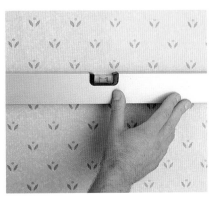

Level match: with some wallpapers the actual match is free, but the paper design of each length needs to be level with the previous one. Once a length has been applied, use a level to check that the whole design remains constant and in the correct position on the wall.

INTERNAL CORNERS

A s all rooms have internal corners, learning how to deal with them is an important part of basic papering technique. However square an internal corner is, never try to bend a full length of paper around it because the paper will always wrinkle along the junction, producing an unsightly finish. The best technique is to cut a single length in two and rejoin it precisely along the corner junction.

1 Measure the exact distance from the last full length to the corner junction. Check this distance along the entire length to make sure there are no slight variations along the junction. Add 12 mm ($\frac{1}{2}$ in) to this measurement, and cut the next length of paper into two pieces accordingly.

2 Paste the first length of wallpaper, and pattern match it as usual to the previous length.

3 Brush it into place, allowing for the 12-mm ($\frac{1}{2}$-in) overlap to bend around onto the adjacent wall.

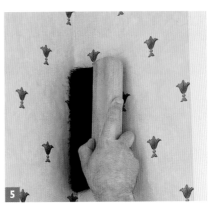

4 Paste the other half of the length of paper and position it on the adjacent wall, matching the pattern as well as possible. Undulations along the corner junction may mean that the match is not exact in some places. However, the length must be hung vertically, so use a spirit level to make sure that it hangs in the correct position on the wall.

5 Make sure that the edge of the second half of the length is firmly stuck down, especially along the corner junction. Trim off any excess paper, as required.

6 Use a clean, dampened sponge to wipe away any excess paste from both the surface of the wallpaper and also from the ceiling and the skirting board, respectively.

7 To ensure that the corner stays stuck down—especially vinyl paper—pull back the edge and apply overlap adhesive along the junction. Push the paper back in position.

EXTERNAL CORNERS

The technique for dealing with external corners varies considerably from the one for internal corners. Where these corners are square, it is possible to bend wallpaper around them and continue along the wall as usual. However, in most cases, a length will cease to be level as it rounds the corner, and an alternative technique is required.

1 Bend the wallpaper around the corner and trim to fit as well as possible. Be careful not to let the wallpaper tear at ceiling or skirting board level.

2 Apply a second length of paper, overlapping the first, matching the pattern on the overlap close to the corner. Trim the length to fit.

3 Hold a spirit level vertically in the centre of the overlapping lengths, and cut through both pieces of paper using a craft knife. Continue the cut from ceiling to skirting board.

4 Peel back the second length of paper and then remove the two excess strips of wallpaper that have been produced by the cut with the craft knife.

5 Smooth back the second length of paper to produce a perfect butt-joint. It may be necessary to use a seam roller along the joint to produce a perfect flat match.

6 This technique can be very messy and results in a lot of paste getting onto the wallpaper surface. Be sure to remove all of this residue with a clean, damp sponge.

EXTERNAL CORNER CONSIDERATIONS

- Cutting: the most important thing to consider is where to create the overlap before cutting through the lengths. This will depend on how far the first length of paper bends around the corner and the most appropriate place to match the pattern. For papers with an open background, it is best to cut through the background rather than the main part of the pattern. For wallpapers with a more complicated or busy design, it is less important where you overlap and cut.

- Keeping level: when matching the second length to the first one, there may need to be some compromise between exact pattern matching and keeping the paper vertical. Ensuring that the paper is precisely vertical is the first priority; after that, join the pattern as accurately as possible, paying particular attention at eye level. Use a level to make sure that the edge of the second length is vertical and can then act as a good starting point for papering the rest of the wall surface.

PROBLEM-SOLVING

Most papering problems are due to poor application and general technique, though sometimes a particular paper can be difficult to hang. Whatever the reason, most problems can be overcome or any damage can be repaired—things that require extra work to correct, represent a good lesson for future projects.

Lifting seams: in any room, it is likely that some seams will dry out and come away from the wall. Simply reapply some paste to the area and stick the paper down again; remove excess paste.

White seams: where dark colours are joined, the lining paper will show through if the seams do not match precisely. Use a fibre-tip pen the same colour as the paper to touch-in these areas.

Tearing: wallpaper is vulnerable to tearing just after it has been applied, while it is still wet. Most tears look worse than they are; it is usually possible to tease the paper back in place and stick it down.

Shiny seams: this is the result of overbrushing the seams during application and/or the presence of paste along the seam. Wash seams with a mild detergent and then rinse with clean water.

Poor pattern match: it may be the case that the paper has stretched so the pattern matches in some areas but not in others. Most small mistakes will not be noticeable, but be more careful in the future.

Bubbles: bubbles occur when wallpaper has not been left for the correct soaking time before applying it to the wall. Small bubbles can be split open and stuck down. Large areas will need to be stripped.

5
PAPERING
AWKWARD
AREAS

Having mastered basic wallpapering techniques,
dealing with more complex obstacles on a wall
surface becomes progressively easier. Most obstacles
require trimming around, and this tends to be the
difficult part. The secret of wallpapering these areas
is precise trimming, which in effect means taking a
little extra time. Creating clear, sharp edges and
accurate seams will make the end product far more
impressive. For those areas of the home that are an
awkward shape, such as stairwells, taking your time
is, again, the crucial factor. This way
you can keep to the correct work
sequence, which, in turn, will
produce the best finish.

DOORS AND ENTRANCES

A ll rooms have a doorway of some description, so it is essential to know the best way of papering around them. Most doors have a frame or casing, which makes papering much easier; however, some entrances have no doors or frames and these require a different technique altogether.

DOORS

Always ignore the door itself and concentrate on the frame because this has a precise edge to paper up to, which makes papering a straightforward exercise in cutting and trimming.

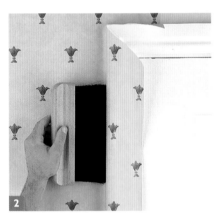

1 Let the length of paper flop loosely over the corner of the frame, being careful not to tear the paper. Make a diagonal cut back to the corner.

2 Use the paperhanging brush to crease the paper carefully into the frame/wall junction both at the side and above the door.

3 Trim the excess paper with a craft knife, and remove residual paste from the paper and door frame with a damp sponge.

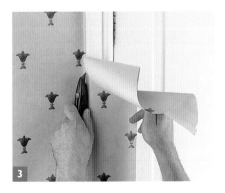

ARCHES

An entrance that does not contain a
door or frame is more difficult to
paper around, especially if it is a
curved one, such as an arch. As long
as the correct technique is followed,
however, it is possible to paper an
archway very successfully.

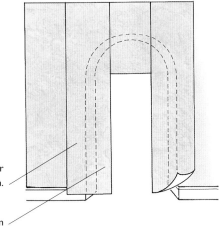

Let lengths of paper on the main wall go over
and beyond the edge of the arch.

Trim the paper back to 2.5 cm (1 in) from
the edge of the arch.

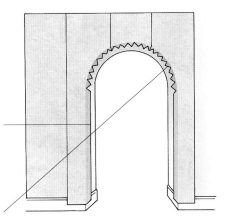

On the straight edges of the arch, bend the
paper around the edge, allowing it to stick
on the internal wall of the arch.

On the curved edges of the arch, make a number
of cuts in the paper at right angles to the edge in
order to bend the paper around the edge. The
small flaps can then be stuck to the internal edge
of the curve.

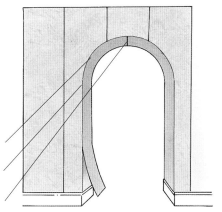

Cut two pieces of paper to run inside the arch.

Ensure a straight edge along the corner junction.

Join the two pieces at the top of the arch.

WINDOWS

W indows that are not recessed into the wall, and therefore have no deep sill, can be treated in a similar manner to doors, since the wallpaper is simply trimmed up to the window frame. However, where the window is recessed, the papering technique needs to be adjusted to take into account the edges and corners.

RECESSED WINDOWS

Recessed windows, which are present in many homes, vary in shape and in size, but the technique used to paper around them is the same whatever the shape. Following the correct work sequence and cutting precisely is all that is required to overcome these obstacles.

1 Let the wallpaper go across the recess, making sure that it is also stuck firmly in position on the wall. Use scissors to make a horizontal cut back to the corner of the recess precisely along the top edge of the recess.

2 Make a similar horizontal cut along the bottom edge of the recess, back to the corner of the window sill. It may be necessary to use a craft knife to cut around the corner of the sill to release the required flap of paper above.

3 Bend the flap of paper around the external corner of the recess, creasing it into the frame edge junction. Trim it with a craft knife to fit accurately.

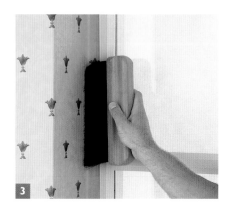

4 Apply another length of paper overlapping the previous length. The second length should be just long enough for the bottom edge of it to reach the window frame in the recess when it has been trimmed to fit. Match the pattern very carefully all along the overlap.

5 Use a craft knife and a straight edge (a level is ideal) to cut diagonally through the overlapping lengths of wallpaper, back to the recess corner.

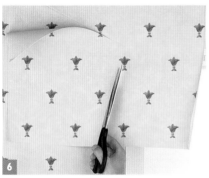

6 Use scissors to trim the bottom section of the second length back to the recess corner and the diagonal cut made in Step 5.

7 Peel back the second length of wallpaper and remove the excess paper below it (the top section of the first length).

8 Smooth the first length back to create a perfect butt-joint and fold the bottom part of the second length under the recess, then trim to the frame, as required. Finally, sponge off excess paste with a damp sponge. Continue along to the other end of the window and repeat the process around the other side of the recess.

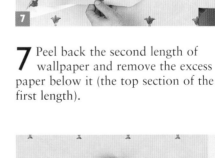

WALL SWITCHES AND SOCKETS

E lectrical wall switches and sockets are common obstacles in most
rooms so it is important to know the most appropriate technique
for wallpapering around them. The technique for wallpapering around
switches and power points is the same. As with all electrical fittings,
make sure that the power is turned off at the electrical distribution box
before you begin to work around them.

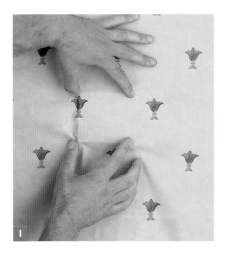

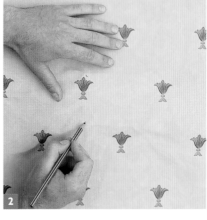

1 Let the paper hang over the front
of the switch and carefully mould
the paper to its outline, being careful
not to make any tears or rips across
the paper surface.

2 Make a pencil mark slightly in
from each of the four corners.

3 Use scissors to cut four diagonal
lines from the centre of the
switch plate out to the marks. This
creates four triangular flaps.

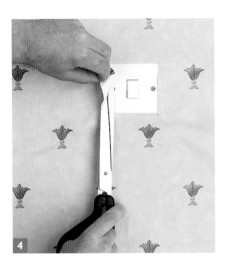

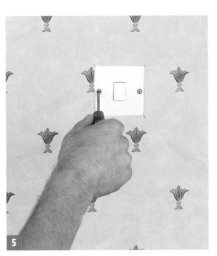

4 Cut away each flap to reveal a square hole in the wallpaper, slightly smaller than the switch plate itself.

5 Loosen the retaining screws on the switch plate until it comes free from the wall surface.

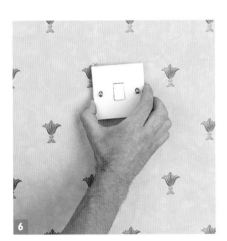

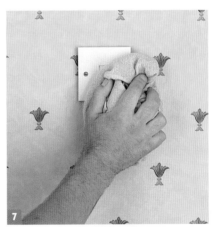

6 By carefully moving the plate into a diagonal position, it is possible to pull it through the square in the wallpaper, allowing the cut edges of the wallpaper to be hidden behind the plate.

7 Tighten up the retaining screws, making sure that the switch plate is level. Use a dry rag to remove any excess paste. Do not turn the electricity back on until the switch is totally dry.

WALL OBSTACLES

M ost obstacles encountered along a wall surface can be overcome using the techniques already demonstrated, or by combining techniques. If at all possible, try to remove the obstacle.

DEALING WITH RADIATORS

Radiators are an awkward shape to paper around and they require ingenuity and patience. Remember that the seam behind a radiator will not be seen; the areas to concentrate on are those directly around and just behind the edge.

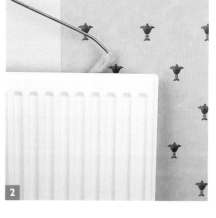

1 Let the length of paper hang loosely over the front of the radiator. Cut slits in the paper to correspond with the brackets that support the weight of the radiator.

2 Use a small, long-handled roller to push the paper behind the radiator, positioning it so that the cut in the paper coincides with the position of the supporting bracket.

RADIATOR REMOVAL

Radiators should only be removed if you have some plumbing experience. If a radiator is taken off, remove the brackets but replace screw fixings. Use the paperhanging brush to smooth the paper over the screws, letting them pierce the paper. Unscrew the screws and reattach the bracket; repeat with the next length.

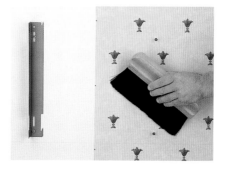

MISCELLANEOUS OBSTACLES

For all the other obstacles that may be encountered, common sense and planning are the best tools for successfully wallpapering around them. The guidelines below deal with some of the more common ones.

COMMON OBSTACLES

- Lights: if possible, remove wall lights, paper the area and refit the lights. Remember to turn off the electricity before disconnecting the light.
- Hooks: it is always best to remove hooks before wallpapering, unless you are certain that pictures will be hung back in the same place. A new pattern or design often leads to a different choice of picture, and starting afresh after wallpapering is usually the best policy.
- Phone sockets: these can be treated in the same way as electrical sockets (see page 264–265). Carefully undo the front plate from a phone socket, then undo the retaining screws that secure it to the wall. Be careful not to dislodge any wires when carrying out this procedure.
- Fireplaces: these are nothing more than intricate mouldings, the next stage on from papering around a door frame. Make cuts in the paper at right angles to the fireplace profile then the paper will mould easily around its edge and make it easier to trim with a craft knife.
- Toilets: the tank usually has a curved edge which makes it difficult to trim around accurately. Take the top off the tank, if possible, then apply the paper before replacing the top. This produces a very neat edge at this level. For the sides, trim the paper to slightly less than what appears to be the correct size. The excess paper can then be pushed into the curved junction, creating a neat finish.
- Sinks: these are similar to toilets. However, bear in mind that it is never sensible to wallpaper directly above a sink, since water splashes will soon damage the paper; it is best to tile these areas.
- Wall cabinets: try and remove any wall cabinets before starting to paper, as trimming around them can be a difficult and time-consuming job. Remember to mark fixing holes so the cabinets can be put back once papering is complete.
- Kitchen cabinets: these can be treated in a similar way to wall cabinets since most kitchen wall cabinets can be taken down and repositioned after papering. Floor cabinets are generally permanently fixed. The area directly above worktops is best tiled; if it is wallpapered, the paper will deteriorate rapidly.

STAIRWELLS

Working in stairwells has the problem of access and safety. It is essential to construct a stable, safe platform so that you can reach all those areas that would otherwise be inaccessible. In addition, there are a number of other factors that you need to take into consideration if you are going to achieve the best possible results when wallpapering a stairwell.

STAIRWELL CONSIDERATIONS

- Types of pattern: stairwells are by nature tall and relatively narrow, so consider what effect the wallpaper pattern will have on such an area. Vertical stripes, for example, will make the stairwell appear even taller.
- Two people: the ideal setup for papering a stairwell is to have one person positioning the paper at the top while a second person holds the paper away from the wall at the bottom. You can do it on your own but having two people makes the job a lot easier.
- Using a level: when applying the first length in a stairwell, use a spirit level to check that the paper is vertical up and down the entire length. Long lengths have a tendency to swerve at the bottom even if they are totally vertical at the top.
- Wall bannister: try and remove any bannister or rails from walls that are to be papered, otherwise they will make the task much more difficult. Reattach them

once the papering is complete.
- Adjust the platform: not all stairwell designs are like the one shown opposite. Where necessary, adjust platforms with extra ladders and planks to account for turns in the staircase, or more complicated designs than a simple straight run of stairs.
- Soaking times: be accurate and consistent with the time you leave the wallpaper to soak after it has been pasted and before it goes on the wall. Fluctuating these times from length to length can cause pattern matching problems, which will be accentuated over the long seams in a stairwell.

THE STAIRWELL SETUP

Designs vary, but safety should always be the primary concern when building a platform in a stairwell. Make sure that all the equipment you are using is in good condition and able to withstand the stresses that will be put on it.

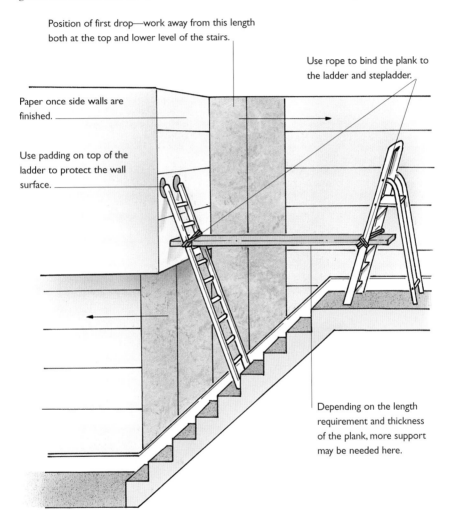

Position of first drop—work away from this length both at the top and lower level of the stairs.

Use rope to bind the plank to the ladder and stepladder.

Paper once side walls are finished.

Use padding on top of the ladder to protect the wall surface.

Depending on the length requirement and thickness of the plank, more support may be needed here.

BORDERS

Borders add a decorative edge to a wall finish. They can either be
an addition to the wallpaper design itself or they can be applied
on a plain painted wall to add a patterned frame to the overall finish.
Application methods vary according to where the border is being used.

CEILING LEVEL

Ceiling level is the easiest place to hang a border because the ceiling junction
can be used as a guideline when positioning the border itself. All borders
should be pasted using proprietary border adhesive, which is stronger than
standard paste and adheres much better to the wall surface.

1 Continue the ceiling colour
slightly onto the wall surface so
that if there are any undulations in
the ceiling junction it will not be
possible to see any wall colour above
the border when it is applied—this
gives the appearance of a precisely
level ceiling edge.

2 Fold up the border in a similar
way as to when hanging
wallpaper. Apply the border using
the ceiling junction as a guide to
positioning the top edge of the
border. Use a paperhanging brush to
smooth the border and remove any
air bubbles from under its surface.

Applying on wallpaper: the
advantage of applying a border on
wallpaper is that it is usually easy to
keep the border level by following a
line in the actual pattern of the
wallpaper. Where there is no ordered
pattern to follow, draw a pencil
guideline, as shown opposite.

PICTURE AND DADO BORDERS

Applying a border in one of the central areas of a wall is a simple process as long as the border is kept precisely level. When dealing with internal corners, never try to bend a single length around the corner as it will invariably shrink slightly as it dries and pull away from the corner junction. Use a single length of border per wall; join each length, matching the pattern along the junction.

1 Make a pencil mark on the wall at the required level and use a spirit level to draw a line around the entire perimeter of the room.

2 Use the pencil line as a guide for hanging the border. Crease the border firmly into the corner and trim it so that it overlaps slightly onto the adjacent wall.

3 Apply a second length of border so that it overlaps onto the first, being careful to match the pattern precisely. Draw a pencil guideline along the junction, peel the border back and trim with scissors.

4 Smooth the border back in place and remove the excess paste with a clean, damp sponge.

TRIMMING CORNERS

Use scissors to trim the border at the corner instead of a craft knife. A craft knife blade might cut through both strips of border, which would mean that once the borders were brushed back in place, the ends would not meet at the corner.

COMBINING PAPERS

R ather than using just one wallpaper to decorate a room, it is possible to combine different papers to create an interesting and varied effect. Many manufacturers produce papers with this idea in mind and coordinate borders to be used with specific papers. You can either follow their guidelines or you can create your own individual schemes.

Using a border divide: using two different papers on the same wall surface requires some sort of border to divide the two patterns. A paper border acts as an ideal dado divide, separating the designs while adding a decorative feature.

Solid borders: a solid wooden dado rail can be used to divide different papers. This provides a pronounced finish and a clear-cut edge to both the wallpapers.

Framing: borders and wallpaper can be combined to create framed areas along a wall surface. The technique for creating mitred corner seams in borders is explained on page 284.

6
COMBINING PAPER AND PAINT

A successful decorative finish depends on a good combination of colour and design. By blending paper and paint together you can produce a very attractive and balanced decorative scheme. Texture and colour can each create stunning results, and by combining the media of paint and paper, the options for experimentation are increased. There are many ways in which they can be combined and this chapter illustrates just a few of them, so you can go on to develop your own original ideas for all kinds of interesting and unique finishes.

WHAT TO USE WHERE

Different paint and paper combinations can be used in particular areas of the home to create highly decorative effects. However, it is worthwhile bearing in mind that some combinations and effects are better suited to certain areas than others.

SUITING DIFFERENT AREAS

- Stairwells: these tend to receive a lot of wear and tear at the lower levels but not at the top. This makes them an ideal area to have a wooden dado trim dividing two papers, or to have paper above the trim and paint below. Then, when the bottom level becomes worn, it can be redecorated while the top level is left as it is.
- Child's bedroom: in a similar manner to stairwells, the bottom level of the wall surface tends to get damaged more quickly. Having a wooden dado trim divide or a paper border means that the bottom level can be redecorated while the top level is left untouched. A paint effect below the dado trim can also help to disguise blemishes and make the finish last as long as possible.
- Alcoves: these offer the opportunity to create a feature within a room, and can be treated differently from the rest of the decoration in the room. If the main walls are wallpapered, the back of the alcoves can be painted a light colour. This gives the effect of greater depth and provides an ideal background for displaying ornaments.
- Paper panels: paper panels can be very effective on walls,

but they are less common on wooden surfaces. However, panel doors offer an ideal opportunity for using wallpaper in a different way since the central area of each panel can be wallpapered to match the walls while the rest of the door is painted to match the other woodwork in the room.
- Decoupage: this technique involves cutting out attractive designs or shapes from wallpaper, or other sources, and sticking them to the wall to create a collage effect. It is a good way of faking images, which is usually the domain of faux or trompe l'oeil artists.
- Painted borders: using paint as a border is another alternative to wooden dado trim or paper borders. Painted borders can be stencilled at any level to produce a frame for a particular feature.

PAINTABLE PAPERS

Textured and paintable papers are the crossover between the wallpapering and painting worlds. These types of paper usually have an embossed surface, which adds depth to the finish once the paper is applied to the wall. The textured pattern is excellent for covering up rough wall surfaces since the undulations are obscured by the thick embossed nature of the paper. Some textured papers can be left unpainted, although most will benefit from being painted in either light or dark colours.

Adding colour: textured papers can be painted bold colours to enhance their features while at the same time creating a very solid look. Painted with vinyl emulsion, this effect is very hardwearing and easy to clean. Using the paper above the dado level also breaks up the wall surface, providing greater character and impact.

Basic texture: woodchip paper is one of the most common of all the textured papers and is extremely good for covering old, uneven walls. On its own, the effect can be very ordinary, but with the right accessories, woodchip paper can become an attractive integral part of a decorative scheme.

HANGING TEXTURED PAPERS

Textured papers are hung in a similar way to standard wallpaper, but with one or two subtle differences in technique. Because they are generally heavier, the soaking time for textured paper tends to be slightly longer, and the paste is usually mixed to a stronger, thicker consistency.

EMBOSSED PAPERS

Embossed papers have a relief pattern that raises the design, giving a much greater feeling of depth to the paper finish. When applying these types of wallpaper, care must be taken not to flatten the relief pattern and damage the textured effect.

1 Check the ends of each roll of wallpaper to make sure that the edges are not damaged.

2 Once the paper has been pasted and left to soak for the manufacturer's recommended time, apply it to the wall using a paperhanging brush. Be careful not to brush the paper too much, especially along the seams.

3 Trim the lengths with scissors— the coarse texture of the paper tends to blunt craft knife blades very quickly, and a blunt blade can lead to the paper being torn.

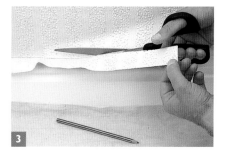

WOODCHIP REPAIRS

Textured woodchip paper is ideal for old, uneven walls because it covers and disguises imperfections in the surface. As with embossed papers, use scissors for trimming—the small pieces of wood fibre in the paper are difficult to cut through with a craft knife. The most versatile property of woodchip paper is that it is very easy to repair damaged areas simply by patching and repainting.

1 Use a scraper to remove the loosely stuck down edges of the damaged area of woodchip paper.

2 Cut a piece of woodchip paper slightly larger than the hole. Hold it against the damaged area, tearing around the circumference of the hole as accurately as possible.

3 Apply paste to the new patch of woodchip paper and stick it in place over the hole.

4 Once the patch has dried, paint over the whole area to complete the repair job.

PAINT EFFECTS ON TEXTURED PAPERS

Textured papers offer the opportunity to create excellent paint effects since the raised surface adds an extra dimension to the finished product. Applying the effect to the high points will give an entirely different finish from applying it to the low points of the paper.

COLOUR WIPING

Colour wiping is a method of colouring the low points of a textured paper. It gives the appearance of the base colour being ingrained with the glaze colour that is applied to create the effect. Use a vinyl silk emulsion as the base coat for this paint effect.

1 Apply the glaze generously in all directions across the surface of the textured paper.

2 Use a clean, damp sponge to wipe down the paper in long vertical sweeps. This technique is best used on papers with a dominant vertical pattern, as shown here; however, for an all-over design, the sponge can be wiped across the surface of the paper in any direction.

LEAVING THE PEAKS
The finished effect leaves the peaks on the textured wallpaper surface clear of glaze so that the base coat colour shows clearly on these raised areas.

COLOUR HIGHLIGHTING

The aim of highlighting is to accentuate the peaks in the paper with the glaze colour, rather than the troughs. The glaze is applied to the peaks and left in place, rather than being wiped away as with the colour wiping technique. A base coat of vinyl silk emulsion paint should be used for this effect as well.

1 Once the brush has been dipped in glaze, dry off the excess from the bristles with a clean rag.

2 Use light sweeping horizontal strokes across the surface of the paper, letting the bristles touch just the top of the relief pattern.

3 Build up the depth of colour to the level you require before moving on to the next area on the paper surface.

TEXTURE WITH HEIGHT AND DEPTH
The result looks as if the paper texture has both height and depth—very different from the effect of colour wiping, even though the same glaze, paper, and base coat have been used to achieve this highlighting.

HANGING WALL PANELS

Wall panels are thicker than wallpaper and require a heavy-duty paste in order to stick them to the wall. To produce the best possible finish, walls should also be lined before applying the panels. Most panels are designed to be applied at dado level around a room. It is usually possible to apply whole panels and reduce the need for cutting and trimming.

1 Soak the back of the wall panel with warm water, and leave for 20 minutes before applying paste. This lets the panel expand, and will prevent any bubbles from appearing in its surface later.

2 Apply paste generously to the panel, ensuring that it covers all areas including the edges.

3 Apply the panel to the wall, ideally starting in an internal corner. Use a spirit level to ensure that the panel is vertical.

4 Brush out any air bubbles in the paper using a paperhanging brush. Be careful not to damage the panel surface during this process.

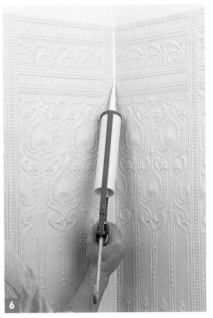

5 Once one wall is complete, begin the adjacent wall. Start, and therefore join, the design at the internal corner.

6 Run a bead of decorator's caulk along internal corners to produce a perfect neat finish.

CUTTING REQUIREMENTS

When smaller panels are required, use a straight edge and craft knife to cut the panel to the correct size before pasting.

WALL PANEL BORDERS

You can enhance the wall panel effect by adding a border or dado rail above it. Paper borders are not ideal for this purpose as they tend to be overshadowed by the depth of the wall panels themselves. The solution is to use a border made from the same heavy-duty material as the panels. This should be applied using the same adhesive as that used for the wall panels. The alternative option is to apply a wooden dado rail around the top of the wall panels. This provides a very solid and substantial edge to the complete panel effect. A wooden dado rail can either be painted or stained, according to personal taste.

PAINT EFFECTS ON WALL PANELS

W all panels can be painted in a single colour or they can be used for various paint effects. In the example below, an impressive verdigris effect has been created by colour wiping and highlighting.

1 The texture of wall panels means that both colour-wiping and highlighting techniques are ideal to use on them. Clean all the panels with mineral spirits, then let them dry before applying any paint. With ornate panel textures, such as the one shown here, pay particular attention to all the details in the pattern, so that all impurities are removed from the surface. Wear protective gloves to protect your hands.

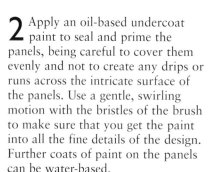

2 Apply an oil-based undercoat paint to seal and prime the panels, being careful to cover them evenly and not to create any drips or runs across the intricate surface of the panels. Use a gentle, swirling motion with the bristles of the brush to make sure that you get the paint into all the fine details of the design. Further coats of paint on the panels can be water-based.

3 A pale green base coat is the ideal colour to begin a verdigris effect. As with the undercoat paint, it should be applied all over the wall panel surface. Water-based emulsion paint is the the best choice. It means that two coats can be applied in one day. Once the second coat is dry, you can begin applying the verdigris effect.

4 Load a mini roller with dark green paint, then remove the excess on a piece of scrap paper. Run the roller very gently across the panel surface, just touching the high points and peaks of the pattern. Do not apply too much pressure, otherwise the paint will be forced into the deeper troughs that make up the texture of the panel.

5 Using the same technique as in Step 4, add another coat of paint—with a rusty red being the ideal choice of colour. Again, be careful not to apply too much pressure. Try to vary the intensity of the colour by applying slightly more paint in some places than in others.

6 Mix a dark green glaze and brush it over the entire panel surface, giving a translucent top coat to the finished effect. Make sure that the entire surface is evenly coated.

THE VERDIGRIS EFFECT
The finished panel effect can be stunning, providing the perfect background for furniture and ornaments alike. Extra coats of glaze can be applied to create greater depth and texture.

BORDERS

Paper or stencilled (see page 234) borders can be effective for framing walls or door frames. In addition to the standard technique for borders, it is necessary to make mitred seams. Choose the borders carefully, since some border patterns are not suitable for doing this.

PAPER BORDERS

1 Apply two lengths of border so that they overlap at the corner. Allow a generous amount for the overlap. This allows you enough room to manoeuvre the two strips into the best position for matching the pattern and mitring the corner.

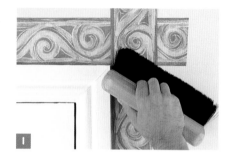

2 Use a craft knife to cut through the overlap at a diagonal angle, beginning at the inner corner and finishing at the corner cross section of the two lengths of border. Be careful to avoid cutting the painted wall with the craft knife.

3 Peel back both strips of border and remove the excess pieces of paper created by the diagonal cut. These two pieces are now excess to requirements and can be discarded.

4 Smooth the two strips back into position to produce a neat mitred seam. Remove excess paste with a clean, damp sponge. Use the same technique to deal with the opposite corner of the door frame.

PART THREE: TILING

SUCCESSFUL TILING

Tiles have been used to provide decorative and durable surfaces for walls and floors for hundreds of years. Their influence continues to grow due to the ever-increasing choice and easy availability for the amateur home decorator. In years gone by, tiling was considered the domain of the professional, and most homeowners would not have dreamed of attempting to tile a sink splashback, let alone an entire room. Nowadays, many home decorating superstores have a special tiling section, and modern products and tools are much easier to use. Tiling is now a job in the home that anyone can take on and achieve a good result. This section of the book guides you through all the necessary techniques for any tiling project, showing you how to solve problems along the way and produce a professional result that will enhance your home for the enjoyment of your family and the admiration of your friends.

GETTING STARTED

Taking it slowly is the secret of good tiling. When results fail to live up to expectations, it can usually be attributed to rushing, rather than any errors in technique. It takes more time to grasp the methodology of tiling than that of other home do-it-yourself tasks that can be done quickly, with an instant result. To build up confidence with tiling tools and materials, you have to be patient and work slowly—it is far better to take longer with preparation and execution than regret a poor finish for many years to come. Enjoy the process of tiling—don't look on it as a chore. Aim to improve your technique and, above all, be creative with patterns and designs, because it gives great personal satisfaction when all your effort produces a truly individual look. By all means look through magazines for ideas, but adding your own personal touch is always the most pleasing part of any home improvement project—and tiling is no exception.

BEING PREPARED

Preparation is an essential part of
any home improvement project and
can make the difference between an
average finish and one that you can
be proud of. Although preparation
can be the least enjoyable part of any
decorating task, it must be carried
out thoroughly to ensure good
results. Chapter 1 takes you through
the entire process of planning and
preparing, from choosing tiles to
the preparation of surfaces for tile
application. There is plenty of advice
on how to treat different surfaces
and what techniques will produce
the best results.

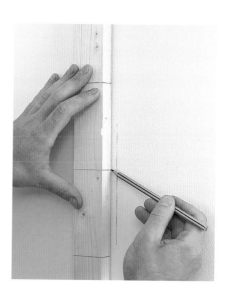

ESTABLISHING A SOUND TECHNIQUE

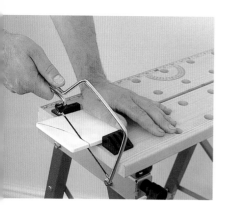

A good tiling technique is built on a sound
understanding of basic rules and methods.
Establishing good working habits with basic
techniques from the start will stand you in good
stead when you come to carry out the more
demanding tasks. Chapter 2 explains the basic
tiling technique, from laying first tiles through to
developing a sound method for simple tile cutting.

DEALING WITH AWKWARD AREAS

Awkward areas are really defined by the fact that
they require more planning or, in most cases,
intricate tile cutting. What they really involve is
just a more intricate application of the same basic
tiling technique. Chapter 3 guides you through a
variety of awkward situations that you might come
across, providing the solutions and demonstrating
that keeping to a simple system makes it possible
to overcome any obstacle when tiling.

ADVENTUROUS TILING

Expressing individual preferences is
an important part of enjoying tiling,
and Chapter 4 shows you how to
stray away from the more traditional
looks and create your own unique
designs. The basics remain the same,
but some additional techniques for
combining tile sizes and producing
different patterns are outlined in this
chapter, adding to the fundamental
skills learned earlier in the book.

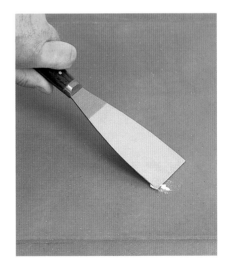

TILING FLOORS

Many of the techniques used on a vertical wall
surface can be transferred to floor tiling, since the
general appearance of the tiles remains the same.
However, because of their function, floor tiles
need to be more durable, and this means that the
methods of preparation and application do vary
slightly. These subtle changes in approach are
explained in detail in Chapter 5, enabling you
to extend your tiling repertoire to the household
floors as well as walls.

MAINTAINING SURFACES

As with all decorated surfaces, it is
important to know the best methods
of maintenance and how to carry out
minor repairs. By design, tiles are
extremely durable and have an
appreciable life span, whether on
the walls or on the floor. Chapter 6
demonstrates how to keep tiles
looking as good as possible and gives
advice on how to lengthen their life
span with little effort.

PROGRESSIVE TILING

This section of the book caters to both the novice and the more experienced tiler, teaching the beginner all the basic techniques while enabling the more skilful to fill in any gaps in their knowledge before progressing to new and exciting challenges. Much of the fundamental knowledge and understanding used for other forms of decorating can be carried over into the tiling field; this helps the process of forming ideas, solving problems, and adapting to different situations. After all, the decorator is concerned with improving the look of a room, and applying tiles is no different in this respect from applying paint or wallpaper. The concise and accurate instructions given in the following chapters, linked with the variety of ideas and choices they provide, make this section of the book an invaluable tool for helping you to create the perfect tiled finish and enabling you to integrate tiled surfaces into the rest of the decoration in your home.

1
PLANNING AND PREPARATION

Careful planning of a tiling project is the key to producing a good overall finish. Choosing patterns, designs, and colours are all important, as is the actual tiling technique, but making sure that surfaces are well prepared and a logical sequence is followed are the essential ingredients of any tiling project. Tiles are expensive, and starting off with the wrong strategy can prove costly. The whole tiling experience should be thought out and done slowly, not rushed. Tiles are relatively permanent once applied and require major work to change their appearance, unlike changing one coat of paint for another, so taking a little extra time to make important choices and following the correct procedures will ensure a finish to be proud of.

PLANNING A SCHEME

P lanning a scheme of tiling is an area that combines personal
preference with practicalities. Although most tiles can be applied
anywhere in the home, you need to consider how the tiles will fit into
a particular scheme in a room and how practical they will be.

Covering surfaces:
tiles are very decorative
and they can be used to
cover any of the wall
surfaces in a room. A
tiled wall surface can
be very impressive,
whether the tiles are
highly patterned or a
plain design. A tiling
project of this size
requires plenty of time
to plan it properly and
a certain amount of
skill when it comes to
tile application and
starting in the correct
place on the surface to
be tiled.

Creating a dado: tiling
up to dado level allows
the tiles to have an
equal standing with the
rest of the room's
decoration. Combining
paper and paint with
tiles requires a certain
amount of imagination
to coordinate the whole
scheme, and it puts a
greater emphasis on
matching texture and
finish in order to get
the desired effect.

Covering the floor: floor tiles combine the highly practical function of being the most hard-wearing of floorings with huge decorative appeal. It is vital to keep tiles aligned and level for a good effect; careful preparation and accurate tile application are essential if you want to create a desirable floor tile finish.

Smaller areas: the simple tiling of a splashback can effect the whole feel of a room. The splashback's colour, size and pattern all combine to give the room a finished look. Because smaller areas of tiles tend to come in for more scrutiny, the neatness and accuracy of the tiling is vital.

PLANNING IDEAS

- Colour: whether complementing other decorations, or forming the main theme, always obtain samples from your supplier before making a final choice, then the tiles can be compared and tried in the actual room that is being decorated. Make sure you compare paint colour swatches with tiles, as well as carpet and wallpaper samples, if necessary.
- Size: there are no hard and fast rules on the best size of tiles for a particular room, but it is worth remembering that large tiles are more awkward when it comes to making fiddly cuts, and smaller tiles take longer to apply.

- Pattern: often a few patterned tiles within a decorating scheme produce the best results—too many highly patterned tiles can be overwhelming, especially in a small room, and may spoil the overall look.
- Expense: almost without exception, the more expensive the tiles, the more attractive and better quality they will be. However, combining more expensive tiles with cheaper alternatives can often work very well in a scheme. It is also worth considering how long you are likely to stay in the house, and whether the extra expense will be beneficial in the long term.

TYPES OF TILE

There is a vast range of tiles to choose from, which means that in most cases it is possible to find the exact size, finish, and colour required. To help you choose, many manufacturers provide large tiled display boards to show off their products, and most produce catalogues illustrating tiled interiors. It is a good idea to use whatever aids are available to help narrow the choice and pick the finish you want.

STANDARD TILES

This group of tiles includes the more traditional-looking tiles that come in a wide range of relatively simple colour themes and patterns.

Handmade and painted tile

Picture tile

Relief picture tile

Rectangular wall tile

Glazed terracotta tile

Unglazed terracotta tile

BORDER TILES

The choice of border tiles is constantly increasing, with different sizes, types of pattern, and variety of textures, all adding to the large range already available.

Relief border tile

Standard border tile

Dado border tile

Mitred quadrant tile

Relief tile slips

ALTERNATIVE TILES

Nonstandard tiles are becoming increasingly popular, with sizes varying from small mosaics to larger wall tiles, making all manner of different effects and finishes possible.

Octagonal tile

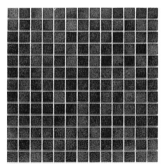

Marble tile

Sheet mosaic   Tiled scene   Inset tiles

FLOOR TILES

Floor tiles are thicker and more durable than wall tiles. The range of tiles is slightly more limited, but the manufacturers are constantly coming up with new ideas to increase the variety of finishes.

Marble floor tile

Quarry tile   Mosaic floor tile

Standard floor tile   Slate floor tile

ORDER OF WORK

I t is always difficult to decide where to start on a particular wall, since many of them are not perfectly square and obstacle-free. Instructions for dealing with particular situations are dealt with in other chapters; however, it is worth taking time at the planning stage to consider any obstacles that will have to be taken into account, what the most common problem areas are likely to be, and how they are best overcome.

BATHROOMS

The bathroom is the one room in the house that is often totally or partially tiled, and it will undoubtedly contain areas that need considerable planning before you can begin to tile. A simple bathroom scenario is outlined below and gives some valuable pointers on the most suitable order of work.

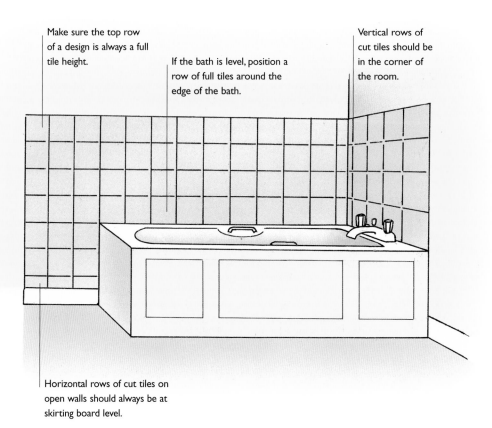

Make sure the top row of a design is always a full tile height.

If the bath is level, position a row of full tiles around the edge of the bath.

Vertical rows of cut tiles should be in the corner of the room.

Horizontal rows of cut tiles on open walls should always be at skirting board level.

KITCHENS

Kitchens provide many similar obstacles to those found in bathrooms, with additional problem areas such as sockets and switches. This example also shows the need for careful planning around windows.

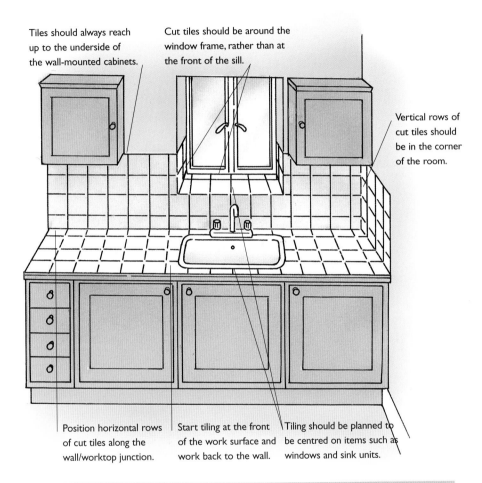

Tiles should always reach up to the underside of the wall-mounted cabinets.

Cut tiles should be around the window frame, rather than at the front of the sill.

Vertical rows of cut tiles should be in the corner of the room.

Position horizontal rows of cut tiles along the wall/worktop junction.

Start tiling at the front of the work surface and work back to the wall.

Tiling should be planned to be centred on items such as windows and sink units.

ESTIMATING QUANTITIES

There is no secret to estimating the quantity of tiles required for a job—it is all a matter of simple mathematics. Measure the dimensions of the area to be tiled in order to attain the surface area. Divide the surface area of one tile into this figure and this will give you the number of tiles required. It is always worth adding on 10 percent extra to account for cutting errors and breakages. To make measuring easier, it is worth breaking down complicated surfaces into smaller areas so that the calculations are more accurate.

PREPARING WALLS

Creating a sound, level surface on which to tile is essential. Not only will this produce better results when new tiles are applied, it will also make the actual tiling process much easier. A new wall surface is the ideal starting point for tiling, but it is often the case that an old tiled surface is being replaced.

EXISTING TILES

A previously tiled surface can be tiled over if it is sound and level. If the old tiles are firmly stuck to the wall, new tiles may be applied directly over the top of them. Some minor repairs may be necessary to ensure that the surface is totally sound. Remove any loose old tiles before beginning the preparation.

Filling space: fill the space left by the removal of old tiles with an all-purpose crack filler. Before applying the filler, dust out the hole thoroughly to ensure good adhesion. Build up the filler until it is level and flush with the surrounding tiles.

Using old tiles: an alternative to using filler in the space left by loose old tiles is to use old tiles of the same size as those on the wall. Simply apply some adhesive to the tile, and use it to fill the hole. Again, make sure that the tile surface is flush with the surrounding area of tiles.

Sanding tiles: after the old tiled surface has been filled, wash it down with soapy water, then rinse well. Sand the entire tiled area with silicone carbide paper; this will scratch the glaze and help provide a key for the adhesive. Make sure that you sand each tile to get the best possible adhesion of new tile to old.

WALL REPAIR

When an old tiled surface is badly damaged or loose, it cannot be used as the base for retiling and must be totally stripped away. Although this is a longer process than simple repairs on existing tile surfaces, you will reap the benefit when the new tiles are applied.

Removing old tiles: old tiles are best removed using a hammer and cold chisel. Try not to dig into the wall with the chisel, as this will damage the surface of the wall. Position the chisel point exactly on the junction between tile and wall before hitting it with the hammer. Wear safety goggles to protect your eyes from flying tile splinters and debris.

Removing old tile adhesive: once tiles are removed, there is often a large amount of residual old tile adhesive left on the wall. A steam stripper is ideal for softening the hard adhesive before removing it with a scraper. Steam strippers vary, so be sure to read the operating and safety instructions before use.

Patch plastering: where walls are particularly rough, it may be necessary to skim some areas with a coat of multipurpose plaster to make the surface level enough for tiling. Seal the wall area with a PVA solution (five parts water to one part PVA) before applying the plaster.

PREPARATION ESSENTIALS

- Never tile over wallpaper since the weight of the tiles will gradually pull the paper away from the wall surface. Wallpaper must be stripped before tiling.
- Gloss-paint surfaces must be sanded before tiling over them, to provide a key for the new tiles.
- Old and new plaster surfaces must be sealed with a PVA solution (five parts water to one part PVA) before they are tiled.

CREATING A FRESH SURFACE

I n many situations, such as working around baths or tiling up to dado level, it is easier to create a totally flat fresh surface on which to tile. The simplest way of producing a new surface is to use a flat building board such as water-resistant medium-density fibreboard (MDF), which is economical and easy to work with. Always wear a dust mask when sawing MDF to prevent inhalation of dust particles.

FLUSH PANELLING

MDF is useful when gaps around the bath make tiling difficult. It makes a nice neat junction between the bath and the tile surface. The fibreboard can be applied directly to the wall to create a very smooth flush base on which to tile. Board thickness should be around 9 mm (⅜ in).

1 Cut the sheet of board to the required size and position it on the edge of the bath. To create a waterproof seal, apply general-purpose sealant to the board/bath junction.

2 Once positioned, drill pilot holes through the board using a wood drill bit, and switch to a masonry bit once you hit the wall. Or, if you are using concrete anchor screws, an all-purpose drill bit will be supplied with the screws. Increase the entrance size (see below).

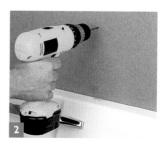

3 If using standard screws, insert a wall plug into the hole before inserting the screw. Concrete anchor screws (shown here) can be inserted directly into the wall. Insert screws every 30 cm (12 in), in both horizontal and vertical directions, until the board is secured.

INCREASING THE HOLE SIZE

Use a countersink bit to increase the entrance size to the drilled hole. This will allow the screw head to sit flush with the MDF surface once it is screwed in.

PANELLING ON A FRAME

Where wall surfaces are very uneven, you may need to attach sheets of water-resistant medium-density fibreboard to a frame on the wall. This will cover any large depressions in the wall surface and give an even surface for tiling. Use concrete anchor screws for this wood/masonry combination.

1 Secure 5-by-2.5-cm (2-by-1-in) battens vertically to the wall, up to the height that is to be tiled. Place the battens 30 cm (12 in) apart, ensuring that they are vertical by checking with a long spirit level.

2 Pack uneven areas in the wall by hammering in wedges of wood behind battens that do not sit flush with the wall surface. This will ensure that the battens are vertical to the floor and also to the actual wall surface. Secure the wedges in place with a nail if they start to slip.

3 Place a cut sheet of board on the wooden framework, then mark vertical pencil lines on the board surface to show where it should be secured. These vertical lines should correspond with the battens secured to the wall. Nail along each line every 25 cm (10 in) to secure the board to the frame.

4 Nail another length of batten to the top of the framework to give a neat fixed level to tile up to. The vertical pencil guidelines on the board surface will show where the securing points are. A decorative dado border can be used instead of the batten, or a moulding can be attached to the front of the batten when the tiling is finished.

BOXING IN

A s well as wall surfaces, there are other areas that may require preparation before you can start tiling. Unsightly pipes, for example, can be boxed in and then the box can be tiled to create a decorative surface.

SIMPLE BOXING

Boxing in requires a combination of wooden battens and building board to build a sturdy framework around the pipes. Water-resistant medium-density fibreboard 18 mm (¾ in) thick is ideal, with 5-by-2.5-cm (2-by-1-in) battens as support. Boxing is best screwed together to provide stronger joints. To ensure a flush surface for tiling, countersink the drill holes (see page 300).

1 Attach a batten to the wall directly above the pipes and secure another batten to the floor. Make sure the floor batten runs parallel to the wall surface, and that it is positioned farther away from the wall than the pipe. Use screws that do not go below the level of the floorboards otherwise you may damage pipes or cables below floor level, or, even more importantly, you may injure yourself.

2 Cut a sheet of board to the correct size. The height should be the same as that of the top edge of the wall batten. Screw the sheet in place at floor level, allowing the screw to go through the board and into the floor batten.

3 Cut a second piece of board and attach it to the wall batten and first sheet of board. Make sure that the corner joint is precise in order to achieve a neat finish. Continue until the pipes are totally boxed in and the box is ready to tile.

BOXING-IN TIPS

Boxing in is not always completely straightforward, and you may need to take the following considerations into account when covering up areas of wall. Although accuracy is important, remember that the boxing will be covered, so a perfect finish at this stage is not essential.

Cutting curves: use a jigsaw to cut curves in the board where you need to allow pipes to protrude through the boxing. When using a jigsaw, always follow all the manufacturer's safety recommendations and never place your hand in front of the blade of the saw or in the direction you are cutting the board.

Leaving access: many pipes have shutoff valves, stopcocks, or inspection joints, depending on the particular function of the pipe. You need to make inspection hatches in the boxing to allow access to these points. Cutting in a small hatch and fitting it with magnetic catches is the ideal solution.

Corner boxing: corners may be either boxed in as shown on the opposite page, but vertically, or a single panel can be used to cover the corner, as shown at left. This method requires making a mitred cut through a length of batten to provide a 45-degree angle for attachment of the batten to each side of the corner junction. A thin building board such as water-resistant plywood can then be cut to fit across the corner. Attach the plywood to the battens using brads or small screws.

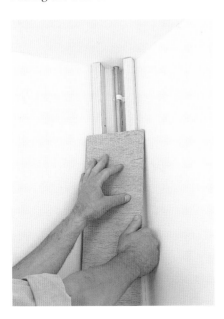

FINAL PLANNING

Before starting to tile, prepare the working area and make sure that all the tools and equipment you need are at hand. There are a few final preparations that will make life much easier, speed up the tiling process, and lead to a better overall finish.

Breaking up spacers: tile spacers are usually manufactured in sheets and need to be broken into single units before they can be used. It saves a great deal of time if several sheets are broken up before tiling starts, then you can achieve an easy rhythm of applying a tile with one hand and fitting a spacer with the other.

Shuffling tiles: there can be slight colour differences between tile batches, and sometimes even within the same box shades may vary slightly from one end of the box to the other. Mix or shuffle tiles from different boxes before starting, so that any variations will be "diluted" across the whole wall surface. Although this problem is most common with strongly coloured tiles, even white tiles should be shuffled to ensure an even finish.

BE PREPARED

- Have a bucket of clean water and cloth at hand, so surfaces can be kept clean at all times.
- A second bucket of clean water can be used for temporary storage of tools during breaks. This prevents adhesive on items like notched spreaders from going hard, which would make further application to the wall more difficult.
- Protect sinks, baths, furniture, and any fixtures with dust sheets. Adhesive splashes can be difficult to remove from any surface once they have hardened, so it is best to prevent them in the first place.

2
TILING TECHNIQUE

Tiling requires a methodical approach with attention to detail. Once you have established a sound basic technique, you can attempt more difficult tiling projects. As with all decorating tasks, speed comes with practice. It is important to take your time rather than rushing to finish the job quickly. Even the most experienced tilers can always improve their technique, and professionals are always trying to achieve the perfect tiled surface. This chapter shows you how to tile walls and demonstrates the few simple rules and procedures that are the basis for a sound tiling technique.

STARTING LEVEL

Tiles have crisp straight edges that give a very ordered and precise finish when they are applied to the wall. Although this is one of their attractive characteristics, it also means that poorly applied or crooked tiles stand out, so it is important to start level and tile from a secure, fixed base. Take time to determine the starting point, as mistakes can be difficult to rectify once tiling has begun.

1 A tiling gauge is essential for determining the best possible starting point on a wall surface. Cut a length of 5-by-2.5-cm (2-by-1-in) batten about 1.5 m (5 ft) long, or shorter if you are tiling a small area. Line up a row of tiles along the length of the batten with tile spacers between them. Using a pencil, mark the position of each tile along one edge of the batten.

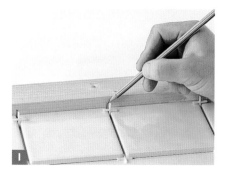

2 Find the central point of the wall, or area to be tiled, by measuring first vertically and then horizontally across the wall. Make sure that the tape measure is level when measuring. Make a pencil mark at the centre. This acts as the point from which to centralize the entire design.

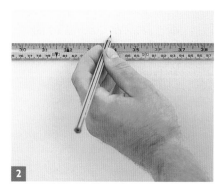

3 Use the tiling gauge to find how many rows of tiles you will need for the area you are going to tile. Hold the gauge vertically against the wall to show where the tile edges will fall once they are applied. Mark the positions along the wall. Then hold the gauge horizontally and mark again. It is unlikely that the tiles will fit exactly into the working area, so you will need to adjust the central point slightly so that any tiles you have to cut will be at the edges not in the centre (see pages 296–297).

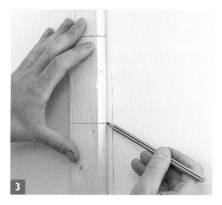

4 It is unlikely that the top of the skirting board is exactly level, or that the tile gauge has demonstrated that the best position to start tiling is directly on top of the skirting. The bottom row of tiles will probably require cuts. This means that the starting point is where the first row of full tiles will be applied, and this is where a length of batten should be secured to provide a solid base. Ensure that the batten is level.

5 Once the horizontal batten is secured, attach a vertical batten to provide the starting point across the other wall dimension. Secure the batten where the first column of vertical tiles will begin, using a level to make sure that the batten is completely vertical. Alternatively, the vertical batten can be positioned at the central point of the area to be tiled, and tiling can progress toward the corner, rather than away from it. Either way is acceptable, as the sole purpose of the vertical batten is to maintain a rigid vertical line to butt the tiles up against.

6 Attach the wall battens with nails, but do not drive them all the way into the wall. Leave a good length of the nailhead showing, so that the nails can be removed with a claw hammer and the battens taken off once the tiles have been applied and the adhesive has set. Long masonry nails usually work well, but on dry-lined or stud walls it may be easier to use screws.

APPLYING ADHESIVE

Tile adhesive must be applied evenly to ensure that the tiles sit correctly on the wall surface. You can use ready-mixed adhesive, or powder that needs water added to it. Both types are equally effective and there is no difference in technique when applying them.

SMALL AREAS

In small intricate tiling areas, it is easier if you use smaller tools. You can apply the adhesive to the wall or to the back of the tiles. Adhesive starts to harden once it is exposed to the air, so applying it to a small area at a time reduces the possibility of it drying before the tile has been applied to the wall.

Applying adhesive to tiles: use a small notched spreader to apply adhesive directly to the back of tiles, removing any excess. The jagged teeth of the spreader create an even layer of peaks and troughs along the adhesive surface, which improves adhesion when the tile is applied to the wall.

Getting in corners: a small notched spreader is the ideal tool for getting adhesive into tight corners. This is especially useful when laying the first tiles, which will need to be tight against the supporting frame. Beginners will also find that a small notched spreader is easier to use and creates less mess than a large one.

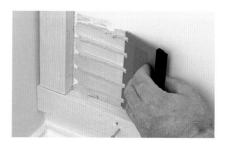

ADHESIVE IDEAS

- When taking a break, always keep the lid on the tub of tile adhesive to prevent it from drying out.
- If tiling a large area, use tile adhesive that requires mixing, as it is usually cheaper than ready-mixed varieties.
- For very small areas of wall, use "tile and grout" adhesive since, as the name suggests, this can be used as grout as well as adhesive. Although it tends to be expensive, it is very economical in small areas as it eliminates the need to buy both an adhesive and a grout, which are difficult to buy separately in the small quantities you would need.

LARGE AREAS

On large open expanses of wall, tile adhesive can be spread over greater areas of the wall surface and the tiles can be applied relatively quickly. Use a large notched spreader since it covers a large wall space much more quickly than a small spreader.

1 Use the flat broad surface of the notched spreader to dig adhesive out of its tub or bucket, then use a pressing, sweeping motion to apply it to the wall. Do not try to apply too much at a time as the adhesive will simply fall away around the sides of the spreader and onto the floor.

2 Draw the serrated edge of the spreader across the surface of the adhesive, creating furrows in its surface. Apply enough pressure for the points along the spreader's edge to touch the wall surface, but not enough for them to gouge into it. This creates an even coat that is the ideal surface to twist the first tiles onto, producing a firm bond between wall and tiles.

3 Do not cover more than one square metre (yard) of the wall at a time because the tiles must be applied while the adhesive is still wet and workable. It is better for beginners to start by covering an area half this size and gradually build up to the larger area.

APPLYING THE FIRST TILES

The first tiles are the most important in any tile design because they provide the starting point and base for the whole tiled area. Poor application at this stage can affect the entire finish, so you need to take great care when positioning the first tiles.

1 Place the first tile tight into the corner made by the horizontal and vertical frame edges. Use a slight twisting motion when pressing the tile onto the adhesive surface to ensure good suction between the back of the tile and the adhesive.

2 Continue to apply tiles in a row along the top of the horizontal frame edge. Apply spacers between every tile to ensure uniform gaps for grouting. Because of the wooden frame, the spacers at the base of the first row of tiles have to be positioned pointing out from the tiled surface. These can be removed when the adhesive has set, whereas other spacers on the wall surface are left in position to be grouted over.

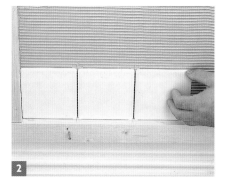

3 After every two rows of tiles, check that the level is being maintained. Use a short level, held across three tiles at a time, to make sure that no tiles have slipped out of position. Take care not to get any tile adhesive on the level—clean it immediately if you do.

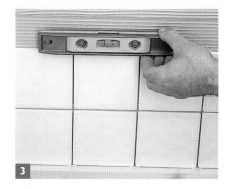

4 Once a larger block of tiles is complete, hold a long strip of wood across the tiled surface, to check that they are all sitting flush. Any sunken or protruding tiles will be obvious and then any necessary adjustments can be made.

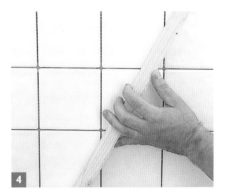

5 Adjustments to tile position must be carried out while the adhesive is still wet. Lever out sunken or protruding tiles with a scraper, being careful not to scratch or chip the tile surface.

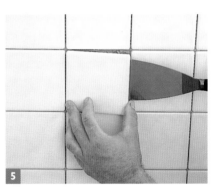

6 For a sunken tile, apply more adhesive to the back of the tile with a small notched spreader. Reposition the tile on the wall, again using the wooden batten to check that it is now sitting flush with the surrounding tiled surface. For a protruding tile, simply remove some of the adhesive and reapply the tile to the wall.

WATCHPOINTS

- Use a damp rag or sponge to clean excess tile adhesive off the tiled surface as you go.
- Tile up to one metre (yard) high, then allow the adhesive to set before applying any more tiles.
- Once the whole area has been tiled, the wooden frame must be left in place until the adhesive has set. Then remove it and use cut tiles to fill the gaps.

CUTTING TILES

To complete almost any tile design, you will need to cut some tiles to fill gaps. Cutting a straight line across a tile is relatively easy and you can use one of two tools—either a simple hand-held tile cutter or a tile cutting machine. Both will produce the same result.

SIMPLE CUTTING

Using a hand-held tile cutter is the more traditional method of cutting tiles. Their simple design combines a handle with a cutting spike that scores the tile as it is drawn across the tile surface. It is worth spending a little extra to get a good-quality tile cutter as these produce the cleanest cuts.

1 Measure the distance between the edge of the tile and the corner junction to determine the size of tile needed to fill the gap. Take 3 mm (⅛ in) off the measurement to allow for grout.

2 Mark the measurement on a full tile with a fibre-tip pen. Using another tile as a straight edge, score along the marked line with the tile cutter, applying a firm but even pressure. This will cut into the glazed surface of the tile, leaving a clearly defined scratch.

3 Place the scored tile on two matchsticks so that the "cut" line is positioned on the centre of each matchstick. Apply even downward pressure on each side of the scored line in order to snap the tile along the "cut" line.

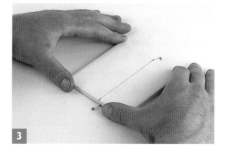

MACHINE CUTTING

Tile cutting machines are a more recent innovation. Although they produce the same result as a hand-held tile cutter, they tend to be quicker to use and, with practice, generally provide a more efficient way of cutting tiles. The same "scoring" principle is used, except the cutting blade is circular rather than a single cutting point.

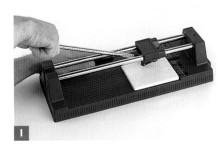

1 With a fibre-tip pen, mark where the cut is required and position the tile on the cutting machine so that the cutting wheel sits directly on the fibre-tip line when lowered onto the tile. Applying an even downward pressure on the machine handle, push the cutting wheel along the full extent of the fibre-tip line, scratching the tile surface.

2 Clamp the tile between the bracket above the cutting wheel and below the two sliding rails. The scored line on the tile must be positioned centrally between the rails—most machines have a pointer on the cutting machine bracket so you can line it up accurately. Push down on the cutting-machine handle to snap the tile along the scored line.

3 Most tile cuts will be clean and precise; if there are any rough edges or bumps, they can be removed with a tile file.

INTERNAL CORNERS

Internal corners are the most common obstacle when tiling—quite simply because all rooms have them. If tiles are being laid on more than one wall in a room, you will have to deal with a corner. Tiling a corner is straightforward as long as you follow a few simple rules.

SIMPLE CORNERING

If a tiling plan has been worked out correctly (see pages 306–307), when you arrive at an internal corner you will usually require just under, or just over, half a tile to fill the gap between the last full tile and the corner junction. Cutting straight lines on the tiles is a simple process, and it is easy to produce a neatly tiled internal corner.

1 It is usually easier to apply the tile adhesive to the back of a cut tile, rather than the wall, when positioning the tiles along the corner junction. Make sure that the factory edge of the tile is jointed next to the column of full tiles, and the cut edge is running along the corner junction. Continue up the corner junction, filling the gap with more cut tiles.

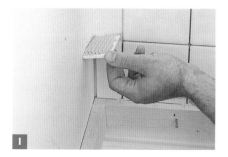

2 Tile the adjacent wall up to the corner junction. This will also need to be finished with a column of cut tiles. It is important to cut these as neatly as possible, as the cut edge of these tiles will overlap the column of tiles on the first wall. Remove any rough edges with a tile file.

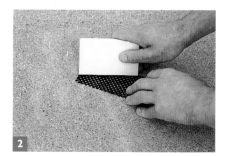

3 Position the cut tiles along the corner junction and continue until the whole internal corner is tiled. Apply adhesive to cut tiles one at a time—don't try and apply it along the entire corner junction.

KEEPING TILES LEVEL

It is important to keep a constant check that tiles are level when dealing with an internal corner. Since cut tiles are just as likely to slip out of position as full tiles, making sure that they stay in the correct place is essential for a neat finish. You need a spirit level and spacers to help you maintain the level across a corner.

1 Check that tiles are in the correct position by holding a spirit level across the corner junction. Position the edge of the level so that one end is at the junction between two tiles on one wall while the other end of the level is positioned on the corresponding row of tiles on the adjacent wall.

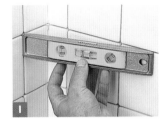

2 Position spacers along the corner so that they span the junction and maintain the necessary gap between, and along, the two columns of cut tiles.

CUTTING SLIVERS

Sometimes small gaps along a corner will require thin slivers of tile to fill them. Because tiles are brittle, cutting a sliver using the usual cutting technique may break the tile. You need to use a slightly different technique, which puts a greater, more even pressure along the scored cutting line.

1 Measure the cut requirements as normal, then score the line with a hand-held cutter or tile cutting machine.

2 Rest the edge of the tile on top of another tile, making sure the scored line is positioned directly above the edge of the tile below. Apply even downward pressure on the main body of the scored tile until the sliver snaps off.

EXTERNAL CORNERS

Internal corner joints overlap and are easy to conceal, while external joints are more prominent and expose any mistakes far more readily. Tiling an external corner is an exercise in concealment, which requires a slightly different tiling technique.

PLASTIC QUADRANTS

The greatest aid to producing a neat external corner is plastic quadrant lipping. It creates a smooth defined edge to tile up to, as well as protecting the corner from being knocked or chipped. Always try to plan your tiling strategy so that full tiles are used to tile away from the external corner.

1 Cut the quadrant to the required length with a hacksaw. Apply adhesive to one wall surface and align the quadrant precisely along the external corner edge. Make sure there is enough adhesive along the edge of the corner to hold the quadrant in position.

2 Tile the one wall, positioning the first tile next to the quadrant, and butting it up tightly against the quadrant lip. Continue to apply tiles. Insert tile spacers along the quadrant/tile junction perpendicular to the tile surface, as the quadrant edge will not allow them to be laid flush against the wall surface. (These spacers can be removed when the adhesive is set.)

3 Once one wall is complete, apply adhesive to the adjacent wall and continue to tile that wall in the same way.

STANDARD OVERLAPPING

For a more traditional finish when tiling an external corner, you can make an overlapping tile joint. Tiles with a glazed edge (as shown here) will maintain the tile colour along the corner; tiles with an unglazed edge can be used for a more rustic finish.

Creating the junction: tile the first wall so that the edges of the tiles run precisely along the corner junction. When tiling the adjacent wall, allow the tiles to overlap onto the edges of those previously laid, creating a tiled external corner.

CREATING CURVES

Ceramic quadrant tile strips can be used to create a smooth, curved edge on an external corner. These are particularly suitable around window recesses, where the external corners run horizontally as well as vertically. Ceramic quadrant borders give an attractive finish to a window sill.

1 Tile the wall up to the edge of the sill. Use some old broken tiles to build up the actual sill surface, to allow for the height of the quadrant tiles when they are applied. Make sure the broken tiles are firmly stuck down, and provide a level surface.

2 Apply the finishing tiles on top of the broken-tile base, positioning them so that they are set back from the sill edge. The distance they are set back should be the same as the width of the quadrant tiles being used.

3 Carefully position quadrant tiles along the sill edge, maintaining gaps with spacers as usual. You may need to apply more adhesive than usual to the back of each quadrant tile to hold them firmly in place.

GROUTING AND POLISHING

O nce the tile adhesive has dried, you need to fill in the junctions between the tiles with grout to make the tiled surface water-resistant. As well as being practical, grout provides the overall finish, effectively framing the tiles and highlighting their decorative appeal.

APPLYING GROUT

Grout can be bought either ready-to-use, or in a powder form that requires mixing with water. Both will produce the same result, although it is usually more economical to buy the powder form.

1 Mix grout in a clean bucket with cold water. Proportions will vary between manufacturers, but try to achieve a smooth workable paste. If you mix by hand, it is easier to break up any lumps in the mixture. Always wear protective gloves since prolonged exposure to grout can cause skin irritation.

2 Apply the grout to the tiled surface using a grout spreader or squeegee. Use broad sweeping movements in all directions to ensure that the grout gets into every joint. Grout only one to two square metres (yards) at a time since there is a fairly short working time before the grout starts to go hard, and it can be tricky to remove grout from the surface of the tiles once it has dried.

3 Remove the excess grout from the tiles with a damp sponge. Build up a rhythm of wiping off tiles and rinsing the sponge in clean water. Continue until all the grout is removed from the surface of the tiles, leaving just the grout in the junctions between the tiles.

4 Run the rounded end of a grout shaper along all the tile junctions to give the grout a final smooth surface, making each grouted joint into a perfect, slightly concave trough.

FINISHING OFF

Once the grout has dried, you need to check to make sure that the surface is watertight and that there are no grout splashes. It is almost inevitable that the odd area will need some minor attention, or that some grout will have found its way onto the tiled surface.

1 As the grout dries, air bubbles inside it can come to the surface and create a hole. If this happens, use the end of your finger to apply a small amount of grout to the hole to make the junction waterproof again.

2 Dried grout on the tiled surface can be removed using a scraper, but take care not to scratch the ceramic surface of the tile with the sharp edge of the scraper. Allow the scraper to slide along the surface of the tile, rather than letting it dig down into the ceramic.

3 Finally, polish the tiles with a dry cotton rag to remove any powdery residue created by the wet grout being applied. You may need to do this two or three times on each area of tiles to remove all the residue and leave a clean, bright surface.

SILICONE SEALING

A tiled surface is very rigid, so any slight structural movement within a room, or building as a whole, can cause joint cracking. Grout is flexible enough to withstand this movement on flat open tiled surfaces, but in corners and more specifically around fixtures such as baths and sinks, a more flexible waterproof seal is required. Here, the best thing to use is waterproof sealant, which is sold in tubes.

1 To seal between the tiles and the bath, clean the junction of the tiled edge and the bath with some methylated spirits to remove any surface impurities on the bath edge. It evaporates quickly to provide a clean surface for the sealant.

2 Apply masking tape along both the bath edge and the edge of the tiled surface, making sure that the tape is stuck down along the entire length. Leave the joint of the tile/bath junction exposed.

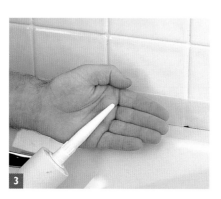

3 Cut off the end of a tube of sealant so that the diameter of the hole will span the joint size created between the two lengths of masking tape. Cut the hole at a slightly diagonal angle—this will allow it to be drawn smoothly along the tile/bath junction.

4 Fit the tube of sealant into a sealant gun. Applying even pressure on the trigger of the sealant gun, draw the cut end of the tube along the tile/bath junction between the two strips of masking tape. Create a bead of sealant large enough to just cover the edges of the masking tape strips.

5 With a dampened finger, carefully smooth across the surface of the bead of sealant in one continuous, steady motion.

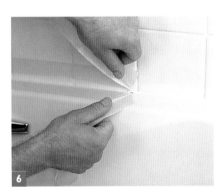

6 While the sealant is still wet, carefully remove the tape to leave a neat siliconed joint. If any area of the joint pulls away as the tape is removed, carefully smooth the sealant back in position with a dampened finger.

ALTERNATIVE SEALS

Although silicone sealant in a tube is the most commonly used and versatile system of waterproofing a joint, there are other alternatives.

- Sealant dispensers: silicone sealants in a range of colours to match the most common bathroom suites are available in syringe-like dispensers.
- Quadrant tiles: these can be applied along a tile/fixture junction, using a silicone sealant as the adhesive to fix them in place (see page 335).
- Plastic sealant strips: these are applied to a tile/fixture junction using double-sided waterproof tape.
- Wooden strips: as long as the wood has had several coats of varnish, decorative wooden mouldings can be used to seal along a junction, using silicone sealant as the adhesive.

FUNCTIONAL TILES

There is a range of functional tiles available that produce more than just a durable decorative surface. Applying these tiles requires little more than the basic techniques outlined in this chapter.

Mirror tiles: as their name suggests, mirror tiles provide the dual function of a tiled surface with the normal properties of a mirror. They are ideal in bedrooms or bathrooms and can be used in small areas—as a splashback for example—or to cover larger areas of wall and create an expansive effect. You can apply mirror tiles in the same way as wall tiles except that you need to butt them tight against each other (with no spacers) for the best effect. Some manufacturers recommend their own adhesive for attaching the tiles to the wall.

Worktops: a tiled worktop surface in the kitchen is a popular alternative to a veneered or wooden finish. Heat-resistant tiles can be used to provide an area where you can place hot pots and pans; ordinary ceramic tiles are no good for this purpose. Fix the tiles with the usual tile adhesive, but use epoxy grout, as it is more hygienic and hard-wearing.

Soap dish tiles: these tiles have a soap dish fitted in them. They are top heavy compared to a normal tile and need to be supported with masking tape until the adhesive has set.

3
TILING
AWKWARD
AREAS

Once the tiling basics have been mastered and a slightly more complicated tiling project is planned, it soon becomes apparent that most rooms have more than just flat walls to deal with. This chapter shows you how to cope with the most common awkward areas found on wall surfaces and explains the most efficient methods of dealing with them. However daunting some surfaces may appear, the same basic rules apply, with the emphasis on cutting tiles accurately and keeping them level. Patience and taking your time is the key to success—speed will come with experience.

CUTTING AROUND ELECTRICAL FIXTURES

E lectrical fixtures are the most common obstacles when tiling in kitchens, where sockets are required above the worktops to supply household electrical appliances. However, wall lights, switches, and other electrical sockets and outlets can be found in all manner of places in the house and it is important to use the correct techniques to deal with them.

WALL FIXTURES

Tiling around fixtures such as wall lights cannot be done while they are in position. The best method is to remove the fixture from the wall, leaving the supply wire as the only obstacle. If you are doing this job yourself, make sure that the electricity is turned off at the electrical distribution box before removing the fixture. Draw a wire plan on a piece of paper, so that you can attach the fixture to the wall supply again once tiling is complete.

1 Wrap electrical tape around the end of the supply wire. This will protect the wire and prevent it from splaying out, which would make it difficult to thread through the drilled tile later on.

2 Measure the point at which a hole is needed in the tile to thread the supply wire through. Holding the tile firmly on the workbench, use a tile drill bit to make a small hole, and then change to a masonry bit to expand the diameter of the hole until it is large enough to accommodate the supply wire.

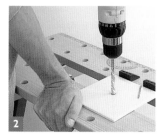

3 Check that the wire threads through the tile before applying adhesive and fixing it to the wall. Once the surrounding tiles have been applied, remove the tape from the wire then the electrical fixture can be rewired and repositioned on the tiled surface. Do not turn the electricity back on until the fixture is safely secured in place.

SOCKETS AND SWITCHES

Wall-mounted sockets and switches do not need to be completely removed from the wall in order to tile around them. But you must turn off the electricity supply at the electrical distribution box since the socket plate will need to be loosened by unscrewing the two retaining screws.

1 Hold a full tile in position over the face of the socket plate. Mark off the portion of tile that needs to be removed, adjusting the measurement so that it appears to encroach onto the socket plate by about 3 mm (⅛ in).

2 Score along the longer of the measured lines with a tile cutter, taking care not to extend the cut any farther than the junction with the shorter line.

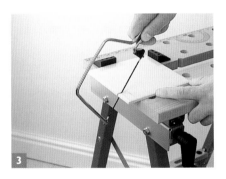

3 Use a tile saw to cut along the shorter line, back as far as the junction with the longer line.

CAUTION

Always turn off the electricity supply at the consumer unit before working around electrical fixtures. If in any doubt, contact a qualified electrician to carry out the work.

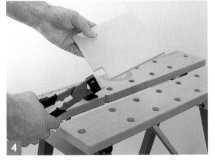

4 Break off the small portion of tile by applying an even pressure along the scored line with a score and snap tool. Loosen the retaining screws on the socket plate and position the tile with the cut edges behind the socket plate to give a neat finish. Reattach the socket plate, using slightly longer screws, if necessary, as the depth of the tile may not allow the original screws to reach their previous fixing point.

CUTTING AROUND PIPES

P ipes are a common problem when tiling. The ideal solution is to
box them in before tiling (see pages 302–303), but this is not
always possible. Pipes that are left exposed need to be dealt with in as
simple a manner as possible. Although pipes may appear a daunting
obstacle, accurate measuring and cutting are the only skills required.

MEASURING THE CUT

Pipes are easiest to deal with when they span the junction of two tiles (as
shown here), even though this means that two tiles need to be cut. It is
important to be very precise when measuring around pipes as there is little
room for error and any mistakes will be noticeable.

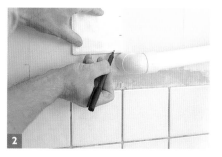

1 Hold the tile to the side and up
against the pipe, and mark off
the diameter of the pipe on the edge
of the tile. Make sure that the tile is
held in the right position to allow for
the correct gap between it and the
row of tiles below.

2 To find how long the horizontal
cut on the tile needs to be, hold
the tile above the pipe, making sure
that the vertical edges of the tile are
aligned with the corresponding edges
in the row of tiles below. Mark how
far the edge of the pipe extends onto
the tile.

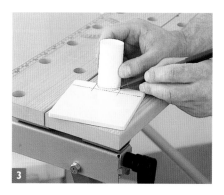

3 Extend all three markings on the
tile to map out a rectangular
portion on the pipe side of the tile.
Position a scrap piece of pipe so that
it fills the rectangle as completely as
possible, without crossing the three
marked lines. Draw around the edge
of the pipe to produce a perfect
guideline for cutting. If no scrap
sections of pipe are available, use a
compass to produce the same
diameter as the pipe.

CUTTING

Because the portion of tile that needs removing before the tile can be fitted around the pipe is curved, it is impossible to cut it out with an ordinary tile cutter. A tile saw is the ideal tool for cutting curves.

1 Clamp the tile securely to the workbench and carefully saw around the curve, taking care to keep to the guideline. Once you have reached halfway around the curve, start sawing again from the other end of the curve until the two sawed cuts meet and the unwanted portion of tile is removed.

2 Use the curved face of a tile file to remove any rough edges from the cut section of tile.

3 Apply adhesive to the back of the tile and position it around the pipe. Repeat the process to fit the adjacent tile around the other side of the pipe.

CUTTING ALTERNATIVES

- When a pipe is in a position to protrude through a single tile, measure as before, but score and snap the tile through the centre of the marked hole before using the tile saw. Saw the two semi-circular areas and reunite the two halves of tile around the pipe. The cut will not be obvious across the surface as a whole.
- For small pipes, it may be easier to use a large drill bit to form the circular cut for the pipe.
- Use a profile gauge—a tool for copying the shapes of objects—to determine the required shape to cut out of a tile.

INTERNAL WINDOW RECESSES

Recessed windows present more of a planning problem than a cutting problem when they are tiled. On walls that have a window, it is essential to try and keep a balanced layout, especially when using patterned tiles. A little extra time spent planning with a tiling gauge will be beneficial to the overall finish of the room.

TILING THE WALL FACE

Try and plan the tile layout so that it is centred on the window. That way any necessary cuts are balanced and are the same size on each side of the recess. It is unlikely that the window dimensions will allow for whole tiles to fit exactly around its border, so you will need to cut some tiles. Tiles at the top edge of the window reveal will also require temporary support with a wooden batten while the adhesive dries.

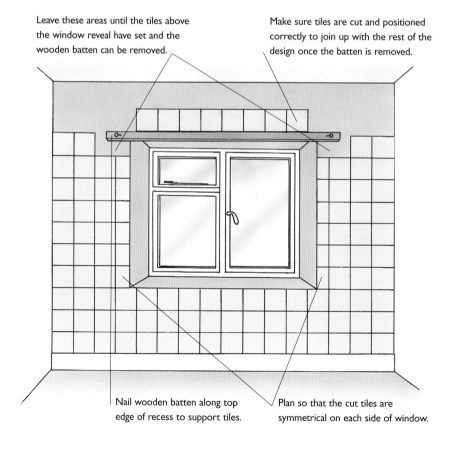

Leave these areas until the tiles above the window reveal have set and the wooden batten can be removed.

Make sure tiles are cut and positioned correctly to join up with the rest of the design once the batten is removed.

Nail wooden batten along top edge of recess to support tiles.

Plan so that the cut tiles are symmetrical on each side of window.

TILING THE REVEAL

Once the wall face is complete, the window recess can be tiled. Always work back from the edge of the recess toward the window, so that the cut tiles butt up against the window frame. Tile the top of the recess first, so that a wooden slat can be used to support the tiles while the adhesive dries. If the sill was tiled first, the base of the supporting planks might damage tiles laid on the sill. Tile the sill next, then tile the recess sides after the sill has dried.

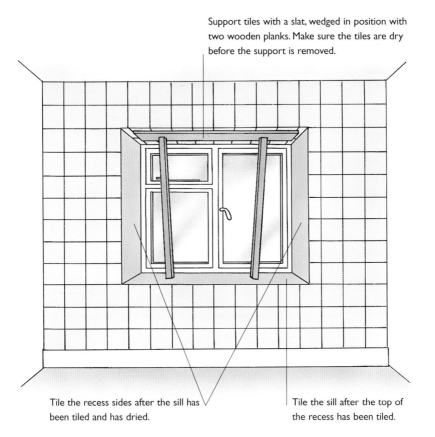

Support tiles with a slat, wedged in position with two wooden planks. Make sure the tiles are dry before the support is removed.

Tile the recess sides after the sill has been tiled and has dried.

Tile the sill after the top of the recess has been tiled.

Laying the recess tiles: position the tiles in the recess so that they slightly overlap those on the wall surface. Alternatively, create a rounded edge using quadrant tiles (see page 317).

MAKING AND TILING A BATH PANEL

T iling a panel for an inset bath has the effect of integrating the bath into the rest of a tiled scheme. As well as their decorative appeal, tiled bath panels make easily wipeable, durable surfaces, which are suited to such a busy area of the home. Use water-resistant medium-density fibreboard to make the panel itself—it is easy to cut to size and provides an excellent base for tiles.

MAKING THE FRAME

A bath panel must be mounted onto a strong frame, otherwise the panel will have too much flexibility, which may cause cracking along tile joints and ruin the finish. Use a framework of 5-by-2.5-cm (2-by-1-in) wooden battens to make a solid base for attaching the panel to.

1 Cut a piece of batten the same length as the bath. Position it on the floor parallel with the bath rim. Hold a scrap piece of MDF (the same height as the bath panel will be) running from underneath the bath rim down to the floor batten. Use a level to make sure the MDF is vertical, and mark along the edge of the batten making a pencil guideline on the floor.

2 Position the wooden batten along the pencil guideline and screw it into the floor. Make sure that the screws are long enough to secure firmly to the floor, but do not go all the way through the floorboard and risk damaging service pipes or wires below floor level.

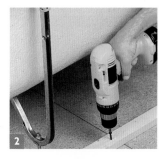

3 Cut shorter lengths of batten to act as vertical supports, and fix them securely at their base. Most bath designs will accommodate the batten beneath the bath rim, although in some cases it may be necessary to fit another length of batten under the rim to attach to the vertical supports.

4 Finally, fit diagonal supports to make the frame totally rigid. Take care when measuring the lengths required, as you will need to mitre the ends of the battens to ensure that they sit flush against the vertical supports.

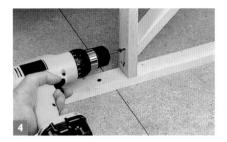

MAKING THE PANEL

A well-fitting bath panel should create a good decorative effect, so it is important to take your time cutting the MDF sheet to size. Some bath rims have a slightly undulating profile, and this must be taken into account when measuring the fibreboard.

1 Take precise measurements from under the rim to the floor surface, all the way along the bath. Use these measurements to cut the MDF to size. Fit the panel under the rim, and run a pencil along the edge of the rim, making a guideline on the MDF panel.

2 Remove the panel and lay it flat on the floor. Lay out the dry tiles on the MDF. Do not tile above the pencil guideline or the panel will not fit under the rim when it has been tiled. Once the tiles have been laid out, they can be stuck down with tile adhesive. Attach the panel to the frame using magnetic catches, or screw it to the wooden frame using a tile drill bit and mirror screws.

A PATTERNED PANEL
For a unique bathroom feature, use patterned tiles to create your own colour combinations and design.

TILING AROUND SINKS

S inks tend to have curves and straight edges, which can create problems when tiling around them. The easiest solution is to ease the sink away from the wall and tile behind it. If this is not possible, you can make a paper template of the shape of the sink.

"MOVABLE" SINKS

Because sinks are plumbed into the water supply they cannot simply be moved out of the way before tiling. However, in some cases it is possible to ease a free-standing sink away from the wall slightly. You can then slide tiles behind the sink without the need for complicated tile cutting.

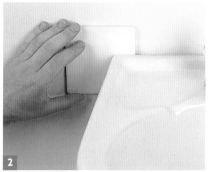

1 Most free-standing sinks are attached to the wall with retaining screws. Carefully loosen these screws with two or three turns of a screwdriver. Make sure that the sink remains well supported on its pedestal.

2 Try sliding a tile between the back of the sink and the wall, to check that the sink has been moved far enough away from the wall. If there is room, it is now simple to tile around the sink. Slip the edge of tiles behind the sink rim to give an extremely neat finish. Once tiling is complete, the retaining screws can be tightened to fix the sink securely in place once more.

CAUTION

Pipework below sinks can be very rigid: easing a sink away from the wall can put joints under stress and risk rupturing them. If in any doubt, do not try this method of tiling around a basin, but use the method shown opposite.

MAKING A TEMPLATE

Using a paper template is an effective way of cutting tiles around curved edges, such as those found on sinks. Cut a number of pieces of paper to the exact size of one of the tiles.

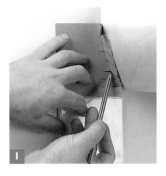

1 Using scissors, cut a number of slits in the paper template. Hold the template against the side of the sink as if it were a tile, allowing the strips of paper to mould into the shape of the sink. Mark a pencil guideline along the crease created.

2 Cut around the pencil guideline, then place the remainder of the template on a tile. Next, draw the outline of the cutout on the tile with a fibre-tip pen.

3 Clamp the tile securely to the workbench and saw along the marked guideline. The tile may then be fitted in place next to the sink. Continue to cut and fit tiles around the rest of the sink.

OTHER AREAS FOR USING A TEMPLATE

- Toilet cisterns: these are often held in position with retaining screws and it may be possible to ease them away from the wall very slightly, as shown on page 332, but proceed with caution and never risk

damaging the pipework. A template can be used just as effectively.
- Shower wall units: if possible, tile before a shower wall unit is fixed. Otherwise, use templates to make the required tile cuts.

TILING A SPLASHBACK

A splashback behind a sink protects the wall from water splashes and is easy to clean. Tiling a splashback is far easier than tiling all the way around a sink, requiring few, if any, cuts. However, it is essential to make sure that a splashback is centralized and maintains a balanced appearance in relation to the sink itself.

POSITIONING A SPLASHBACK

Decide on the exact dimensions of the splashback. Two to three tiles high is the normal vertical requirement. Along the horizontal line, it is a matter of personal choice—tiles can extend exactly to the sink edge, or protrude farther onto the wall surface. This decision may be dictated by tile size, and what looks the most appropriate.

1 Measure the exact centre of the sink, and make a pencil mark on the wall above.

2 Draw a vertical line up from this mark, and use this as a guide to positioning the first tile. Support the tiles on spacers wedged between the tile edge and the sink itself.

3 If the last tile extends farther than the basin edge, support it on a nail hammered into the wall precisely below the bottom edge of the tile.

FILLING THE GAPS

When tiling a splashback behind a sink, it is essential to make a waterproof seal between the tiles and the sink. Sealant can be used (see pages 320–321). Alternatively, ceramic quadrant tiles can be fitted, using a silicone-based sealant as the adhesive for them.

1 Apply a generous bead of silicone sealant to the back of a quadrant tile along its whole length.

2 Position the tile at the splashback/sink junction. Continue to apply tiles until the junction is covered. Manufacturers often supply quadrant tiles which are shaped at one end, and these give a finished look to the tiles at each end of a splashback junction. Once in place, grout all the tiles.

APPLYING A BORDER

A tiled splashback can be decorative enough on its own, or a border can be added to create extra interest. A number of materials can be used for this purpose, it is really a matter of personal preference.

Applying a hardwood border: the combination of a hardwood strip against ceramic tiles gives a very attractive finish. Mitre the corners accurately and attach them to the wall with a silicone-based adhesive. Varnish the wood to protect it from water splashes before grouting.

TILED BORDERS

D ado edgings and borders can be used to create decorative edges to tiled designs. As border tiles vary in size and pattern, it is possible to create numerous effects with them. Many designs are made specifically to complement a particular tile design. This means you can follow the manufacturer's lead on creating a design, or you can produce a design of your own choosing.

TILING A DADO EDGING

Applying border tiles requires the same technique as for standard tiles, except for dealing with corners. These need a slightly different technique, especially when using relief border tiles, as shown here.

I Apply tile adhesive to the back of border tiles and then position them on the wall. When a corner is reached, measure the distance from the end of the border tile right into the corner junction.

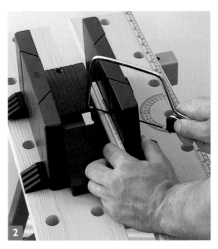

2 Mark this measurement on a whole border tile. Clamp a mitre block to the workbench and place the marked tile tightly against the mitre block edge. Using a tile saw, cut through the border tile at the mark.

3 Apply adhesive to the back of the mitred border tile and position it in the corner. Not all border tiles will require mitring to go around an internal corner. Mitres are necessary with relief border tiles to produce a good finish: flat border tiles or slips can be given simple straight cuts.

BORDER CHOICES

As well as complementing a tiled surface, a border can be used in a "starring" role to create the focus to the entire tiled surface. The look can be traditional or slightly more adventurous. Decisions on the role of border tiles will almost certainly come down to room and surface requirements, combined with the other decorative aspects of the interior.

Half-tile borders: border tiles are usually about a quarter to half the width of standard tiles. These are the ideal dimensions for using them as a dado edging in a half-tiled room.

Full-tile borders: although border tiles are specifically designed for borders, it is not essential to use them when creating a tile divide or border. Full tiles of a different design or colour but similar shape to the main body of tiles can be used equally effectively.

Tile slips: thin tile slips can be used on their own or as part of a larger overall border design. A multilevel tiled border created out of more than one row of border tiles provides an impressive finish.

TILING WORKTOPS

Worktops are far easier to tile than wall surfaces, as there are no problems with tiles sliding. The difficulty arises in producing a perfectly flat finish that will be long-lasting as well as hard-wearing. Standard ceramic tiles can be used on a work surface, but it is better to use tiles specifically designed for worktops since they can withstand hot pans and the general hard wear and tear of a kitchen.

PREPARING THE EDGE

MDF or marine plywood can be used as the worktop base. Whatever is used, the worktop must have a durable edge—a simple tiled edge is prone to being chipped. It is also important to create a decorative edge that fits in with the room scheme. Hardwood lipping protects the tiles and gives an attractive finish.

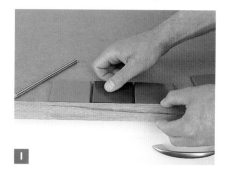

1 Hold a cut strip of wooden lipping along the front of the worktop surface (MDF is shown here). Position some tiles up against the edge of the lipping so that their faces are flush with the top of the lipping. Holding the lipping in position, move the tiles away. Draw a pencil line along the back edge of the lipping where it meets the worktop surface.

3 Position the lipping back on the front of the worktop, making sure that the pencil guideline is still running along the worktop/lipping junction. Secure the wooden strip in place with some brads.

2 Place the lipping on the worktop, with the pencil guideline facing upward. Apply some wood glue along the lipping below the pencil guideline.

APPLYING THE TILES

Once the lipping is fitted, the tiles may be applied. Always work back from the edge of the worktop toward the wall: that way any cut tiles will be against the wall rather than at the front of the worktop. Use tile adhesive and space the tiles in the usual way.

SETTING UP

- Designs: if including a picture or pattern in your worktop design, plan where particular tiles should be positioned for the most effective results.
- Sealing: before tiling, seal the hardwood strip with varnish and allow it to dry. This will prevent any tile adhesive from becoming ingrained in the lipping surface.

1 Seal the worktop surface with a PVA solution (five parts water to one part PVA) and allow it to dry.

2 Spread tile adhesive evenly across the surface of the worktop. The evenness of the adhesive layer is often the secret to producing a level finish, so take time to ensure that it is evenly spread before applying the tiles.

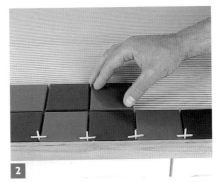

3 Once the tiles have been laid and the adhesive has set, finish the tiled surface with an epoxy-based grout. This is more durable and hygienic than standard grout mixtures. The epoxy-based grout has a short working time, so only work over a small area at a time, wiping the excess away with a damp sponge as you go.

TILING A FIREPLACE

Fireplaces often form the focal point of a main living area. When tiling a fireplace, there are certain constraints on the type and style of tile you can use. If fitting a new fireplace, tiles made specifically to fit that design are sometimes supplied; when refurbishing a period fireplace, it's often a compromise between authenticity and availability.

1 When fitting tiles on a fireplace, you need to vary the tiling technique slightly by beginning at the top and working down—this makes it much easier to centralize the tiles and create a balanced finish with evenly matched cuts where required. Slip the bottom edges of the top row of full tiles behind the metal fireplace surround, so it supports their weight. Make sure that the tiles are centralized. Fix a piece of batten on each side of the metal surround to support those tiles nearest the edge of the fireplace. If there is no metal surround, nail a batten across the top of the fireplace entrance to act as support.

2 Once the tile adhesive has set, remove the batten. Tile down to floor level, inserting spacers and making sure that the tiles do not slip. The final tile nearest floor level on each side of the fireplace will be supporting the tiles above until the adhesive has set, so make sure that these tiles are positioned correctly and supported.

3 Fill in with cut tiles around the edge of the full ones to complete the tiling. Cut some wooden beading to fit around the junction between tiles and fireplace to hide the tile cuts. Paint or stain the beading the appropriate colour, then grout the tiles.

FOCAL POINT
A well-tiled fireplace can complement the decoration in the rest of the room, and an attractive set of fireplace tiles makes such a good focal point that the whole colour scheme for the room can be based on the fireplace tiles.

FIREPLACE CONSIDERATIONS

- Active fireplace: if the fireplace is going to be used, make sure that the tiles are heat-resistant. If surfaces need to be made good before tiling, use fire-resistant cement.
- Finding tiles: to find original tiles, try visiting antique stores to see if they have any period fireplace tiles— it is often possible to find single replacements for broken originals.

- Be extravagant: because relatively few tiles are needed to tile a fireplace, this is one area where you can use more expensive tiles. A well-chosen set of handmade or richly patterned tiles are well worth the extra cost.
- Hearths: always consider the hearth when choosing fireplace tiles. It can be an option to continue the tiles from around the fireplace onto the hearth.

INSERTING A MIRROR

Mirrors make an attractive addition to a tiling scheme, especially when they are framed with border tiles. To make the frame, attach a level supporting batten with masonry nails. Lay the bottom row of tiles along its length. Cut mitres in the tiles so that the top edge of the tiles is the same width as the mirror. Stick them to the wall.

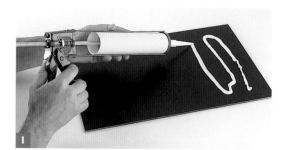

1 Apply mirror adhesive across the back of the mirror, spreading it very liberally to ensure that it will be well stuck to the wall surface.

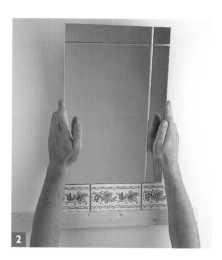

2 Carefully position the mirror on top of the row of border tiles and the supporting batten. Leave until the adhesive on the mirror has dried before applying the rest of the border tiles.

3 Continue applying border tiles around the edge of the mirror until the frame is complete. Try to cut the mitres in each corner so that the cuts correspond to similar areas of pattern. If the border tiles on the sides begin to slip, attach vertical battens to the wall to support them while the adhesive sets.

4
SIZE AND PATTERN COMBINATIONS

The wide choice of tiles means it is possible to produce all manner of patterns and designs when tiling a surface. In addition to using border tiles to break up uniform tile surfaces, the great variety of shapes and sizes of tiles makes it easy to create designs that do not conform to the traditional appearance of a tiled surface. You can experiment with different-sized tiles to achieve your own very individual look, using tiles uniformly across a wall, or combined with each other to create different patterns and effects. The technique for applying different-sized tiles is basically the same as that for same-size tiles with a few minor modifications.

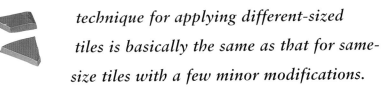

TILED SCENES

T iled scenes are one of the most common uses of specially painted or patterned tiles. They can be used to create a picture or an overall design integrated into the main body of a tiled surface. It is important to make sure that the scene appears at the right level on the wall. A large tiled scene on an open wall is best positioned at eye level, whereas groupings or smaller scenes can be spread more randomly across the wall surface.

1 Lay out the tiles on a flat surface before applying them to the wall, to make sure that you have all the tiles required to complete the design. This also shows you the actual size of the design and helps you work out the best position for it on the wall.

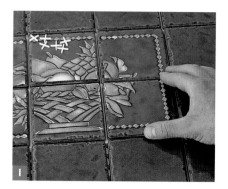

2 Use a coloured grout that complements the main colour on the tiles. This creates a more continuous look, rather than the sharp contrast created by traditional white grout.

TILING SEQUENCE

For some tiled scenes, the tiles will need to be applied to the wall in a specific sequence to produce the desired finished picture. It is very important to take a little extra time and plan the tiling carefully before applying the tiles.

ADDING CHARACTER
A tiled pattern such as this can combine with the surrounding decoration to add character and even humour to a room, accentuating the room's features as well as providing a focal point.

DESIGN IDEAS

There are a number of ways in which picture tiles, or complete scenes, can be used to create a decorative finish. It is worth considering different ideas before making a final decision.

- Commission your own scene: many tile firms offer a service whereby your own scene design can be reproduced on tiles. Although fairly expensive, this is one way of producing a very individual look.
- Groupings: using a combination of small tiled scenes can be an effective way of adding interest to a large tiled surface.
- Single scene tiles: the occasional single picture tile above a countertop, or surrounding a bathtub, can enliven a plain finish.

- Using texture: relief tiles are especially effective in a tiled scene, adding an extra dimension to the picture as a whole.
- Framing: simply framing a tiled scene alone on a wall can create an attractive finish. Use wooden beading or border tiles as the frame.
- Tile transfers: these can be applied to plain tiles to create a picture of your own design. This is an inexpensive way of enlivening a plain tiled surface.
- Painting: use ceramic paints to produce your own picture on the tiles. The design need not be complicated, and it is often the most simple brush strokes that create the most dramatic effect.

SHEET MOSAICS

Mosaic tiles can cover entire wall surfaces, or be used in smaller areas, depending on the required effect. Because they are so small, mosaic tiles tend to be stuck to a net backing that holds them together in blocks. These blocks or sheets are usually about 30 cm (12 in) square. For tiling the wall, a whole sheet is applied at a time, making progress far quicker than it would be if the tiles had to be applied individually. Some mosaic tiles are covered on the face with a sheet of paper to hold them in position, rather than being backed with netting. This paper is soaked with a damp sponge and removed from the tile surface once the mosaic block has been applied to the wall and the tile adhesive has set. The mosaics shown below are the more common type with a net backing.

APPLYING MOSAIC TILES

Keep sheet mosaics as flat as possible before applying them to the wall, as this makes them easier to pick up and handle. There is no need to use spacers as the individual tiles are held in the correct position by their net backing. Because mosaic sheets are not rigid like a normal tile, they can be difficult to maneuver into position. The secret is to begin by applying the bottom of a sheet to the wall first and work upward to the top row of tiles on the sheet. Because the sheet is made up of so many small tiles, it can be difficult to apply even hand pressure to all the tiles. To make sure that they are firmly stuck down, run a mini paint roller back and forth over the mosaic surface, creating an even pressure to bed the tiles into the tile adhesive below.

1 Apply adhesive to the wall before unrolling the mosaic sheets onto the wall. Apply the bottom of a sheet to the wall first and work upward to the top row of tiles on the sheet.

2 Run a mini paint roller over the surface of the mosaic tiles, rolling it back and forth with an even pressure to bed the tiles into the tile adhesive below.

CUTTING AND GROUTING

Sheet mosaics can be cut down to size to fill gaps along corners and junctions, though this tends to be an intricate job. Try to plan a design so that it will not involve cutting the tiles themselves—mosaic tiles are so small that it is difficult to cut them.

1 Measure the number of tiles required to fill the gap, then cut through the net backing of a mosaic sheet, using a craft knife. Cut as cleanly as possible, taking care not to tear the netting as this will loosen the mosaic tiles.

2 Roll the cut sheet into position, again working from the bottom up. Use the mini paint roller to bed in the tiles and even out the joining with the adjacent mosaic sheet.

3 Once the mosaic is complete and the tile adhesive has set, grout the tiles. Make sure that the grout gets into every tile junction. Sponge off and polish in the usual way.

COLOURFUL MOSAIC FINISH
Combining a variety of mosaic colours and designs makes an impressive finish in any room setting.

BROKEN MOSAICS

S heet mosaics are designed to speed up the way in which a mosaic can be completed and produce a very even, uniform finish. A more authentic rustic effect can be produced by using single, randomly shaped mosaic tiles. Applying these tiles is time consuming, but the technique can be used in small areas to make a pictorial design to stick on the wall on its own, or amalgamate into a larger tiled surface. Single mosaic tiles can be purchased in bags containing a wide range of colours and sometimes different textures. However, you can easily make your own mosaic tiles from old or broken tiles.

1 To make a small mosaic picture, cut a sheet of thin water-resistant exterior-grade plywood to size. Draw a design on it with a pencil, or trace a design from a book onto it.

2 Place some old tiles in a bag or wrap them in a cotton rag. Hit them firmly with a hammer to break up the tiles. Although the bag should stop any splinters of tile flying about, wear goggles to protect your eyes.

3 For more uniform mosaic tiles, cut small sections out of larger tiles with a score and snap tool or tile nippers.

4 Apply adhesive to the tiles one at a time, using a filler knife or scraper. Position the tiles on the design, ensuring that they are firmly stuck in position.

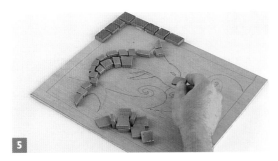

5

5 Vary the colour and pattern to build up the finished picture. Try to keep uniform gaps between the tiles to allow for grouting.

NATURAL EFFECT
A mosaic of broken tile fragments on the wall surface adds a natural effect to an otherwise formal room. The mosaic can complement the colours of furniture and fixtures, or provide a complete contrast.

DESIGN IDEAS

As you can create mosaics in all sorts of shapes and sizes, the rules for making them are fairly flexible. The following guidelines, however, will help you to produce the best possible finish.

• Thickness: try to use tiles of the same thickness—this makes it much easier to produce a mosaic with a flat surface.

• Using other materials: add interest by using different materials within the mosaic—ceramic tiles, broken china, and coloured glass can be added to the tiled design. Take care when applying these, and don't leave any sharp edges protruding from the mosaic surface.

• Keeping it simple: the most effective mosaics tend to be those with simple, unfussy designs. Do not be too extravagant when drawing the initial plan.

• Using borders: tiled or wooden borders make excellent frames for a finished mosaic and turn it into a design feature.

USING LARGE TILES

W hen applying larger than standard tiles, accuracy is essential because any mistakes are magnified by the size of the tile. The same adhesive can be used, along with standard spacers in most cases. Keeping tiles level and very precise cutting are vital for a quality finish.

LARGE TILE IDEAS

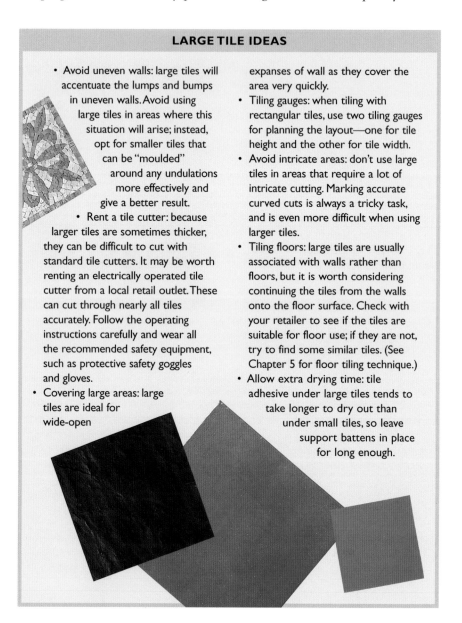

- Avoid uneven walls: large tiles will accentuate the lumps and bumps in uneven walls. Avoid using large tiles in areas where this situation will arise; instead, opt for smaller tiles that can be "moulded" around any undulations more effectively and give a better result.
- Rent a tile cutter: because larger tiles are sometimes thicker, they can be difficult to cut with standard tile cutters. It may be worth renting an electrically operated tile cutter from a local retail outlet. These can cut through nearly all tiles accurately. Follow the operating instructions carefully and wear all the recommended safety equipment, such as protective safety goggles and gloves.
- Covering large areas: large tiles are ideal for wide-open expanses of wall as they cover the area very quickly.
- Tiling gauges: when tiling with rectangular tiles, use two tiling gauges for planning the layout—one for tile height and the other for tile width.
- Avoid intricate areas: don't use large tiles in areas that require a lot of intricate cutting. Marking accurate curved cuts is always a tricky task, and is even more difficult when using larger tiles.
- Tiling floors: large tiles are usually associated with walls rather than floors, but it is worth considering continuing the tiles from the walls onto the floor surface. Check with your retailer to see if the tiles are suitable for floor use; if they are not, try to find some similar tiles. (See Chapter 5 for floor tiling technique.)
- Allow extra drying time: tile adhesive under large tiles tends to take longer to dry out than under small tiles, so leave support battens in place for long enough.

MARBLE TILES

Marble tiles produce a special effect by attempting to create the look of a natural surface, rather than the manufactured appearance of standard ceramic tiles. They are applied in a slightly different way than any other type of tile. Card is used instead of tile spacers to give a narrow grout joint between tiles, adding to the effect of a totally uninterrupted marble surface.

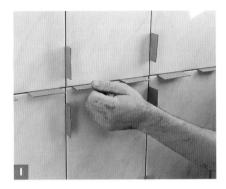

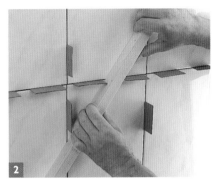

1 Apply marble tiles to the wall using ordinary tile adhesive, but use thin pieces of card to space the tiles. Remove the card spacers once the adhesive has set.

2 After each block of tiles has been applied, hold a wooden batten across the surface to check that all the tiles are sitting flush. Adjust any before the adhesive sets.

LUXURY FINISH
A completely marble tiled bathroom is both stylish and luxurious.

MARBLE TILE IDEAS

- Always use an electrically operated tile cutter on marble tiles (see page 350).
- Mitre external corner joints to produce a crisp marble edge.
- Use abrasive silicone carbide paper to sand any cuts that are not perfectly smooth.
- The attractiveness of a marble tiled surface depends on it being flat, so it is important to check that the tiles are sitting flush before the adhesive sets.

COMBINING SIZES

U sing different-size tiles within a design allows you to experiment with all sorts of patterns and colours. Some manufacturers produce different-size tiles that are designed specifically for use with one another: small insert tiles, for example, which can be used at the corners of larger hexagonal tiles. However, it is not necessary to take the lead from the manufacturer, and your own experiments can produce more individual designs.

DESIGN IDEAS

Simply taking two or three different colours of tiles, in two different sizes, allows for numerous possibilities when building up a design. Make sure that the dimensions of the small tiles divide into the dimensions of the large tiles, otherwise it will be difficult to create a pattern.

Simple rows: alternating rows of large tiles with rows of small tiles creates a simple but extremely effective design. Alternating the colours as well adds extra interest.

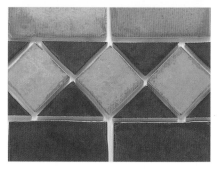

Checkerboards: arranging large tiles with groups of four smaller ones creates a lively variation on the standard checkerboard theme.

Diamonds: a diamond-shaped border running through the main body of larger tiles requires more cutting than the other designs, but is well worth all the extra effort when the tiling pattern is complete.

PLANNING

Once the design has been chosen, planning the actual tile application is important. A more extensive wall plan than usual is required, as it saves a great deal of time if the tiles are positioned in the correct place the first time.

Drawing the design: draw a reduced version of the design on graph paper, showing colours, shapes, and appropriate spacing of the tiles.

TILING A MULTI-SIZE DESIGN

It is important to be methodical and have an ordered approach while applying tiles in a multi-size design. When tackling more intricate areas, it is often easier to apply adhesive to the back of tiles and position them singly, rather than applying adhesive to large areas of the wall at a time and then rushing the tile application before the adhesive sets.

1 Attach supporting battens and apply the larger tiles in the usual way, following your design plan.

2 Gradually build up the smaller tile design, using plenty of spacers to maintain the gaps. Keep a constant check on the tiles to make sure that none have slipped.

3 Once the pattern is finished and the tile adhesive has set, remove the supporting battens and fill in the edges of the design.

DIAMOND PATTERN

Making a diamond pattern is an easy and effective way of
varying a tile design. Colour can be kept the same across the
entire surface or two or more colours can be used. Whichever look
you prefer, the tiles are applied in the same way but there is some
variation from the standard tiling procedure. Starting off correctly is
essential—the first tile forms the starting point for the entire design,
and small mistakes at the base will be accentuated as more tiles are
applied up the wall. The vertical batten provides a vital support, as it
prevents any tiles from slipping sideways as the rows are built up.

1 Attach the supporting
battens. Use a short
level to make sure that the
first tile is exactly vertical.

2 Gradually build up the tile levels, ensuring
the overall level is maintained. Once the
main body of tiles have dried, remove the
battens and use cut tiles to fill the gaps.

STRIKING PATTERNS
A diamond-pattern tile design
has a dramatic effect in any
room, adding character and
interest to surfaces.

BRICK BOND PATTERN

B rick bond patterns, as their name suggests, mimic the staggered look of building blocks or the jointing system of bricks in the structure of a house. Standard square tiles can be used, but rectangular tiles often provide a more authentic look. White or cream tiles provide a wonderfully minimalist finish, suitable for entire wall surfaces or use in smaller, detailed areas. Colours can be used, if preferred. Spacers need to be cut into a "T" shape to fit into the tile joints.

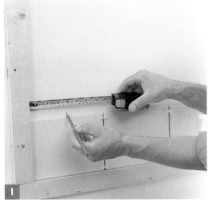

1 Apply the first row of tiles as usual. Measure halfway along the first tile and make a pencil mark on the wall. This gives the position for placing the first tile on the next row to produce the staggered effect.

2 Continue applying rows of tiles, measuring the starting point for each row as shown in Step 1. Once the adhesive under the main body of tiles has set, remove the battens and use cut tiles to fill the gaps.

ORDERED LOOK
Brick bond tiling produces a very ordered look on a wall surface. Here, the neutral colour scheme and large windows create an airy, modern effect.

HERRINGBONE PATTERN

Herringbone patterns, with their very distinctive interlocking
blocks, are usually associated with floor tiling or even outdoor
driveways. However, their decorative appeal looks equally good inside
the home. Rectangular tiles are used to create a herringbone pattern,
and, as with brick bond designs, spacers need to be cut into "T"
shapes to fit into the joints. Triangular supports have to be made to
support the first row of tiles. These are best made from plywood,
although any other thin building board can be used.

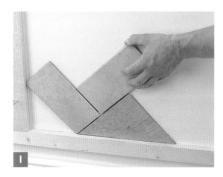

1 Nail the first triangular support
in place on the wall and build up
the herringbone design on top of it.

2 Continue along the wall surface,
interlocking the tiles and adding
triangular supports as required. Once
the design has been built up, leave
the adhesive to set, then remove the
battens and supports. Use cut tiles to
fill in around the edges.

DISTINCTIVE DESIGNS
Once you have mastered
the herringbone design, you
can go on to create all
manner of highly distinctive
designs that will dramatically
change the tiled surface.

5
TILING FLOORS

Tiled floors make an attractive and durable finish in any area of the home. In many ways, floor tiling is easier than tiling walls—there is less likelihood of tiles slipping out of position. However, it is still important that tiles are laid correctly and are not knocked out of position as the design is built up. As floor tiles tend to be larger and thicker than wall tiles, they are more cumbersome to handle, but practice will soon overcome initial problems. Floor tiles have to be hard-wearing as they will be walked on, and some sound subfloor preparation is essential.

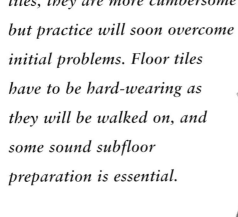

CHOOSING A DESIGN

T he choice of floor tiles is immense, and it can be difficult to decide which tiles are best suited to a particular room. Although many decisions will be influenced by the rest of the decoration in the room, when choosing floor tiles remember that they always create a bold statement and become an integral part of the room. It is important to think carefully before you buy floor tiles—they are expensive and will be on the floor a long time.

Kitchens: a kitchen benefits from a hard tiled floor since it is easy to clean and very durable. Edges can be hidden under cabinet units, making a professional finish easily achievable. The symmetrical design of a tiled floor such as this also complements the organized feel of a fitted kitchen.

ADVANTAGES AND DISADVANTAGES OF TILED FLOORS

It is worth weighing up the advantages and disadvantages before deciding on whether or not to lay a tile floor.

Advantages
- Highly decorative
- Withstands heavy wear and tear
- Low maintenance
- Lasts for years
- Easy to clean
- Practical in areas prone to damp

Disadvantages
- Often expensive
- Cold underfoot (although underfloor heating is an option)
- Easy for breakages to occur
- Cannot be taken with you when you move

Bathrooms: because bathrooms periodically get damp, a tiled floor makes an ideal surface—carpets are prone to rotting.

ESTIMATING QUANTITIES

- The simplest way to estimate how many tiles are needed for the job is to multiply the width and length dimensions of the room to obtain the floor surface area, then divide this figure by the surface area of one tile.
- For irregular rooms, calculations can be slightly more difficult and it may be easier to divide the room into smaller areas.
- Always add on between five and ten percent to the total tile figure to allow for breakages. Cutting around the edges of a room always takes more tiles than expected, as well. It is also useful to have a few tiles to replace any cracked tiles in the future.
- Buy slightly more adhesive than recommended by manufacturers: they often underestimate the amount needed to finish the job.

Other areas: hard tiles need not be confined to just kitchens and bathrooms; they can be used effectively in all areas of the home— their decorative appeal makes them a desirable finish for any room.

PREPARING WOODEN FLOOR SURFACES

Wooden floor surfaces need thorough preparation before tiles can be applied. The floor must be made rigid, as any movement once the tiles are laid will cause the tiles to move and crack the grout joints. The most common way of preparing a wooden floor for tiles is to make good the floorboard surface and lay a plywood or chipboard subfloor as a base for the tiles.

1 Check the entire floor area to see if any boards are loose. Knock in protruding nails with a hammer and punch, and screw down any boards that are not firmly in position.

2 Cover the floor with plywood with a minimum thickness of 18 mm (¾ in). Screw the sheets to the floorboards below, at intervals of 30 cm (12 in) in every direction.

3 Stagger the edges of the sheets of plywood, and make sure that the edges are butted up against each other.

CAUTION

When screwing into the floor surface, make sure that the screws you use are long enough to bite firmly into the floorboards, but not so long that they go beneath the boards and run the risk of damaging any service pipes and wires below floor level.

DEALING WITH FLEXIBILITY

However firmly fixed down a wooden floor is, there is always a danger that there will still be enough movement to put tile joints under stress. Some manufacturers recommend a specific system for dealing with flexible floors. The best course of action is to use a proprietary flexible floor adhesive for applying the tiles. Alternatively, some manufacturers now supply a proprietary tile sheet that is sandwiched between layers of adhesive and applied as shown below. Available in a variety of shapes and sizes, the sheet can be trimmed to size with a craft knife, if necessary.

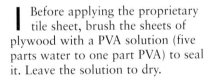

1 Before applying the proprietary tile sheet, brush the sheets of plywood with a PVA solution (five parts water to one part PVA) to seal it. Leave the solution to dry.

2 Apply tile adhesive to the floor, then, while it is still wet, unroll and stick down a proprietary tile sheet on top of the adhesive. Allow to dry, then apply adhesive over the sheet. Lay the tiles on top.

ADJUSTING OTHER LEVELS

Floor tiles raise the floor level, so you may need to consider other areas in the room that could be affected by this change.
- Doors: you may need to cut a little off the bottom of doors so that they will be able to open onto the newly tiled surface.
- Skirting: shallow skirting will look even smaller once tiles are applied to the floor. It is often better to remove the skirting before tiling and refit it when the floor is finished. This has the added advantage of covering the cuts around the edge of the room.
- Thresholds: as well as adjusting the door, it may be necessary to fit a threshold strip to make a clean dividing step between the tiles in one room and the floor covering in the next room.

PREPARING CONCRETE FLOOR SURFACES

C oncrete floor surfaces need less preparation than wooden ones—
there is no need to worry about the rigidity of a concrete base, as
it is far less prone to movement than wood. The main emphasis is on
making sure that the floor is level and clean, and that there are no
impurities on the surface that could react with the adhesive and affect
its ability to stick the tiles.

REMOVING OLD FLOOR COVERINGS

It is essential that you take up old floor coverings—carpet, vinyl, and other
miscellaneous coverings—before applying tiles. The only exception is when
there is a well-established old tiled floor as a base. These existing tiles must be
firmly stuck down and all polish or sealant coatings removed before new tiles
can be applied.

1 Use a spade to pry underneath
stubborn old linoleum or vinyl
flooring that has been glued down.
Scrape it away from the concrete
surface below.

2 Once all the old flooring has
been taken up, remove any
remnants of old glue with a scraper.
Use a proprietary glue remover to aid
this process, if necessary.

3 Brush and thoroughly clean the
whole floor. When it is clean,
apply one coat of proprietary floor
sealer to the entire area and leave it
to dry before tiling.

FILLING HOLES

Years of wear and tear can take their toll, so there may be some areas of an old concrete floor that require extra preparation before tiles can be laid. It is important to fill in any cracks and holes so that the entire surface is level. Failure to fill holes will make tiling more difficult and waste adhesive. Dust out holes and dampen them before filling them.

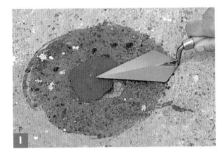

1 Fill large holes with a standard sand and cement mix (one part cement to four parts sand, mixed with water to a stodgy consistency). Smooth the filled area with a trowel.

2 For more undulating floors, it is necessary to return the concrete screed to a level base. Mix up some proprietary self-levelling compound and pour it onto the floor surface.

3 Using a steel float, spread the compound across the entire floor. It will find its own level, gathering more in any depressions in the floor. Once dry, the compound produces a perfectly level finish.

NEW CONCRETE SCREEDS

With a new concrete surface, or screed, a little care has to be taken before tiling, even though the surface may be perfectly level.
- Damp course: the screed must be laid over a damp course membrane, otherwise rising moisture will lift a tiled surface.
- Priming: always seal new screeds with a proprietary sealer.

- Checking dryness: even when a screed appears to be dry, it is worth using a damp meter to check that this is the case. Depending on depth, some screeds can take weeks or even months to dry out fully. Ask your tile supplier what the optimum damp meter reading should be before you use a particular type of tile on a new concrete screed.

WHERE TO START

A s with all tiling projects, it is essential to begin in the right place. No room is completely square, so it is never possible to start in one corner and tile around the room. Instead, you have to find the centre of the room and make your calculations based on this point so that all the cut tiles will be around the edge of the room.

FINDING THE CENTRE OF A ROOM

Finding the centre of a relatively square or rectangular room is fairly simple. For more awkwardly shaped rooms, the principle of measuring the centre of wall dimensions is still the same.

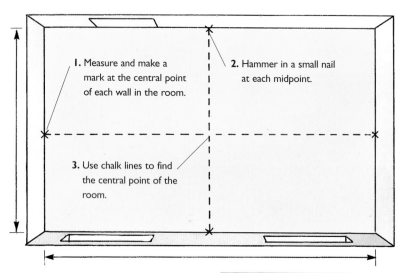

1. Measure and make a mark at the central point of each wall in the room.

2. Hammer in a small nail at each midpoint.

3. Use chalk lines to find the central point of the room.

Snapping a line: attach a chalk line between two of the nails on opposite walls. Making sure that it is tight, lift the line above the floor surface, and then let go to allow the line to "snap" onto the floor. When the line is removed, a chalk impression is left behind to provide a precise guideline across the centre of the room. Attach the line to the other two opposite nails and repeat the process. The second line will bisect the first and thus give the exact central point of the room.

PLANNING THE LAYOUT

The easiest method—laying tiles from the centre of the room outward—can trap the tiler in a corner. The best plan is to use the central line as a guide, and move this guideline toward the wall farthest from the door. Tiles can then be applied continuously toward the door, allowing the tiler to get out of the room without walking on setting tiles.

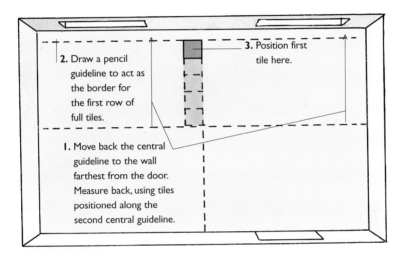

2. Draw a pencil guideline to act as the border for the first row of full tiles.

3. Position first tile here.

1. Move back the central guideline to the wall farthest from the door. Measure back, using tiles positioned along the second central guideline.

3. Once the full tiles have dried, fill in around the edge of the room with cut tiles.

1. Work away from the first tile toward the far corner of the room. It is often easier to apply two rows of tiles at a time.

2. Work away from the other side of the first tile and continue in rows until the door is reached and all the full tiles have been laid.

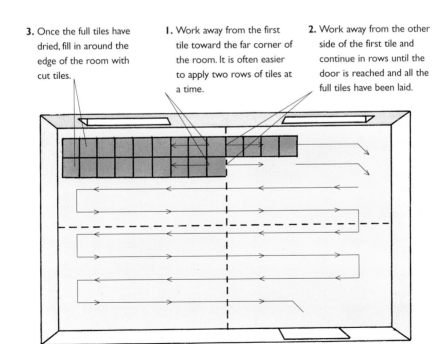

LAYING THE FIRST TILES

B efore laying the first tiles, make sure that all tools are at hand and that the floor surface is free of any obstructions. The first tiles are the cornerstone of the whole floor and must be positioned correctly. Apply tile adhesive evenly and keep tools, hands, and tiles as clean as possible while tiling.

GUIDELINES

Although a pencil line acts as a good guideline for placing tiles in position, it is very easy to accidentally knock tiles out of position, and this may go unnoticed until the adhesive has set. It is safer to nail a wooden batten along the pencil guideline, then the first row of tiles can be butted up to this batten.

1 Nail a wooden batten along the pencil guideline for the first row of tiles to butt up against.

2 Apply tile adhesive to the floor in areas of one square metre (yard). This should provide enough adhesive coverage for two rows of tiles to be applied at a time.

3 Press the first tile into position tight up against the batten, making sure that the tile is also aligned with the central guideline of the adjacent wall.

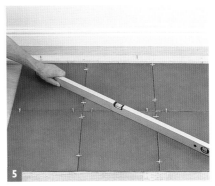

4 Fit spacers perpendicular, or upright, to the tile surface rather than flat on the floor between tiles (see below, right).

5 Once a block of six or more tiles has been laid, check that the tiles are level; adjust adhesive levels if any are sticking out or have sunk.

6 Sponge the tile surface with clean water as you progress across the floor, to keep it clean and free of any adhesive.

SPACERS

Spacers are fitted perpendicular to the tile surface rather than flat on the floor between tiles so that they can be removed when the adhesive has set. Because the floor surface must be durable, the grout needs to be as deep as possible. Spacers left in place, reduce the depth of grout and create a weakness.

CUTTING TILES

F loor tiles are cut in the same way as wall tiles with a few minor variations. Use a good quality hand-held tile cutter, or tile cutting machine, and make sure that you measure and cut accurately. If you have a lot of thicker floor tiles to cut, it may be worth renting an electrically operated tile cutting machine.

1 Where the tiles on the floor and the skirting run parallel, place the tile to be cut on top of the adjacent tile, butting the edge of it against the skirting or wall. Mark where it needs to be cut, allowing for spacers and therefore grout.

2 Where the distance between the last full tile and the wall surface is not consistent all the way along the wall, measure the distance with a tape measure and transfer the measurements to the tile before cutting it.

3 Clamp the tile in the tile cutting machine. Applying downward pressure on the cutting wheel, push it across the tile surface to score it. Position the tile above the cutting wheel and below the sliding rails, and snap down with the machine handle to cut the tile.

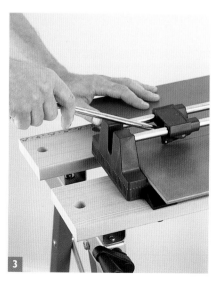

4 Use the tile file to remove any jagged edges along the cut tile. Larger lumps and bumps can be nipped away with tile nippers.

5 Check that the tile fits the gap before applying adhesive directly to the back of the tile.

6 Position the cut tile, making sure that the factory edge is jointed with the main body of tiles and the cut edge faces the skirting or wall. Use spacers in the usual way.

Using a profile gauge: this is the ideal tool for producing a precise outline of intricate areas, such as a door architrave. The gauge is adjustable and moulds around any surface. The outline can be transferred onto a tile and used as a guide for cutting with a tile saw.

MAKING TEMPLATES FOR FLOOR TILES

Tiling a floor inevitably involves some intricate cutting. Profile gauges (see page 369) can be used in some areas, but a paper template is often the best way of dealing with awkward areas. Make sure that the tile saw blade is sharp enough to cope with intricate cuts.

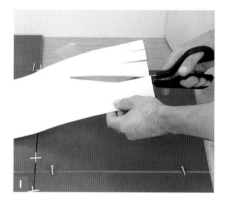

1 Cut a piece of paper to the size of tile needed, as if there were no obstacle for cutting around. Cut slits along the edge of the paper to correspond with the obstacle that needs cutting around.

2 Position the paper as if it were a tile, allowing the slits to lap up onto the obstacle (a sink pedestal is shown here). Crease the slits along the floor/pedestal junction and mark along the crease with a pencil.

3 Remove the paper, flatten out the slits, then cut along the pencil guideline to produce an exact template of the pedestal profile.

4 Holding the template firmly in position on the tile to be cut, draw along the curve of the template with a fibre-tip pen.

5 Clamp the marked tile in the workbench. To prevent the cut portion from snapping off before the cut is complete, saw halfway along the fibre-tip line, then turn the tile and saw the other half. Support the cut part with your other hand once it nears breaking away.

6 File away any rough edges, then apply tile adhesive to the back of the tile and position it next to the pedestal. Insert spacers between the tiles in the usual way.

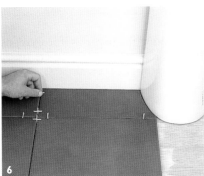

TEMPLATE GUIDELINES

It is hard work sawing through a floor tile, so always double-check the template measurements and the guideline on the tile to make sure that they are correct before starting to saw. For intricate shapes, it may be necessary to cut more slits in the template so that it can be moulded accurately around the obstacle.

GROUTING FLOOR TILES

U nglazed tiles must be sealed with a proprietary sealer before
grouting, to prevent grout from becoming ingrained in the tile
surface. However, most tiles are already glazed and grouting can take
place as soon as the adhesive has set. Remove the spacers before
grouting. Always use grout that is specifically designed for floors—wall
tile grout is not as durable. Floor grout has a coarser texture, so it is
essential that it is well mixed with no dry or lumpy areas.

1 Put the grout in a bucket and
gradually add cold water until
the mixture is a firm but pliable
consistency. Wear protective gloves
since prolonged exposure to grout
can cause skin irritation.

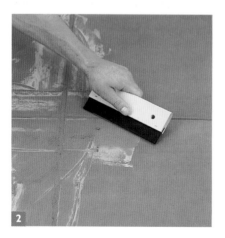

2 Apply the grout to the tiles with
a grout spreader, working the
spreader in all directions across the
tile joints to ensure that every joint is
filled with grout.

3 Using a damp sponge, wipe away
the excess grout from the tiled
surface after every few tiles have
been grouted—it is much harder to
remove grout from tile surfaces when
it has set.

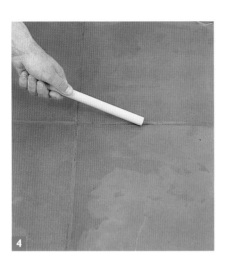

4 Smooth the grout joints with a piece of wooden dowel, making each grouted joint into a concave trough shape. Wipe away excess grout with a damp sponge.

5 Once the grout has dried, polish the tiles with a dry cotton rag to remove the thin cloudy residue of dilute grout. Each tile will need to be wiped two or three times to remove all the residue.

6 Replace the skirting board if it was removed before tiling the floor. The skirting board will hide the cut edges of the tiles.

GROUTING COLOUR

Because floor grout is produced in many different colours, you can choose a suitable grout for the tiles you are using. It is normally best to use a dark complementary grout colour because light contrasting colours show the dirt more easily, and stains in the grout will be more noticeable. Darker colours tend to be the more hard-wearing option.

WOOD-BASED TILES

C ork and parquet panels are attractive floorcoverings, providing relatively hard-wearing surfaces that are easy to clean. Traditional parquet floors are made from individual wooden blocks; today, there are tile-size panels available that are easier to lay.

LAYING CORK TILES

Make sure that cork tiles are laid out dry in the room to be tiled for two to three days before application, so that they can become accustomed to the atmospheric conditions of the room. Find the centre of the room (see page 364) and measure back to one of the farthest walls to find the best starting point, then draw in the starting line, as required. Only apply adhesive to an area of the floor large enough for a working period of about 20 minutes at a time.

1 Apply adhesive to the floor using a notched spreader. Leave it for 30 minutes until it is "tacky." Apply the first tile at the junction between the starting line and the bisecting room line.

2 Continue to lay tiles, butt-joining the edges. Cork tiles can be cut, as required, using a craft knife and a straight edge. Fit cut tiles around the edge of the room, as needed.

3 Once quite a few of the tiles have been laid, use a rolling pin across the tile surfaces to ensure that they are all well bedded into the adhesive and that they are level.

FINISHING THE FLOOR

Some cork tiles have a prefinished surface, and they require no extra treatment once laid. However, in other cases, it will be necessary to seal the surface once it has dried, using the varnish or sealant that the manufacturer recommends. No preparation is required, it is simply brushed onto the cork tiles.

LAYING PARQUET PANELS

As with all wooden floorcoverings, parquet panels should be allowed to acclimatize to the atmospheric conditions within the room before they are laid. The period of time should be weeks rather than days, if possible, because the jointing system of parquet panels requires time to adjust completely before they are fixed in place.

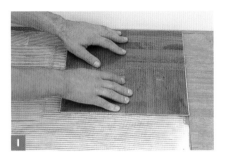

1 If the room dimensions allow for it, and the wall adjacent to the starting line (see page 364) is relatively square, begin laying panels along a starting line that is the width of the cork expansion strips away from the wall (see below). This distance is usually 12 mm (½ in). As with cork tiles, allow the adhesive to go "tacky" before applying the panels.

2 Parquet panels are joined using an interlocking tongue-and-groove system. Build up the rows of panels until the floor is complete. Using an ordinary handsaw, cut panels to fit the edges, as required. Finish around the edge of the whole room, next to the wall, by inserting cork expansion strips.

3 Cover the expansion strips by nailing a piece of quadrant beading around the floor perimeter. Secure it in place by knocking in brads through the quadrant and into the skirting. The quadrant can then be stained to match the floor finish, or painted to match the skirting. Alternatively, remove the skirting before applying the panels, then replace them afterward, covering the cork expansion strips.

CORK EXPANSION STRIPS

Flexible cork expansion strips are a necessary requirement for parquet panel floors. They absorb any slight movement by the floor panels.

LAYING HEAVY-DUTY TILES

The most common heavy-duty floor tiles are quarry tiles. Although smaller in size than most floor tiles, they are considerably thicker and require laying on a bed of sand and cement (mortar), rather than being stuck down with standard floor-tile adhesive.

1 Nail a support batten parallel to the wall. Measure out a section to be battened off, using some tiles laid dry and including spacers. Nail in two more battens to section off the area. Remove the tiles.

2 Mix the mortar, using four parts sand to one part cement. Stir them together then gradually mix in enough water to make a stodgy consistency.

3 Pour the mortar into the area that is sectioned off with battens and spread it with a trowel, getting it as level as possible at a depth of about 12 mm (½ in).

4 Lay tiles on the mortared surface and give them a tap with the butt end of a hammer to bed them in. Fit spacers perpendicular to the tile surface.

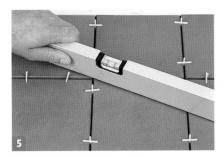

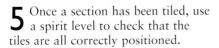

5 Once a section has been tiled, use a spirit level to check that the tiles are all correctly positioned.

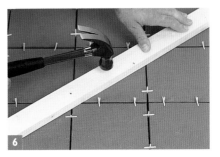

6 Hold a wooden batten across the tiled surface and give it one or two taps with a hammer along its length to ensure that the tiles are well bedded in and level. Allow to set, then remove the battens and spacers before tiling another section. Some tiles will need to be cut to finish around the edge of the room. A standard tile cutter will cut some varieties; however, it is easier to rent an electrically operated tile cutter if the tiles are particularly hard.

WORKING IN SECTIONS

Once the usual support batten has been nailed parallel to the wall, you need to nail in two more battens at right angles to act as barriers that will prevent the mortar from spreading too far across the floor. Sectioning off areas also makes it much easier to keep the mortar and the tiles level.

GROUTING HEAVY-DUTY TILES

Quarry tiles can be grouted with ordinary floor tile grout, but heavier flagstones and natural stone tiles need to be grouted with a sand/cement mix (mortar) to create a long-lasting seal. In both cases, the aim is still to fill all joints as neatly as possible.

Grouting quarry tiles: follow the normal floor tile procedure and spread the grout across the surface, making sure that it gets into all the joints. Clean off the excess with a damp sponge as you proceed across the floor.

Grouting flagstones: use a pointing trowel to press mortar into the gaps between the stones. Gently smooth over the mortar with an old paint brush, creating a well-defined edge to the junction between mortar and stone.

RUSTIC FEEL
Natural stone floors are the most durable of all floor coverings and give a lovely rustic feel to a room.

6
REPAIRING AND RENOVATING TILES

However well tiled a surface is, it is likely that at some point you will need to carry out repair work—it is much better to replace a single damaged tile than the whole surface. Old tile surfaces can be renovated, and sometimes even the shabbiest of floors can be given a new lease on life. This chapter deals with the many areas related to working on existing tiles, either improving their look or changing their appearance to suit the required need.

REPLACING DAMAGED TILES

The most common repair to any tiled surface is replacing a cracked or broken tile. Although tiles have a hard surface, they can be cracked by too much physical abuse. In some cases, they simply have a weakness that causes cracking over time. Replacing a tile is a relatively simple procedure that can be carried out without damaging any of the surrounding tiles.

REMOVING AN OLD TILE

In some cases, a damaged tile may lift out of place easily; unfortunately, most of the time they need far more persuasion—although the tile may be broken, the adhesive holding the various pieces is as strong as ever.

1 Loosen the grout around the edge of the cracked tile with a grout raker, running the blade up and down the joint quite vigorously. Take care not to damage the edges of surrounding tiles.

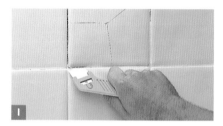

2 Wearing safety goggles to protect your eyes from any flying debris, drill a number of small holes across the surface of the broken tile to break up and weaken the entire tile.

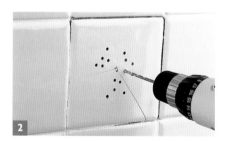

3 Use a hammer and cold chisel to knock out the broken up tile, taking care not to dig the point of the chisel into the wall surface underneath (see below).

BROKEN PIECES

As broken pieces of tile are gradually removed, it becomes easier to position the chisel in a levering position behind the fragments of tile to remove them. Always wear protective goggles while carrying out this procedure.

Inserting The New Tile

Compared with removing broken tiles, inserting a new tile is a relatively simple procedure. Tile replacement is a good reason for keeping a few spare tiles after each new tiling project is finished, rather than trying to buy a matching tile at a later date.

1 Use a scraper to make sure that all the old adhesive and splinters of tile are removed from the wall, leaving a relatively smooth surface for the new tile.

2 Apply tile adhesive to the back of the new tile and carefully position it in the hole.

3 Hold a wooden strip across the new tile and the surrounding tile area to check that the new tile is positioned flush with all the other tiles. Adjust the new tile before the adhesive sets, if necessary.

4 Apply spacers perpendicular to the tile surface to maintain the required gap around the new tile. Once the adhesive has set, remove the spacers and grout around the joints of the replacement tile.

DRILLING TILES

A dding a new fixture to tiles poses the problem of attaching it. Although there are many self-adhesive hanging mechanisms available, by far the most secure system always involves screw fixings and brackets. Drilling into tiles to anchor such screw fixings is a straightforward process as long as the correct procedure is followed.

1 Position the fixing bracket in the centre of a tile. Make a mark with a dark-coloured fibre-tip pen to show the required fixing points, using a level to keep the bracket precisely vertical.

2 Stick a piece of masking tape over the fibre-tip marks and redraw the bracket position. (Masking tapes are generally transparent enough to make this re-marking possible.)

3 Using a tile drill bit, drill holes into the tiles at the marks. Hold the bit against the tile surface before starting it, to prevent the drill from jumping across the tile. The masking tape prevents the bit from sliding.

4 To reduce mess, hold a vacuum cleaner nozzle under the holes to catch the dust that comes out as they are drilled. Red brick or concrete dust could discolour the grout.

5 Remove the masking tape and press a wall plug the same size as the drill bit into each hole—tap them with the butt end of a hammer, if necessary.

6 Screw in the fixing bracket, checking that it is level. Make sure that the screws bite firmly into the wall plug as they are screwed in.

7 Attach the fixture to the bracket. This usually requires tightening a small set screw found at the base of the fixture.

CAUTION

Try to avoid positioning fixtures too near the edge of tiles as it spoils the aesthetic look, and drilling near the edge of tiles runs the risk of cracking or chipping them.

CHANGING GROUT

G rout deteriorates over time, becoming stained. To keep the tile surface looking clean and bright, you may need to regrout the tiles at least once during the life span of the surface—particularly in areas that are constantly under attack from water, such as shower cubicles and splashbacks.

REGROUTING

Although regrouting is time consuming, it can totally rejuvenate the tiles and is far more economic than complete tile replacement. A grout raker is the ideal tool for removing the old grout, or the edge of a scraper can be used.

1 Use the grout raker along all the joints on the tiled surface. Take care not to scratch the edges of tiles, and be sure to remove as much of the old grout as possible.

2 Regrout the whole surface using the normal technique (see pages 318–319), taking care to work the grout into all the joints.

KEEPING GROUT CLEAN

There are a number of ways of lengthening the life span of grout.
- Polish the surface with a silicone-based spray. This cleans the tiles as well as sealing the grout, making it much more difficult for water to penetrate it.

- Make sure that bathrooms have extractor fans, so the damp air is not allowed to linger in the room.
- Rinse down the tiles in a shower cubicle after use, and make sure that dripping shower heads or taps are fixed as soon as possible.

CHANGING COLOUR

Grout does not have to be white, and regrouting provides the opportunity for a colour change. A contrasting colour to the tiles can be used, or, as shown here, a similar colour gives a very even and coordinated surface. Proprietary coloured grouts often have different mixing systems; however, in most cases it is possible to vary the colour intensity of the grout and produce a colour that matches or complements the tiles.

1 Wearing protective gloves, mix up the powdered grout in a bucket, adding enough water to make a smooth creamy consistency.

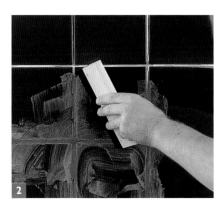

2 Apply the grout over the entire surface with a grout spreader, taking care to work the grout into all the tile joints.

3 Remove the excess grout from the tiles with a damp sponge. Allow the grout to set, then polish the tiles in the usual way.

MAINTAINING GROUT AND SILICONE

In many cases where the grout is stained it is possible to perform a general maintenance job, rather than complete replacement of grout. Silicone seals may need renewing if they are discoloured or if the seal has broken and is letting in water.

CLEANING GROUT

Partially discoloured white grout can often be revived by simple cleaning with a diluted bleach solution. This has the effect of removing dirt and grime, and bringing the grout back to its original colour.

Using a toothbrush: apply the diluted bleach solution to the grout with an old toothbrush, scrubbing vigorously along all the joints. Wear protective gloves, and rinse the tiled surface thoroughly with clean water after cleaning with bleach.

GROUT CLEANING KITS

Small kits produced specifically for cleaning white grout can be used very successfully. These literally "paint" the grout in order to bring it back to its original bright white finish.

1 Use a fitch brush to apply the grout cleaning solution along all the tile joints. Leave it on for the recommended time.

2 Once the grout has dried, remove the excess fluid from the tiled surface with a clean, damp sponge.

REAPPLYING SEALANT

As well as improving the overall look, reapplying sealant renews the water seal between tiles and other surfaces. Most reapplications are required around basins, in shower cubicles or, as shown here, around the edge of a bath.

1 Using a craft knife, cut away the old silicone seal. Cut into the junction to avoid scratching the surface of the bath.

2 For areas of tough sealant, apply a proprietary solvent and allow it to soak in for the time recommended by the manufacturer.

3 Use a scraper to remove the residue, taking care to keep the blade flat on the bath surface to avoid scratching it.

4 Run masking tape along each side of the junction and then apply a new bead of sealant (see pages 320–321). Remove the tape as soon as the sealant is applied.

PAINTING TILES

Tiles can be given an alternative finish by painting them. The finish of painted tiles will not be as durable as the ordinary glazed surface but, as long as the painted tiles are not under constant water attack, they have a good life expectancy.

PRIMING THE TILES

Changing the entire surface colour of tiles requires thorough preparation to make sure that the paint adheres to the tiled surface. Before beginning, ensure that any gaps in the grout are filled and any broken tiles are replaced.

1 Clean the tiled surface with a mild detergent solution and then rinse with clean water. Allow the whole surface to dry.

2 Rub down the surface with abrasive silicon carbide paper. This scratches the glazed surface of the tiles and provides a key for the paint. Once sanded, wipe down the area again with a damp sponge to remove any dusty residue. Allow the surface to dry.

3 Paint the entire tile surface with proprietary tile primer and leave it to dry. This paint is specially formulated to provide a sound base for the application of coats of finishing paint.

CREATING A DESIGN

Most types of paint can be used to produce the desired colour or finish, as long as they are sealed with varnish after they have been applied. As an alternative to one solid colour, any number of different tile patterns can be created—the checkerboard design below is one simple, yet effective example.

Painting a checkerboard: paint the entire primed surface with white latex paint then paint alternate tiles with black latex paint. Use a fine paint brush to produce neat straight lines. Leave the paint to dry, then varnish the entire tiled surface to protect the finish.

USING CERAMICS

For the more adventurous decorator, small hand-painted designs can be applied to tiles with ceramic paint. Again, this paint finish should only be used in areas that are not under regular water attack.

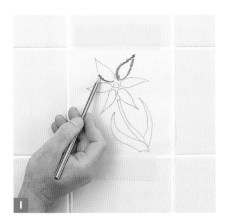

1 Trace a design from a book using a pencil. Stick the image to a tile with masking tape, making sure that it is centrally positioned on the tile and the penciled side of the tracing paper is against the tile surface. Scribble over the outlines to transfer the pencil image onto the tile.

2 Remove the tracing paper, and carefully fill in the design, using ceramic paints. Allow the paint to dry, then varnish the entire tile surface to protect the design.

TRANSFERS AND STENCILS

Transfers and stencils are excellent decorations for transforming the look of tiles, especially when an old surface needs reviving, rather than totally replacing. Although transfers give a less hard-wearing surface than the standard glazed tiles, they are becoming more durable and are therefore perfectly acceptable to use on tiles.

APPLYING TRANSFERS

Transfers are fairly delicate, and they require a great deal of care when moving them from their backing paper onto the tile. Manufacturers' guidelines vary, but this method is typical of the procedure recommended for most types.

1 Clean the tile that is going to have the transfer applied to it with a mild detergent, then rinse with clean water. Leave it to dry.

2 Soak the transfer (on its backing paper) in warm water for about 20 seconds, then apply directly to the tile, as close to the required position as possible. The transfer should slide off the backing paper smoothly—the dampness of the area allows for final positioning of it before evaporation secures the image in place.

3 Using a dry rag, very carefully dab the surface of the transfer to remove any small air bubbles and excess moisture.

STENCILLING TILES

Most paints can be used to stencil on tiles—it is the method of protecting the finish that is the secret of making sure that a stenciled image is long-lasting. Tiles can be primed first (see page 388), but it is not essential for such detailed painted areas. Make sure that the tiles are cleaned and allowed to dry thoroughly before applying the stencil.

1 Stick the stencil securely in position on the tile surface using masking tape.

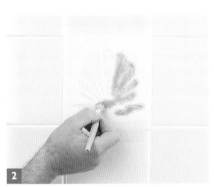

2 Apply paint with a stencil brush, using short dabbing motions and keeping the angle of the bristles as perpendicular as possible to the tiled surface. Remove the excess paint from the brush before applying it, otherwise the paint may seep under the edges of the stencil and distort the finished picture.

3 Remove the stencil carefully and leave the paint to dry. Meanwhile, wash the stencil and dry it thoroughly. Tape the stencil directly over the dried painted image on the tile, and apply some ceramic varnish, using the stencil brush. Make sure that all areas of the image are covered. Remove the stencil and allow the varnish to dry, producing a well-protected stencil image.

RESTORING AN OLD TILED FLOOR

I ndividual taste and preferences vary greatly, and what suits one person might not suit another. This means it is quite common for people to restore or expose areas within the home that previous owners felt were unattractive—old tiled floor surfaces that have been covered with carpet by one person, provide an ideal restoration project for another.

1 Lift and remove the old carpet. Much of the poor condition of the tiles below the carpet will be due to discolouration or old adhesive and dust from the carpet.

2 Use a scraper to remove any large areas of glue and carpet backing that is partially stuck down. Keep the scraper blade flat with the tile surface to avoid scratching.

3 Wash down the surface with clean water, using wire wool to remove any stubborn areas of dirt or grime. If necessary, use a proprietary tile cleaning solution to remove any ingrained dirt.

4 Finally, run a window scraper along all the grout lines and in any small depressions on the tiled surface to remove the last specks of dust and debris, and ensure the surface is as smooth as possible.

5 Clean down the entire surface once more with a mild detergent solution, then rinse thoroughly with clean water.

6 Apply a proprietary floor sealer to give the cleaned tiles a hard-wearing finish and to prepare them for everyday traffic.

RESTORING ORIGINALS
An old restored tile floor tends to have more character than a newly laid equivalent. Colour variations and time create a greater feeling of texture and authenticity.

REPAIRING A DAMAGED FLOOR

B oth old and relatively new floor tiles may need repairing or replacing at some point. As with wall tiles, repairs are relatively simple and far more economic than replacing the entire surface. However, floor tiles are much tougher than wall tiles, and this must be taken into account when doing repairs.

REPLACING A FLOOR TILE

Floor tiles sometimes crack because they were laid poorly, or there may be a weakness within the tile that can lead to cracking over a period of time. Whatever the cause, a cracked tile needs to be replaced since it is not possible to repair it successfully.

1 Wearing goggles to protect your eyes from any flying debris, drill a number of holes randomly across the entire tile surface to weaken it. Loosen the grout around the edges of the tile with the corner of a scraper.

2 Use a hammer and bolster chisel to break up the tile surface. Do not position the chisel near the edge of the tile or you may damage the surrounding tiles. Remove the broken pieces of tile.

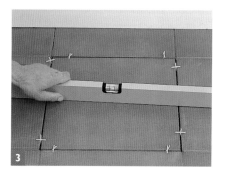

3 Clear any debris before applying the new tile on a fresh bed of tile adhesive. Use spacers in the joints, and hold a spirit level across the tile to check that it sits flush with the surrounding area. Allow the adhesive to set, remove the spacers, and grout the tile joints.

MAKING GOOD DAMAGED AREAS

Small chips or dents don't really warrant full tile replacement—they can be dealt with in a less dramatic manner. Most marks on tiles are superficial and can be wiped away with a proprietary cleaning solution; however, if a heavy item has been dropped on the tile and chipped the surface, some camouflage work is required to hide the damage.

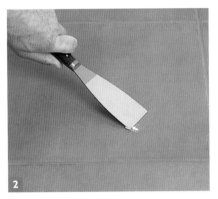

1 Brush away any dust or loose chips from the damaged area of the tile. Blow gently to remove any dust from the bottom of the hole, if necessary.

2 Mix some stainable filler and press it firmly into the hole with a filler knife. Make it as neat as possible so that it does not require sanding once dry.

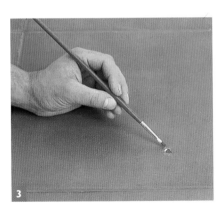

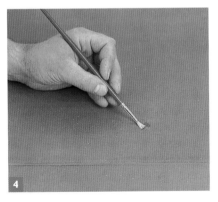

3 When the filler is dry, paint the repaired area with an oil-based paint that matches the surrounding tile colour.

4 Allow the paint to dry, then protect the repair by applying some proprietary floor-tile sealant to the immediate area.

RENOVATING SLATE FLOORS

The texture of riven slate tiles makes them more prone to picking up dirt than the flatter surface of normal ceramic tiles, and this means that slate floors require more attention than standard tile floors. From time to time, they need rigorous and thorough cleaning in order to keep the slates looking in the best condition possible.

1 The ideal tool for cleaning slate tiles is a wallpaper stripper with the broad stripping plate removed to leave just the steam supply pipe. Directing the steam at ingrained areas of dirt aids the removal process and leads to a much cleaner floor. Always wear protective gloves and goggles when using a steam stripper, and follow the manufacturer's instructions for use.

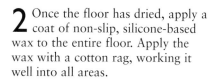

2 Once the floor has dried, apply a coat of non-slip, silicone-based wax to the entire floor. Apply the wax with a cotton rag, working it well into all areas.

3 Allow the wax to dry, then buff up the surface to give a highly polished finish. An electric buffer is ideal, but a broom with a cloth pad attached works just as well.

RENOVATING FLAGSTONES

Flagstones are generally the most heavy-duty form of home flooring, and they can require occasional maintenance. Periodic application of sealant and making minor repairs will keep flagstones in excellent condition and looking good for many years.

1 Joint failure within the flagstone can cause areas to flake away from its surface. Where these become deeper holes, use a hammer and cold chisel to remove the loose chips of stone. Wear gloves and goggles to protect your eyes and hands from any flying debris.

2 Dust out the area and dampen with a little water. Mix up some exterior filler or sand and cement. Adjust the amount of filler/cement added to the mix to achieve a reasonable colour match with the surrounding stones. Press it firmly into the hole.

3 Clean the remainder of the flagstones thoroughly, then apply a proprietary sealer to cover the repaired area as well as the rest of the stone.

CAUTION

Where flagstones have been laid without a damp-course membrane, underneath them they often allow the damp up through them to evaporate into the atmosphere. Sealing the stones is not appropriate in this case, as the sealant itself will not adhere to the flagstone surface and applying it will also upset this natural drying process.

QUICK MAKEOVERS

R eplacing tiles is an effective way of changing the look of a room, but it can be a time-consuming operation. Fortunately, there are options other than full replacement of the tiles—it is possible to give a tiled surface a different look by adding some extra decoration. Also, if some of the tiles on a surface are damaged, individual tiles can be replaced, rather than have to retile the whole area. If you do decide to retile, remember that as long as the old tiles are stuck down firmly, they can be used as a base for the new tiles. This will save a lot of preparation time and speed up the project quite considerably.

TILING MAKEOVERS

If retiling is not an option, it is possible to refurbish existing tiles and create a totally different look with any of the following ideas.

- Borders: adding border tiles to an existing design can have the effect of revitalizing the whole surface. There are various options when choosing borders—even using full tiles of a contrasting colour will provide a fresh looking finish.
- Paint: old tiles can be painted as long as they are prepared properly. Use either a tile primer or a proprietary surface preparation compound on the tiles before applying any coats of paint.
- Reviving grout: many tiled surfaces are let down, not by the look of the tiles themselves, but by the poor condition of the grout between the tiles. Use a grout raker to remove the old grout before regrouting the whole tiled surface. Since it is possible to buy grout in different colours, you can use it to make a decorative contrast with the tiles.
- Replacing sealant: sealant acts as a waterproof seal around tiled areas.

However, it will deteriorate over time. Cutting out the old seal and replacing with new, will give a neater and brighter finish. Alternatively, a decorative wooden moulding can be used as a seal. Paint it first and position it using sealant.

- Stencils and stamps: revive an old tiled surface by using stencils or stamps to paint designs onto the tiles. Use ceramic paints and then varnish the painted tiles. This design technique is not ideal for areas where there is a lot moisture, such as shower cubicles or splashbacks.
- Transfers: tile transfers can be used in a similar way to stencils, to add a picture or design to individual tiles. As with stencils, transfers are not ideal for use on tiles that suffer regular water attack.
- Adding picture tiles: remove a few of the old tiles from the surface (see opposite for the technique) and substitute them with picture tiles.
- Change a splashback: rather than retiling the entire area, simply tiling a new splashback can revitalize the look of the whole tiled surface.

APPENDIX: TOOLS FOR THE JOB

GENERAL TOOLS

It is impossible to carry out a refurbishment without the appropriate tools for the task. Because this book covers so many areas of home improvement, it is not possible to illustrate every tool you may need. Instead, try to build up a general toolbox that will cover most of the jobs in the home. The tools illustrated here are all useful ones to have.

Hot-air gun

Chisels

Electrical tape

Adjustable wrench

Tape measure

Profile gauge

Workbench

Brick chisel

Sander

Staple gun

Short level

Dust mask

Standard handsaw

Cordless drill/driver

Hacksaw

Jigsaw

Hammer

Plastering float

Stepladder

Mitre block

Straight-blade screwdrivers

Cross-head screwdrivers

Plier wrench

PLUMBING TOOLS

N ever make compromises on plumbing tools, since the correct ones are essential for achieving the right result. In addition to a general tool kit, the household plumber needs a few extra items. Most of these can be found in home improvement centres: however, for some items you may need to go to a store for professionals—the bonus of this is being able to get advice from the experts.

Hole saw
For cutting pipe-size holes through walls.

Pipe cutter
Makes cuts through copper or plastic pipe.

Plumbing tape
Makes threaded joints watertight.

Pipe bender
For bending small diameter copper pipes.

Long-nosed pliers
Ideal for detailed work in awkward places.

Pipe wrench
Has movable jaws to grip onto most sizes of pipe.

Adjustable pliers
Has movable jaws for maximum gripping strength.

Sink wrench
Allows easy access to tap connectors below the sink.

Gas torch
For soldering pipe joints.

Plunger
For unblocking toilets and waste pipes.

PAINTING AND WALLPAPERING TOOLS

W hatever the decorating task, the correct tools for the job will help you achieve the best possible finish, so don't compromise on the equipment requirements. Using tools specifically designed for a particular job also makes that job far easier to carry out. Not all the decorating tools are required for every task—a papering and painting toolbox can be built up gradually over time, according to need.

PAINTING EQUIPMENT

Small, long-handled roller

Fine paint brush

Extension pole

Roller handle and sleeve

Mini roller

Paint roller pan

Window scraper

Small paint pad

Triangle scraper

Paint brushes

Filling knife

Paint pad

Paint pad and application handle

Hot-air gun

Glass shield

Dust mask

Paint bucket

Sander

Wallpapering Equipment

Seam roller

Craft knife

Pasting table

Bucket

Wallpaper scorer   Tape measure   Abrasive paper

Pasting brush

Sealant gun

Wallpaper trough

Paperhanging brush   Sealant blade   Sponge

Spirit level

Paperhanging scissors

Rubber gloves

Stepladder

Steam stripper   Protective goggles

TILING TOOLS

H aving the correct tools and equipment is an important part of any tiling project. In addition to the general-purpose tools found in a standard household toolbox (see page 400), there are a number of items, designed specifically for tiling, that you will need. It is always better to buy quality tools—these will last longer than less expensive versions, and will be easier to use and more accurate.

(see page 400)

PREPARATION

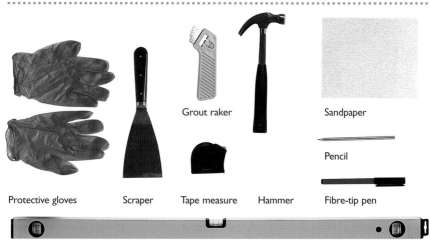

Grout raker

Sandpaper

Pencil

Protective gloves   Scraper   Tape measure   Hammer   Fibre-tip pen

Long spirit level

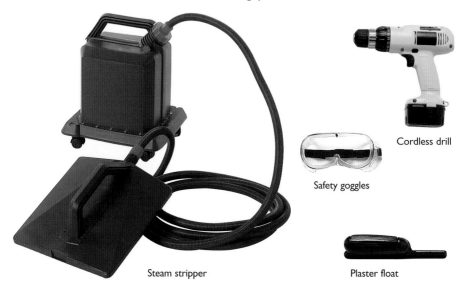

Cordless drill

Safety goggles

Steam stripper   Plaster float

CUTTING

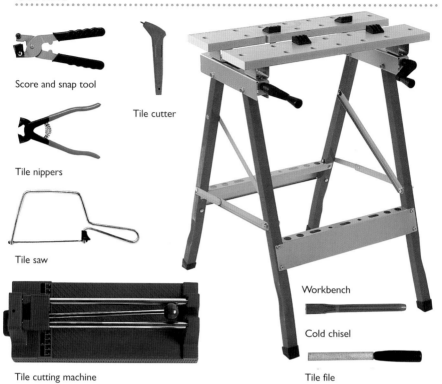

Score and snap tool

Tile nippers

Tile saw

Tile cutter

Tile cutting machine

Workbench

Cold chisel

Tile file

TILING

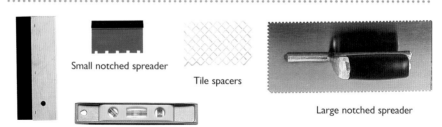

Small notched spreader

Tile spacers

Large notched spreader

Grout spreader

Short level

FINISHING

Trowel

Cotton rag

Sponge

Grout shaper

Sealant gun

GLOSSARY

ACCESS EQUIPMENT Ladders, platforms, scaffolding, and any other equipment used to reach high, inaccessible areas.

AGGREGATE Sand and small stones mixed with cement and water to form concrete.

ARCHITRAVE The moulding that frames a door or window opening.

BALUSTER A post (one of a set) used to support a handrail along an open staircase.

BALUSTRADE The complete barrier installed along open staircases and landings. It consists of the balusters, newels and handrail.

BATTEN A thin strip of wood, typically of 5 cm ׀ 2.5 cm (2 in ׀ 1 in) softwood.

BEAD OR BEADING A type of moulding that has a half round or more intricate profile. It's often used for edging and as decoration.

BEVEL A surface that meets another surface at an angle of less than 90°.

BIND When a door or hinged casement rubs against its surrounding frame.

BORE To drill a hole greater than about 12 mm (½ in) in diameter.

BUTT To fit together two pieces of material side by side or edge to edge.

CARCASE The boxlike, five-sided structure that forms the base of certain types of furniture such as a kitchen cupboard or chest of drawers.

CHAMFER A narrow, angled surface, often at 45°, running along the corner of a piece such as a beam or post.

CONCAVE A surface that curves inward.

CONTOUR The outline or shape of an object.

CONVEX A surface that curves outward.

CORNICE A decorative moulding fixed at the junction between the walls and ceiling, often used to hide cracks.

COUNTERSINK A tapered recess made in the top section of a screw hole to allow the head of the screw to sit flush with the surface of the material.

COVING A prefabricated concave moulding, often used as a cornice.

CUTTING-IN BRUSH A type of brush with bristles cut at an angle to assist painting neatly at an edge such as at a cornice or architrave.

DADO RAIL A decorative moulding, also called a chair rail, installed on walls about waist height, originally to prevent furniture from marring the walls.

DAMP-PROOF COURSE Also referred to as DPC, an impervious material laid in the building foundation to prevent moisture from the ground spreading to the walls or floors of the building.

DAMP-PROOF MEMBRANE Also referred to as DPM, an impervious material laid under a concrete floor to prevent moisture seeping through it.

DOWEL A small cylindrical wooden peg, sometimes with grooves running the length of its surface. It can be used to plug holes or to form a joint by inserting it into holes in two pieces of wood.

EGGSHELL PAINT A paint that dries with a matt finish and is used for interiors.

EMULSION PAINT Used on interior walls and ceilings, a water-based paint with a matt or sheen finish. It dries quickly and is easy to clean off paint equipment.

END GRAIN The fibres in the end of the wood exposed after cutting across the wood.

FEATHER To dull or taper an edge to make it less noticeable, a technique often used in sanding and painting.

FILLET A small, often wooden, piece of moulding with a square cross section.

FURRING STRIP A thin length of wood fixed in parallel strips across a wall or ceiling, forming a framework to which cladding is attached.

GLAZING POINT Or sprig, a small triangular-shaped piece of metal for holding a pane of window glass in a rebate.

GLOSS PAINT A solvent-based paint that dries with a hard, shiny finish. It's suitable for painting interior and exterior wood and metal. This type of paint needs a longer drying time and is harder to clean off paint equipment.

GRAIN The direction of the fibres in a piece of wood.

GROUT A water-resistant paste used to seal the gaps between ceramic or other similar tiles fixed to walls or floors.

HARDWOOD Wood that comes from broad-leaved—usually deciduous—trees such as ash, beech, and oak. This type of wood is typically hard; however, balsa is classified as a hardwood but is a soft, lightweight material.

HEAD The highest horizontal member of a window or door frame.

HEAD PLATE The highest horizontal component of a stud partition wall.

JAMB The vertical side member of the frame that surrounds a door or window.

JOIST A horizontal wood beam that is used to support a heavy structure such as a floor or ceiling.

KERF The groove created in a material when cut by any type of saw.

KEY To roughen a surface, often by sanding, to provide a better grip for a material such as paint or adhesive.

MASTIC A nonsetting compound that seals a joint between two surfaces such as a tiled wall and a worktop, bath, or shower tray.

MATT FINISH A nonreflective finish on a material such as paint or quarry tiles.

MITRE A joint between two bevelled pieces that forms an angle, often a 45° angle.

MORTISE A rectangular-shaped recess cut into wood. It may be used to form a joint by combining it with a tenoned end. Alternatively, it is used to hold a striker box in a door frame for a lock or latch.

MOULDING A narrow, usually decorative, strip of wood or other material. It is available shaped in different profiles. Skirting boards and dado and picture rails are types of moulding.

MULLION A vertical dividing component of a window.

MUNTIN A vertical component between panels; they are used to form a panelled door or wall panelling.

NEWEL Part of the balustrade, the wider post at both the top and bottom of a staircase for supporting the handrail.

NOGGING A short horizonal component between studs in a partition wall.

NOSING The front, often rounded, edge of a stair tread.

PARE To use a chisel, bevel side up, to remove fine shavings from wood—often done to smooth a surface from which wood was removed.

PATTERN REPEAT The distance of a motif before it begins to be duplicated, or repeated.

PELMET A decorative wood unit used to hide the top edge of curtains or a structure such as the track of a sliding door.

PICTURE RAIL A type of decorative moulding that is normally fixed horizontally to the walls above head height.

PILE The fabric raised from a backing—often used to classify a type of carpet.

PILOT HOLE A hole drilled in a material to guide a screw. It should be smaller in diameter than the shank of the screw without its threads.

PLINTH A four-sided base on which a structure, such as a cupboard or chest of drawers, is placed.

PRIMER A liquid substance used to seal a material, such as plaster, plasterboard, wood or metal, before applying an undercoat.

PROFILE The contour or outline of an object.

PROUD When an object protrudes from the surface.

RAIL The horizontal piece of wood that joins vertical pieces in a frame or carcase.

RAISED GRAIN When the wood's surface is roughened by damping, which causes its fibres to swell.

REBATE A step-shaped recess in the edge of a workpiece, often as part of a joint but also used for exterior door frames to prevent the door from swinging through.

REVEAL The vertical side of a window or door opening.

RISER The vertical component of a step or stair.

SASH The structure of a window that holds the glass. It usually opens, either up and down or sideways, but it is sometimes fixed.

SCARF A joint between two pieces of material cut at matching angles—unlike a mitre, the faces of the pieces are flush.

SCRIBE To mark a line with a pointed tool, or to copy the profile of a surface onto a piece of material, which will be trimmed to butt against the surface.

SCORE A line that marks a division or boundary, or the act of making the line.

SECRET NAILING A method of securing components together, such as tongue-and-groove floorboards, using fixings at an angle and punched below the surface of the workpiece.

SHEEN FINISH Also known as a silk finish, the amount of reflectiveness of a painted or other surface, midway between matt and gloss finishes.

SILL The lowest horizontal component of a window or door frame or of a stud partition wall.

SHIM A thin piece of material, such as cardboard or plywood, used as packing to fill a gap between materials.

SIZE A thin gelatinous solution used to seal a surface, such as a plaster wall, prior to hanging wallpaper.

SKIRTING BOARD A wood moulding used horizontally along the walls where they meet the floor.

SPANDREL The triangular material that is used to fill the space below an outside stringer on a staircase.

SOFTWOOD Wood that comes from coniferous trees, including cedar and pine. Although softwood is typically soft in nature, yew is one type that is hard.

SOLE PLATE Also known as a stud-partition sill, the lowest horizontal member of a wood-frame partition wall.

STAFF BEAD The innermost strip of wood that holds a sash that moves up and down in the window frame.

STAIN A liquid that changes the colour of wood but does not protect it. It comes in water-based, oil-based, and solvent-based versions.

STILE A vertical side component of a window sash or door.

STRAIGHTEDGE A length of either metal or wood that has at least one true straight edge. It is often used for marking straight lines or making a surface level.

STRINGER Also known as a string, one of a pair of boards that runs along the staircase, from one floor to another, supporting the treads and risers. If against a wall, it's called an inside stringer; if there is an open side, it's an outside stringer.

STUD A vertical member of a wood-framed wall.

STUD PARTITION WALL A wall constructed with a wood frame, usually covered with plasterboard.

SUBSIDENCE The sinking of the ground that occurs where land has been infilled or when it becomes excessively dry and shrinks. This may be due to a drought or to a large tree.

SUGAR SOAP A strong, alkaline-based liquid that is used for cleaning painted and other types of surfaces.

TEMPLATE Paper, card, metal, or other sheet material formed in a specific shape or pattern to be used as a guide for transferring the shape to the workpiece.

TENON A projecting end of a wood component, which fits into a mortise to form a joint.

TONGUE AND GROOVE A joint between two pieces of material—such as floorboards or cladding—in which one piece has a projecting edge that fits into a slot, or groove, on the edge of the other piece.

TOP COAT The last coat of a finish applied to a surface. There may be several coats underneath it.

TREAD The horizontal part of a step that is walked on.

UNDERCOAT One or more layers of a paint or varnish to cover a primer or hide another colour before applying a top coat.

UNDERLAY A layer of material to provide a smooth surface for laying a decorative flooring. Rubber, felt, or paper may be used under carpeting; hardboard or plywood may be used for other floorings.

UTILITY KNIFE Also referred to as a trimming knife or Stanley knife, a handle that holds a replacable blade, which may or may not retract.

VARNISH A liquid applied to wood materials, it hardens to form a protective surface. It may be clear or coloured.

WET-AND-DRY ABRASIVE PAPER A paper with silicon-carbide granules attached to it for smoothing surfaces. It may be used wet.

VENEER A thin decorative layer of wood applied to a less attractive base material.

INDEX

ACKNOWLEDGMENTS

All illustrations by Chris Forsey. All photographs by Tim Ridley except for the following pages:

l = left, r = right, c = centre, t = top, b = bottom

Page 6b Peter Reid/Houses & Interiors; 8t Camera Press; 8b Nick Huggins/Houses & Interiors; 14 John Freeman; 15 John Freeman; 16 John Freeman; 17 John Freeman; 18 John Freeman; 19 John Freeman; 20 John Freeman; 21 John Freeman; 22 John Freeman; 23 John Freeman; 24 John Freeman; 25 John Freeman; 35c Getty Images; 48cl Redcover; 48cr Redcover; 48br Camera Press; 56b Trevor Mein/Arcaid; 66 John Freeman; 67 John Freeman; 72 John Freeman; 73 John Freeman; 78 Redcover; 79t Roger Brooks/Houses & Interiors; 90br Camera Press; 97b Getty Images; 98 John Freeman; 99 John Freeman; 100t Redcover; 100b Getty Images; 108t Getty Images; 108b Peter Cook/View; 114cr Nick Huggins/Houses & Interiors; 114cl Roger Brooks/Houses & Interiors; 114l Henry Wilson/The Interior Archive; 115l J.T.L Kurtz/Camera Press; 115r Camera Press; 12l Christopher Drake/Robert Harding Picture Library; 128t Robert Harding Picture Library/Trevor Richards; 128b Robert Harding Picture Library/Ken Kirkwood; 129tl Robert Harding Picture Library/Bill Reavell; 129cr Robert Harding Picture Library/Polly Wreford; 129bl Robert Harding Picture Library/Ariadne bottom left; 136 John Freeman; 137 John Freeman; 142l Camera Press; 143t Victor Watts/Houses & Interiors; 143b Corbis; 145b Simon Butcher/Houses & Interiors; 146t Andrew Wood/The Interior Archive; 146c Camera Press; 146b Robert Harding Picture Library/Jon Baldwin; 148 John Freeman; 149 John Freeman; 150r Nick Hofton/View; 151t Christopher Drake/Robert Harding Picture Library; 151b Camera Press; 160c Peter Reid/Houses & Interiors; 160b Corbis; 162 Redcover; 163t Corbis; 164b Camera Press; 165b Camera Press; 169t Camera Press; 169c Corbis; 172t Paul Ryan/International Interiors; 172b Paul Ryan/International Interiors; 176 John Freeman; 177 John Freeman; 188 John Freeman; 189 John Freeman; 194 illustration by Amzie Viladot Lorente; 195 John Freeman; 202 John Freeman; 203b John Freeman; 206 John Freeman; 207 John Freeman; 208 John Freeman; 209 John Freeman; 240t Nick Huggins/Houses & Interiors; 240c John Freeman; 240b Redcover; 272t Robert Harding Picture Library/Flavio Galozzi; 272c Camera Press; 275t Robert Harding Picture Library/Bill Reavell; 275b Redcover; 287b Camera Press; 292t Camera Press; 292b John Freeman; 293tl Dennis Gilbert/View; 293tr Camera Press; 322t Robert Harding Picture Library; 322bl Peter Reid/Houses & Interiors; 331bl Corbis; 336tr Nick Huggins/Houses & Interiors; 336cl Charles E Lamb/Robert Harding Picture Library; 336bl Peter Aprahamian/Robert Harding Picture Library; 341 Getty Images; 345 Redcover; 347br Andrew Wood/ The Interior Archive; 349c Lizzie Orme/Robert Harding Picture Library; 351b Corbis; 354bl Graham Rae/Robert Harding Picture Library; 355b Corbis; 356bl Verne/Houses & Interiors; 358cl Camera Press; 359t Trevor Mein/Arcaid; 359b Fritz von der Schulenberg/The Interior Archive; 378b Tim Beddow/The Interior Archive; 393b Camera Press.

Cover: Tim Ridley (centre top), Paul Ryan/International Interiors (middle left), Camera Press (middle right), Corbis (centre bottom).